Los Desengaños

Memories of a Place

Angela Sanchez Tischler

A Swan Song Book

Los Desengaños

ISBN 10- 0983851913

ISBN 13- 97809838519-1-2

Printed by
E. O. Painter Printing Company Inc.
DeLeon Springs, FL 32130, USA

Table of Contents

Front cover — 1940's photo of ruins of a chimney from Los Desengaños sugar mill.

Back cover — Section of an 1895 map from the Historical map Archive at the University of Alabama.

To my brother's grandchildren

Angelica and Albert Alvarez, and Lucia Sanchez

Introduction

I am here to preserve the memory of a place that ceased to exist. The land is still there, but it is not the same place. It lost its name, it lost its landmarks and it may lose its history when the few of us who know it are gone. The land has not been covered with cement. It may even have a new life. A farmer may be planting crops; a child living near could be making it its own. But the place that was mine is gone.

The place had a name during the time when humans thought they owned it. The name was Desengaños.

I Googled the word "Desengaños"; it yielded many thousands of entries of the words "*los desengaños*" most of them followed by "*amorosos.*" These were tales of broken hearts in poems and other works of literature. When I searched for place names I was surprised at the popularity of the name. There are places named Desengaños in every Latin American country; just in Cuba there were thirteen listed. Only one of them was in the area of interest to me; that was the Embarcadero Los Desengaños, the landing connected with the old sugar mill, of which there was no mention, as expected.

One would think that more places would be named Esperanza, "Hope", but that is not the case. Desengaños, "Disillusions" seem to be more common occurrences. Who would name a sugar mill the Spanish equivalent of "Disillusions", and why? Were these disillusions in love, business, or any of the other aspects of life that tend to go wrong? We will never know.

I use the words Desengaño or Desengaños in Spanish, with either the singular article El or the plural Los, even if the rest of the story will be in English because these, as so many other words, don't bring to mind the same picture in translation.— An English speaker would have used Desengaños without the article in front, but we Cubans like to put articles in front of place names, like "La Habana", where a tourist would just say "Havana." —The accepted use of "disillusion" to me, leaves an "oh shucks" feeling; an "it just didn't work out this time, but go on to something else" situation. Something like Charlie Brown hoping to kick that football every year. Desengaños is sadder. It is the disillusion that comes with the discovery that our life's work was erroneous or had failed in a major way. The loss is so complete that you may never try that again. Of course, when you come right down to it, the meaning of a word is what we personally make of it. For the first twenty-five years of my life the name meant "Paradise." Not until later I wondered why an idyllic place received such epithet.

There is the danger of distorting memory by writing this history or by even talking about the past. Maybe the part of the brain that stores memories is like my computer hard drive: what I put there remains unchanged as long as I leave it alone; when I bring it up and edit it, it is changed. Unlike the computer file, I can't make a copy of my memory to be sure it stays unchanged.

For the earliest part of my story I will have to think of this project as an archeologist working with fragments of an ancient frieze. It will not be honest to cast replacements for the missing parts, but for the whole structure to hold together some improvisations must be made. The restoration is needed to make sense of what has survived. Also, the viewer, and in my case the reader, will be asked at times to use their imagination to fill the blanks in the story line. If I wait to have all the facts, this story will never be written.

Some of it will be written in the past tense as I remember events, but at times, I so completely go there in my thoughts that I can only write in the present as if things were happening right now. I feel the emotions I felt at the time. I will try to use only words that I would have used then and write only of what I knew at the time without using the future as a source of wisdom.

I have used Hugh Thomas' massive book "Cuba, the Pursuit of Freedom" to check the accuracy of names of people and places and the dates of important events, but I will not include a list of sources since this is not a scholarly work. I have not had to research the central facts of my story; either I was there or I heard it directly from somebody who was. A box that moved with me for fifty some years containing hundreds of letters from my parents, my sister, and my aunts, Pepilla and Amelia Sanchez has been my main source of concrete facts. I have translated some from the original Spanish and incorporated them into the story. Later, conversations with my sister have served to bring back into focus faded childhood scenes. Otherwise, these memoirs are based on my recollections. I am writing this near the end of my eighth decade of life taking advantage of a phenomenon of aging that together with my contemporaries I am experiencing: we may forget if we had lunch and the names of friends, but the names of playmates of seventy years ago are coming back. I noticed this with my mother, and now it is happening to me.

The names I used are those of real places and real people and I have made no attempts at disguising them. After all, many of these people are dead and the ones alive have matured enough in the more than fifty years that have elapsed since the events in this story took place to be able to face their life squarely and without worrying about their reputation. We can now laugh about a tyrant that ruled our youth: It was named *el que diran*, the "what would they say." I never knew who the "they" were and why should they care. I will hope that everyone mentioned, including the writer, has put behind that odious *que diran* and nobody is offended by anything they read here.

It has always been acceptable to throw a French word here and there in English writing usually without translation. The educated reader is expected to understand: if they don't, tant pis. I am requesting the same treatment for Spanish words, including those in the title. If *Les Misérables* can do it, why not *Los Desengaños?*

Since I have used so many Spanish words and terms of mostly native origin or local use, I will have to include a glossary. The definitions will be the meaning I and those around me gave those words. The same words may have been used differently a few kilometers down the road. For example, the thatch roofed country houses that somebody in Havana would properly call a *bohío*, the word probably used by the natives, as understood by the first Europeans, we in Camagüey insist on calling *un rancho de guano*. Don't look up guano either; to us it is not bird droppings, but palmettos or Sabal palms and their fronds, used for thatch roofs.

What happened in Cuba in the 1950's was so large and complicated that one single historian cannot grasp all the nuances. Many have told the story from many different angles and with various degrees of impartiality and scholarship. One point of view that has mostly been missing is that of ordinary Cuban citizens, those of us who were neither politicians nor revolutionaries. There were many of us who were not trying to change the country; who were just trying to take care of our lives. I will try to compress those lives into a very small color tile to be added to the large mosaic of the Cuban tragedy.

Silent ruins. The building of the mill

It was fortunate that the bricks could be made on site because tons of them would be needed. The wooden forms covered acres of cleared land. First drying was courtesy of the sun which is reliable even in the late winter at this latitude. For the final drying, the bricks were baked in open fires. Not a very economical system, but wood was plentiful and all the woods would be cleared later anyway when the mill was finished and the sugar cane was planted in all the land for miles in all directions. As the clay was extracted to form bricks, a large pond formed where only a narrow stream ran before. The project overseer had been around Eastern Cuba long enough to know that a dry stream bed can turn into a torrent in a few hours and he was prepared for it. A two-arch masonry bridge was already under construction even before all the catacomb- like ovens and the structures that really determine the nature of a sugar mill: the chimneys that we later referred to as towers.

The available lumber was a builder's dream. Perfect, straight logs of *jiqui* were dragged by teams of oxen from the surrounding forests. That wonderful wood, hard as iron and impervious to water and termites, may be hard to work, but once in place it was as lasting as the bricks. What he didn't know was that those posts will char but will not be destroyed by fire.

This imagined builder had the order of construction worked out. The two wells came first. Then the largest masonry building that must be in place to house the machinery as it arrives and secondary buildings of both wood and brick construction for various uses. African slaves were probably used in the construction but they did not stay in the area once the project was finished. Slaves were freed in Eastern Cuba on 10 October 1868 so they could have stayed as free men but their descendants are not visible in the area as they must have moved to the cities. A construction project of this magnitude and so far from settled areas generates a small community around it. Workers were responsible for their own accommodations. Some brought their families and their animals. Crops were planted, and fruit trees, in the certainty that someone will be here to enjoy them. A road was cleared to the nearest reach of the Nuevitas bay and a small barge landing was constructed. Then imported goods like refractory bricks and boilers were ordered from all over the world and shipped to the deep water port of Pastelillo to be transferred to barges for the trip across the bay of Nuevitas.

We are not even sure if the project was finished before it was destroyed. The ruins and especially the distance between the towers give an indication of the large size. This was a mill unlike the many small ones which ruins dot the Cuban and other Caribbean islands' countryside. Those were put out of business when the giant factory-mills took over the production of sugar. But there is nothing to indicate that this was ever a working sugar mill. If sugar cane had been planted here, there would not be any sign of it after so many years. What was there was an abundance of fruit trees and coconut palms, but those were planted by my mother at a later date. There was one lone coconut palm remaining in my days. It was the tallest coconut palm I had ever seen which to us proved its historic significance.

The only document we had was a hand-drawn map that shows not the sugar mill itself, but the planted fields. More an artistic rendition than a document, it was probably drawn with colored pencils, and showed in neat rows the cane fields and a grove of coconut palms. I only hope that somebody, somewhere, had the sensitivity to see value in that piece of paper and saved it. But I doubt it. In the feeding frenzy that followed the departure of every household after 1959, a kitchen gadget was considered more valuable than a piece of history.

El Desengaño sugar mill was almost certainly destroyed by the Cuban insurgents before 1898. It would have been ironic if my maternal grandfather, Major Miguel Alfredo Agramonte, head of a guerrilla force operating in the province of Camagüey during the last years of the War of Independence —aka the Spanish American War— was responsible for the destruction of the sugar mill. That would have been a good story but it didn't happen. N.G. Gonzales, in his book, "In Darkest Cuba: Two months service under Gomez along the Trocha from the Caribbean to the Bahama Channel", places Agramonte in July 1898 farther west, harassing the Spanish forces near the fort of Marroquin. Small mounted forces were very mobile and covered wide areas. They ranged from organized members of the Cuban Insurgency Army to outright bandits. Together they controlled the whole countryside to the point that the ruling Spanish only controlled the cities. But it is almost certain that this sugar mill was already in ruins at the time of the War of Independence. It more likely was destroyed during the ten year war: (1868 to 1878), fire being the friend of revolutionaries anywhere and a cheap and effective weapon when used to disrupt the local economy. Lacking a reliable account of what happened, we have to ask the ruins themselves and the form of construction indicates an earlier period. For one thing, the square chimneys were of an older building technique than the round ones common a few years later.

1902. A family on the move returns to Cuba

We shall start the story with Pedro Jose Sanchez Dolz not because there is any evidence that he built or named El Desengaño but because even if we don't have a photo, a description or a letter written by him, he is the farthest in the family chain that was remembered by people that I remember. My older aunts and uncles knew him, or knew enough about him to refer to him as "Papa Pedro".

We know that he was the son of Bernabe Sanchez-Pereira y Sanchez-Pereira, a Lieutenant with the Guardia Española, who was born in Puerto Principe (now Camagüey) in a family that had been in that city for many generations. His mother was Joaquina Dolz del Castellar y Lopez de Ganuza, born in Havana. Of course, Bernabe and Joaquina were not Cubans; Cuba was a colony of Spain and they were loyal Spanish subjects. As such, the couple first lived in Mexico where Bernabe may have been sent in some official capacity — or where he had business, we are not sure of this— and where their first child was born. Apparently they soon moved to Spain where three more children were added to the family. Pedro Sanchez Dolz was born in Cadiz, a port city on the southern coast of Spain about 1818.

Next we find Pedro, not surprisingly, in another port city: Nuevitas, on the north coast of Cuba. The Nuevitas where Pedro spent his adult years had, and especially before the railroad reached it in the 1860s, probably closer ties to the ports of New York or even Cadiz than to the rest of Cuba. The arrivals and departures of the brigantines were the pulse of the town. The New York Times regularly printed dispatches from ships at sea as well as arrivals at ports. On February 28, 1860 it reported "Brig Pedro Sanchez Dolz, Fickett (probably the captain), Nuevitas 14 days with cedar and molasses to J. Molina & Co--vessel to Peck & Church. Had a pilot on board 4 days with strong NW gales." There is another dispatch dated March 29 1863 with the same brigantine from Nuevitas arriving at the port of New York with merchandise (mdse). The brigantine may have been owned by Pedro himself or named in his honor by someone else, maybe by his brother Emilio who was known to be in the shipping business. In sailing days, when the winds determined the routes, Nuevitas was a stop for vessels sailing from Cadiz to New York. There is another dispatch on the same newspaper of a bark in port at Nuevitas five days out of Cadiz and on route to New York.

Tradition has it that Pedro traced the streets of the new village; a reason why they are, unlike other old towns in Cuba, in a precise grid. Precision is still a family trait. Was he in some position of authority? We don't know. He was named British Vice-Consul of Nuevitas and Gibara in 1856, an unpaid position. He was also an agent of Lloyds of London.

He must have worn many hats because he also bought or inherited large parcels of land and even a rail line, *Ferrocarril del Baga* that ran from Baga, a place on the south shore of the bay of Nuevitas that is no longer shown on the maps, through the town of San Miguel del Baga and from there east probably to Manati in Oriente Province. Did he also find time to build a sugar mill? In recent times his name has appeared in the Nuevitas web site, Radio Nuevitas as the person who connected Nuevitas with the rest of the island by bringing the railroad all the way into town. The obstacle that had prevented the rail from reaching the town was overcome by cutting through a hill and building a wooden overpass (now replaced by a concrete one) that was locally referred as *el puente*. Whatever else he was, officially he was a merchant, which in his days could mean anything. The waterfront street in Nuevitas where he had his merchant house and probably also his home, is now named after him.

As far as I can determine, he was the first in the family to drop the hyphenated name Sanchez-Pereira, and use his mother's maiden name as his second surname as is the Spanish custom. Pedro Sanchez Dolz married Catalina Adan y Arteaga on the 12 of October 1840 at the Santa Ana church in Puerto Principe. They had two sons and three daughters. The older son, Bernabe by far outlived and outshined his younger brother Joaquin. With business acumen and self-sacrifice he grew the Senado sugar mill into one of the largest and more progressive in the province, and headed a notable dynasty. The daughters were Abisai, whose only son married a cousin and returned to the hometown of Nuevitas; Hortensia and Catalina who married and moved to Spain, losing contact with the Cuban relatives. Pedro Sanchez Dolz must have died before his wife because in the division of Joaquin's property it is mentioned several times that the inheritance came from Catalina Adan.

Joaquin, my grandfather, married Amelia de Miranda y del Castillo in the cathedral of Puerto Principe (now Camagüey) on the 20th of August 1868, and after a few years in Havana where the first child (named Joaquin, of course) was born, they moved to Nuevitas where the other eleven children were born. According to the State Department, he was named U.S. Consular Agent on 12 February 1873 and may have served until 1890 when a new Agent was named. We learn of his complicated business transactions only from the divisionary documents drafted when the widow and children returned to Cuba after his death. My sister insists that he was responsible for the building of El Desengaño. I insist that he inherited ruins. Unless a document or old letter shows up proving otherwise, I will hold on to my theory of an earlier construction.

Joaquin may have been suffering for a long time from the cancer that later took his life because he and his wife made an official will in 1889. At the time they had only eleven children but the will was amended in 1891 when Adolfo, my father, was born. The decision to move the family to New York may have been influenced by Joaquin's illness, but also, many families that could afford to do so went to New York to ride out the war. The Sanchez brothers were definitely not considered patriots. Their political inclinations were not toward the *Independistas* but toward another faction known as the *Separatistas*. Since history is written by the victor, not much is said about the *Separatistas*, but apparently they were working for, or at least hoping for, an amicable separation from Spain.

Another possible reason for taking the older children to New York, and then the whole family, is based on an unconfirmed tale, this one from cousin Cutin Sanchez Calleja who heard it from his maternal grandfather Rosendo (Chendo) Lopez de la Calleja that may explain why the family moved away from Nuevitas. As the story goes, the Guardia Civil was trying to raise money to arm a sort of posse to hunt down a bandit named Mirabal that had been terrorizing the countryside by kidnapping for ransom. Cutin's grandfather refused to put up the money because it would endanger his family. Joaquin financed the whole venture but sent his older children out of the country for their safety.

*

There is a clearer picture of the family members and their relationships when they were away than when they were at home in Nuevitas because we have letters. In 1893 Joaquin took three of the children, Catalina, Oliverio and Armando to the United States, which for them meant New York City. They travelled by steamer from Nuevitas to Havana, Key West and Tampa Bay and from there by train to New York. Oliverio wrote wonderfully descriptive and honest letters to his mother. Armando wrote shorter add-ons. If Catalina wrote, her letters have not survived. It is clear that they had not even been to Havana before but had heard from their father about all the wonders they were about to see. We read trivia like Catalina being seasick and gems from fourteen year-old Armando, "No wonder Papa always said that (Cuba) was still in a semi wild stage." Another family mystery: if to Joaquin this trip was like coming home, and he spoke English, why? When and why had he been in New York before?   Here is from a letter written by Oliverio from a "magnificent" hotel of 36th Street. "Abisais (aunt) took Catalina to a dressmaker; she is having two dresses made. Hortensia (another aunt): is sailing Saturday for Spain. I believe that they will soon be back because Espinoza (Hortensia's husband's last name) doesn't stay put anywhere.

"Pepe (cousin, Hortensia's son) was here last night. Still as pedantic and *españolizado* (Spanish-like, in a derogatory way) as ever in spite of having been here for a year."

Of another cousin, Andres, Abisais' son, there is nothing but praise. "He is sturdy, tall, and has learned English." That cousin also took Oliverio and Armando to an Art Museum.

The two brothers stayed behind probably in a preparatory school, possibly Bethlehem Prep, before entering Lehigh University. Why the Bethlehem connection? We don't know. It may have been on the advice of the family New York business partner George Mosle. The next time the boys saw their father was in 1896 when according to a ship manifest Joaquin (father), Joaquin (son), and again, Catalina, arrived on New York the 11th of November on the Orizaba. Also on that ship were Joaquin's brother Bernabe, his second wife, Elizabeth, Bernabe (son), Catalina, known as Alina, maybe to distinguish her from a cousin of the same age and name, and five minor children. Two more children were born later to complete his dozen. Bernabe, just like his brother, had already left some of his sons in boarding in school in the United States. In his case Alvaro, Pedro and Carlos Sanchez Batista attended the Gunnery School in Connecticut probably to prevent them from joining the rebels or the military. This family was more interested in business than in politics.

Oliverio wrote to his mother from the hotel Marlborough on Broadway about going with their father to a show on the same street and coming out at eleven-thirty. He signs-off with, "love to everybody and a hug from your son who loves you..." They obviously didn't expect to meet as soon as they did. Things must have begun to unravel in Cuba and changes in plans were made in a hurry. Either there is a mistake on the ship manifests, or the oldest son, Joaquin, was dispatched back to Cuba in a hurry to escort his mother, the younger children, and even the servants, to the

United States. They arrived on the Yumuri on the first of February 1897. Once again, faithful son Joaquin turned around and returned to Cuba.

There was a large community of Cuban expatriates in New York. Adolfo remembers going with his sisters to do what they considered their patriotic duty: they spent time at a center sewing uniforms for Cuban rebels. Even a small child like him did something for the cause; he half-heartily sewed buttons on shirts and later wondered about the poor soldier whose clothes fell apart because of him. He attended school; sailed his toy boat on the lake in Central Park just around the corner from the house where they lived at 76 West 90th Street, and adopted English as his language, at least for the time being. Twenty years younger than this oldest brother, he had a special place in the household. His father referred to him in letters as El General. Apparently being strong of character was valued in this family, not only in the boys, but in the girls also. Adolfo remembers an incident when he was attacked by bullies in the park and his treasured sailboat taken away from him. His sister Aurelia came to the rescue, grabbed the boat, and held it high over her head while the band of little hooligans pounded on her.

The eldest daughter, Catalina, married Bernabe Arteaga, a member of the hometown community, just as she would have married if they were back home. The newlyweds sailed back to Cuba. Adolfo remembered how the family went to see them off and arrived just as the ship was moving away from the pier. Oliverio, always Adolfo's hero, pitched the flowers they were bringing and they landed on the deck — one of those isolated images that are engraved in the memory of a child.

While both Oliverio and Armando were attending Lehigh University, Joaquin, the oldest son, rode out the war in Nuevitas. It must have been a strategy to protect property and business, because Bernabe did the same thing, sending his oldest son to wait for the rest of the family in war torn Camagüey as sort of human placeholder. The plan worked somewhat for Bernabe but not for Joaquin. He never returned to Cuba. He died in New York in 1900.

*

The Sanchez Miranda family had left as Spaniards in 1896. Amelia Miranda, returned to Cuba in 1902 with nine of her twelve children after six years in New York. Besides the oldest son who had never left, two daughters had married and had returned before the others. Now they were all Cuban citizens.

Soon after their return, a legal document termed *"Documentos Divisorios"* was drawn to assess what remained of the family fortune and divide it amongst the heirs. Seven of the children were considered minors and were represented by a court appointed trustee. A daughter, Hortensia, turned twenty-three during the procedures and was deemed adult and capable of representing herself. Most of the document is written by hand in the well-formed script used by law clerks of the time, with incredibly even lower case letters and ornate capitals, but typewriters were available because some end notes are typewritten. Apparently the legality of the document required that it be written by hand.

The inventory starts with the cash, dollar value of the Spanish gold given as 3,106.85, followed by an eight page list of bonds, and some shares of stock, from Edison Electric to twenty-four different railroads. They knew how to be diversified, and probably followed the advice of the family partner in New York who was an expert in railroad investing. The total value of the securities was listed as $140,348.50 in 1902 dollars. It is to their credit that they had any money left after years in exile and the fatal illness of the head of the household.

Next is the carefully counted and itemized list of animals. It is sad, but not surprising, that with so much land involved, so few animals had survived. Cattle, horses, donkeys and some sheep, of all ages, are on the list. Of the total of 82 assorted animals, the one assigned the highest value was a breeding ass for $250, while a bull was only $80. Total for all animals was $3,520.

What makes the document so large, and so complicated, is that not only the property of the deceased was being divided amongst his widow and twelve children, but some of it, like the rail line, warehouse, merchant house, home, and other urban property in Nuevitas had still been held in common by Joaquin, his brother and three sisters. It had to be divided five ways before been divided again but, strangely, nothing is said of the two sisters who moved to Spain or their heirs.

Of the properties in Cuba, it is interesting to note what was consi-dered valuable at the time and what wasn't. Of the lumber business there is no mention although there is evidence that it existed. The few animals that survived the revolution were greatly valued, as was the standard gage rail line known as Ferrocarril de El Baga—Baga apparently was a place on the South side of the bay of Nuevitas non-existent even in my earliest recollec-tion but close to the town of San Miguel which was then known as San Miguel del Baga. The several large tracts of land, some owned outright, some in partnerships or some other financial arrangement, seem greatly undervalued. What we later knew as Los Desengaños was then singular, El

Desengaño. Later disappointments, of which there were plenty, must have changed the name to the plural. In page twenty-six of the eighty-three-page document we have the first description of the property, but there is no mention of the sugar mill. If I had not played in the ruins as a child, I would have doubts as of its existence.

It is the first listing under *inmuebles*, real estate. *"La finca rustica potrero El Desengaño con 53 caballerias, 159 cordeles de tierra equivalente a 707 hectareas 84 areas 50 centareas."* A caballeria is roughly 33 acres so the land was a little less than 1,750 acres and not particularly valuable without the sugar mill and no other construction worth mentioning in the document. The location was given as part of *"el fundo subdividido de Nuevitas de Becerra, termino municipal de Nuevitas."* It was described as bordering on the north, east and south with Roma (or Roura?) and on the west with the road to the embarcadero (landing).

The documents didn't give El Desengaño, or even part of it, to my father. The ten year old received one fifth of the animals. El Desengaño went in equal parts to my uncle Ernesto and to my aunt Aurelia. Without knowing more than what is on that document, the division seems arbitrary to say the least.

The document explains that El Desengaño together with another property named La Rosalia were inherited by Joaquin and his sister Abisai from their mother Catalina Adan in a document dated 19 December 1879. Since there is no mention of a mill, which would have made the property immensely more valuable, it can be assumed that even by that date all there was there was land with a pile of rubble on it. The two siblings divided de property themselves leaving Joaquin as the sole proprietor of El Desengaños and Abisai that of La Rosalia. Since Abisai's only child, Andres, married Amelia, one of Joaquin's six daughters, the property was destined to stay in the family. But things were not that simple in 1902. The complications involved in recovering property after a war can only be imagined, and more so, since Joaquin Sanchez, the head of the household, had died in New York. It is not known who was in charge of his investments or if his wife, doña Amelia, knew much about his business.

Did Joaquin build the sugar mill after he inherited the land? Most unlikely. Did his father Pedro Sanchez Dolz, or someone else entirely? The name Carlos de Varona y de la Torre shows up as one-time owners of Las Nuevitas de Becerra, a larger land grant of which El Desengaño had been but a part. He was also listed as the owner of the sugar mill Altagracia. Later there was a town of that name farther south, toward Camagüey, but no sugar mill. There is also a word-of-mouth story in the Sanchez family that one hundred caballerias (3,350 acres) were given to the Marques de Santa Lucia to help settle some ownership question—of which there were certainly many after the war. But that is not part of this story.

On the family's return to Cuba not only their nationality had changed, but the province and city of Puerto Principe had now taken the native name of Camagüey, so they became "Camagüeyanos." The name had changed, but the characteristics of the province remained the same. The 1900 census showed Camagüey with a much lower population density than the other five provinces. Sparsely populated and with a more homogeneous people—after all, the few families of Puerto Principe had been intermarrying for 300 years. The gene pool was increased after the war when many Spaniards chose to stay and make Camagüey their permanent home. This had been a strange fraternal war and in spite of the tales of abuse under Spanish rule, there was no animosity at the personal level. A few North Americans who had come with the transition government also chose to stay, learned the language and became undistinguishable from the locals.

The Sanchez Miranda family moved into a house in Camagüey with the address Salvador Cisneros #12. As some of the siblings married and moved away, the family slowly diminished in size and the widow and remaining children moved to another house at Avellaneda #6 where Doña Amelia lived out her years and daughter Josefa, known as Pilla or Pepilla, the only one to remain unmarried, kept the home address and the upstairs part of the original house until the final exodus.

Adolfo attended a local school; became familiar with horses, at the time, the common conveyance around Camagüey and after a few years sailed back to New York, with his brother Julian, this time to attend school at Bethlehem Prep. Later, Adolfo became the fifth of the brothers to attend Lehigh, but soon Julian broke with family tradition; during a hospital stay he became interested in medicine and transferred from Lehigh to the University of Pennsylvania Medical School. That was followed by an internship at the Lying-In Hospital, a maternity hospital on Second Avenue in New York City before he returned to Cuba to work as a medical doctor. But there was no shortage of engineers in the family: Ernesto had followed Armando and Oliverio who had already graduated from Lehigh University and returned to Cuba to take over family business. The many entries in ship manifests show the movements of the brothers to and from the Port of New York. There was never even a suggestion of an education for the six sisters.

The brothers had made a great impact on the University, and the University on them. Oliverio was well known, not so much by his academic achievements, as by his one arm pull-ups. In the Lehigh yearbook the Epitome, class of 1914 there is a light hearted inquest in which the students were asked to vote for their classmates in categories such as: The Best Looking, The Best Athlete, The Funniest, etc. After each entry there is a second question: Thinks He Is. The name Sanch , Adolfo's school nick-name, appeared several times in that category. That was, of course, in jest, but he did distinguish himself as an athlete. At only one hundred and thirty pounds he tried out for every sport, and was one of their best Lacrosse players at a time and place where the game was immensely popular. He remembers a game in which he played against famed Olympian Jim Thorpe. It must have been of such importance at the time that he kept the newspaper clippings and, if encouraged, would retell the highlights of the game.

Adolfo, my father who later in the narrative I will refer to as Papi, found himself in 1914 with a B.S. in Chemistry and a big decision to make. Not only he divided his loyalty between Camagüey and the North where he had spent so much of his life, but now he had a great job offer in Chile. With his usual lack of modesty, he used to say that he had the best job offer of his graduating class. Some of his classmates received another kind of job offer: they went to fight in Europe in World War I. Of his two closest friends— and Delta Upsilon fraternity brothers—, one joined the Army and eventually rose to the rank of brigadier general, and the other did even better : he became a pilot, every one of whom was treated as a hero at the time. Adolfo considered following them when a letter from his brother Oliverio, who was his father figure, settled everything. He said "Your mother has been separated from you long enough." My father returned to Cuba to stay.

Back in Camagüey he worked as a chemist at a couple of sugar mills during the zafra, first at the Central Daiquiri (the drink originated there or at the copper mines nearby) in Oriente province, and later at Central Francisco, in Camagüey. The sugar mill life was a good transition for somebody who had lived in the United States a great part of his life. He remembers that there was always ketchup on the table for the americanos. The grinding season, or zafra, starts usually in February, lasts only four or five months, depending on the weather and ends when the cane runs out or the rains begin. In the *tiempo muerto*, the "dead season" when there is no need for a chemist at the mills, he tried his hand at other endeavors: he was part owner, with his friend Connolly —who was also the branch manager of the

Royal Bank of Canada — of the colonia Las Josefinas, a sugarcane plantation He also managed a cattle ranch for his sister Catalina who had been living in Atlanta. All those projects must have begun to weigh him down because he asked his sister to send one of her six sons to help him. She did, and he turned over that ranch to her son Armando Arteaga (who later hung himself. By the time the story came to me it was stripped of all tragic elements and it was just a family lore.)

The siblings had been doing some trading amongst themselves and by 1920 the land known as El Desengaño was in the hands of the three younger brothers Ernesto, Julian and Adolfo. Cattle had grazed before on this and other land belonging to the Sanchez family. My cousin Cutin has a copy of a cattle brand given to him by our grandmother. It is a large letter "S" with a smaller "J" inside the top loop and an "A" inside the lower loop which stood for Joaquin Sanchez Adan. She had told him that there was another similar brand with the letter "B" instead of the "J" which was used by Bernabe, the other brother, but he didn't know if a copy of that one had survived. By the 1920's any animal with one of those brands on its flank had long been butchered.

The final ownership of the family property bore no resemblance to that on the Division Documents. Apparently the women were given cash or cash equivalents, and the men took the mortgaged land. The mortgages were held by money lenders or, some, by the sisters themselves,

Julian had also inherited El Guayabito, described in the division document as a small parcel of oceanfront land of approximately 70 acres on the north coast. He had sold that because he was now a medical doctor and wanted nothing to interfere with his practice, According to my mother the division of Los Desengaños was negotiated in her living room and in the presence of a lawyer. Julian, in the Camagüey tradition, planned to farm on the side, but not in such a remote location and not in a land so heavily mortgaged. He let his two brothers have it and bought something else close to town. Adolfo and Ernesto divided the land; Ernesto named his part La Amelia after their mother, and Adolfo, who had already been investing in the property and had built corrales and other structures that were to become the batey was now in sole possession of the site with the ruins, now re-named Los Desengaños, plural.

1921. The making of a cattle ranch. Close encounter with a bull

What Adolfo found in the vicinity of the old sugar mill were some German squatters living in tents. What they were doing or for that matter, if they were really squatters or had some business arrangement, I don't remember hearing. Adolfo himself lived in a tent near the ruins and suffered from Malaria. By that time he had quit working as a chemist and was dedicating all his time and resources to building his finca.

He had put together a group of locals, at least one of whom, Pancho Perez, became his lifelong friend, neighbor and associate. Having lived close to the land all their life,they all had more experience in the kind of work ahead than he did, One of the first tasks at hand was to bring out of the woods the cattle that had lived wild for years, count them and brand them.

They may have already been using the same brand that went on the flank of thousands of animals in the next forty years. The hierro even had a name: El Muñeco, or boy doll. It looked like a stick figure: circle for the head, an ellipse for the body, parallel lines for the legs, one arm down and the other bent at the elbow. Adolfo had found the prototype in the ruins. The original was only about four centimeters long and he had figured that it was used to mark lumber. The larger versions met the requirements for a good hierro: No lines were too close to run together and damage the hide, which in some cases, was the only part of the animal considered of value.

Before the iron burns a Muñeco on the animal's rump somebody has to hold it still which is not easy even with calves, and these were mostly full grown animals. The men were working in the open, with no enclosures or corrales, just horses and ropes. In the excitement and fast pace of the work, even the experts may have underestimated one particularly angry bull. It had been roped by either Adolfo or one of the others working with him, but it apparently had not been secured. Adolfo had dismounted when the bull charged. He was hit squarely on the chest. Instinctively he put up his right hand to protect himself.

Somehow they managed to get the seriously injured Adolfo through roadless terrain to the rail line. One of them must have ridden ahead to Nuevitas to get word to stop the train at some predetermined spot on the track and the victim was almost certainly transported by steadying him on a horse. There was no other way.

Adolfo remembers being conscious lying in a freight car. When he tried to hold his good hand over the hole in his chest, he could see the red bubbles bursting between his fingers with every breath.

The injury to his chest was so obvious — a bull's horn is sharp as a spear and about seven centimeters at the base — that for days nothing was done about his broken hand. He recovered completely from the gouging, which left only the kind of jagged scar you expect to see only in a bullfighter, but the hand injury was with him the rest of his life.

The ship manifest of the Ulna arriving in New York on the 24 July 1921 has him listed as thirty years old and single. His destination this time was the Johns Hopkins Hospital in Baltimore. A tiny triangular shaped wrist bone was out of place in his wrist causing constant pain. The surgeon was not able to repair the damage, only to remove the small bone. The surgery stopped the pain, but his right hand stayed permanently in a semi clenched position which, in a culture that did not cater to sensitive feelings, earned him the nickname of Garabato.

If the name bothered him, he did not show it, not that it would have done any good. He even capitalized on the nickname. The one time he ran for political office he had flyers showing himself using a garabato as a walking stick. Running for office was completely out of character, and can only be explained by his friendship with ex-president Menocal. He was not elected and never tried again.

What is a garabato? It is the inseparable partner of the machete. The machete is wielded on one hand and the garabato held on the other. It is cut from a branch of just the right diameter and with a secondary branch cut short and meeting at about a forty five degree angle near the working end to form a hook. It is usually cut on the spot as needed, although a good one will be saved and put aside for the next job. It is used by cane cutters, by destajeros who clear land on contract and by any guajiro who needs to hold some brush steady to be whacked by the machete. Using a machete without a garabato is dangerous; without the hooked stick to guide him, an inexperienced worker can end up with a nasty cut across his left shin—if he is right handed.

The nickname Garabato was with Adolfo only in town. It did not follow him out of Camagüey. The people at Los Desengaños or his friends up North never heard it. He was Adolfo to the older employees who had been with him through the early years; or he was Don Adolfo to the younger ones. To his friends from Lehigh he was what he had always been, Sanch.

A home and a family. Good and bad times

The first time Adolfo was pointed out to her, he still had his right arm in a sling. Angela Agramonte had surely heard accounts of his accident. Even in a city where horses were regularly tied down near busy street corners and cattle were driven through the outskirts of town, his accident had been noteworthy. They met several times in the next few years but it was a while before they seriously dated. Later they told their children a variety of contradictory and humorous tales about the other's dancing partners, so it is not easy to know facts about the courtship. Camagüey in the 20's must have been a party town. There were dances at the different Clubs: Club Atletico, Tennis Club and even as far as Club Tarafa, near Nuevitas, where Angela visited with relatives.

Angela was anything but a frivolous society girl, although, hers was the time of the flapper and she looked the part, she was a working girl. Her father, Miguel Alfredo Agramonte, died when she was an infant. He had survived the War of Independence only to die from the injuries incurred when he fell off, or jumped off while trying to put out a fire on a thatch roof. Her mother, Consuelo Alvarez, after a few bad business transactions found herself penniless with two boys and a girl. She also was responsible for two orphans sent to them from Havana after the war. (One of them, Ramon, stayed with her all her life). Eventually she remarried; her new husband was Pablo Ronquillo, a widower with five children. Angela and her two brothers spent much of their childhood at the finca Palma Hueca that belonged to their step father's family, surrounded by the step siblings, cousins, friends, and a variety of people with different degrees of blood and other relationships. She ended up with two step sisters practically the same age as she was; one a few months older and the other a few months younger. Her one half-sister, Zoila, was ten years younger than Angela and spoiled by the whole clan.

In town, she was studious, had been tutoring children for pay since she was a child herself. While her sisters were expected to do their share of housework, and even did sewing for others, Angela was excused from that kind of woman's work since she was contributing to the household income with her outside work. That was the reason she always gave for not knowing how to sew, cook or any other domestic skills. She finished Bachillerato with honors, loved to dance, played basketball, and by the time love came calling she was a Math instructor at the Escuela Normal de Maestros. She was known as la Doctora Agramonte although she was still working on her degree, studying por la libre at the University of Havana. She was so well thought of, that her boss, a Doctor Andino, postponed the required competitive opening of the job she was temporarily filling, waiting for her to obtain the university degree that would qualify her for the position permanently. Under that system she went to the University only for exams, staying at the home of her uncle, Aurelio Alvarez, a well-known political figure, who at one time presided over the Cuban Senate, and where she enjoyed the company of another set of cousins and friends.

They were married in 1928 in a simple civil ceremony; the reason given for not having a church wedding was that the groom was in mourning. Amelia de Miranda had recently died of cancer. Angela didn't have the opportunity to spend much time with her future husband's mother, but on one of the few visits, the ailing mother of twelve gave the bride to be her list of household necessities. It included table service for twenty. The wedding trip consisted of a train ride to Nuevitas enhanced by an unexpected party when the train stopped at the Central Lugareño siding and a group of Adolfo's friends boarded the train and toasted the couple with champagne.

In Nuevitas, Amelia, one of Adolfo's six sisters who would be her neighbor and fairy godmother, already had a rented house ready for them. It was on the hillcrest street Maximo Gomez just half a block from Amelia, Andres and their seven children, the only Sanchez relatives left in their former hometown. They had seen to it that the house was fully furnished and outfitted, thanks to Andres' furniture factory and Amelia's great skill as a housewife. The house was one of those houses found only on hillside cities, with the front living room opening to a very ordinary flat street, but the back of the house and its small yard were way down the side of the hill. The view out of the back was that of the Bay.

There is no record of Angela's first impression on visiting Los Desengaños. Just getting there was daunting. It involved crossing the bay in a public launch—which never failed to make her seasick— and then a horseback ride longer than any she had taken before. Once there she found several buildings and the corrales were already finished. There were workers living in the batey and cattle in the field, but the house that would be her home was still under construction. They sort of camped in the unfinished house while work went on around them.

It was Adolfo's dream to have a homestead like the ones he had known in Pennsylvania: full time residence of well-educated gentlemen-farmers equally at home feeding pigs on the farm or attending shows in New York City. Bringing that life style to Los Desengaños would be difficult but he loved every last animal and chore and had no intention of being an absentee landlord regardless of how successful he became. Angela shared his dream. In a way, she was the perfect partner and, at the time, knew more about country living than he did. They both went to work to educate themselves on the ways of modern farming and bringing them to Los Desengaños.

Rural residences in the province of Camagüey had almost without exception been destroyed during the long wars and had not been rebuilt. It had become the norm for ganaderos to have their main residence in the city and only a secondary home at their finca. Only the ones with land very close to town lived full time on the property. Of course, those who farmed in a small scale, whether it was on their own land or somebody else's, lived where they worked because they could not afford otherwise. Moving to the city was not a choice for everyone.

At the time, Cuba was still under the paternalistic umbrella of the United States and promoting modern agriculture was one of their goals. The U.S. Department of Agriculture was very cooperative in supplying Angela with literature on every topic from cheese making to choosing between different breeds of barnyard animals. Chickens were her favorites. After much research, she settled on Plymouth Rocks and ordered the day-old chicks. Incredibly, they arrived in good condition from some source in the Midwest. She placed the little black fuss balls in the brood boxes that, following the instructions from the USDA, she had made out of cut up flannel strips. She bought incubators, cheese making equipment, a cast iron stove. She planted fruit trees.

It is impossible to translate finca as farm or as ranch because it is neither. Or, better said, it is both. Even the largest cattle ranches had smaller animals, fruit trees, and maybe even a planted crop. Beef cattle can also double as dairy cattle. Angela learned to make cheese and butter that was marketed in Nuevitas. For a while the pride of Los Desengaños was its carbide lighting system. Beautiful bright light illuminated the whole batey. But that was a short while, an inherently dangerous system it soon went off with a bang. It could have been worse; nobody was hurt.

For the birth of their first child they forgot about the old fashioned ways and went to the city. They stayed at what was once the Sanchez family home, now the home of Pepilla. Oli was born in the Clinica Agramonte in Camagüey on the 12 of September 1929. He was named Adolfo Oliverio as expected, but with the understanding that he would use the name Oliverio after Adolfo's much admired older brother, who had been a father figure during their father's long illness and death and also during the following years when the family had to remake their life back in Cuba. Oliverio, the brother, had died of appendicitis and his widow, Chea Callejas, had taken their two children to live in Havana, to Adolfo's displeasure.

Angela found the whole process of giving birth so easy that when I came along two years later they didn't bother to go farther than their rented house in Nuevitas and went right back to Los Desengaños where I took my first steps. The porch that surrounds the house on three sides is no place for a toddler; it is four or more feet off the ground and has no railing. Angela would sit on the porch and watch me play on a blanket spread on the ground down below. I learned to walk early before they got around to ordering shoes for me. They didn't bother to register my birth either. A fact that I use in moments of self-deprecation as proof that even then I was a non-entity.

They had married at a time of economic buoyancy. In Cuba the time was known as la danza de los millones. The dance of the millions. The world economy and the price of sugar affected almost everyone. There were tales of colonos, the independent sugar cane planters, who went from humble guajiros to millionaires almost overnight. Supposedly some went on wild shopping sprees. There was the often repeated tale of the new millionaire who bought a grand piano for his two daughters. When he saw them practice together a cuatro manos he said," we are not going to be cheap in this house", and went out and bought a second piano.

Since nothing but the same could be expected in the future, Adolfo saw no problem in borrowing heavily from all sources in order to develop his dream finca. He also had bought more land just on the other side of his brother, Ernesto's, land. La Gertrudis was larger and with even a bigger mortgage. Then almost overnight the situation changed. In 1932 they were on the verge of losing everything. Angela sold some urban rental property in Camagüey that she had bought before she married and bought a finca named El Destino in the South half of the province. It says something about land values of the time when the sale of a house in town was enough to buy a thirty caballeria piece of good pasture land accessible by road all year. They moved from the rented house in Nuevitas to another rented house in San Pablo, in Camagüey. If their only finca was to be the one toward the south, it made more sense to live in Camagüey. Adolfo was preparing to turn everything over to his creditors. Ranchers were losing their land; my mother's step father lost his. Fortunes were changing hands. Oh, yes, my sister Lucy was born that year. The name Lucila coincidentally was that of one of Adolfo's ex-girlfriends, although he claimed that he never suggested it. The middle name was Consuelo, after the maternal grandmother, the only grandparent we were to know.

After Lucy was duly registered, they got around to registering me; my birth certificate says that I was born in Camagüey 15 September 1931. The most likely reason why I was not registered at the time of my birth was that my mother, Camagüeyana to the core, after all, she was an Agramonte, didn't want the world to know that I was born in what to her was the backwaters of Nuevitas. That would have made me a cangrejera (from the word cangrejo, a crab.) They waited after they moved and my sister was born to put my birth in the civil registry. I am in the registry book after her. Also, I was born the 16th, or so I was told, but they thought it was cute for us both to have the same birthday. So now I share a birthday with my sister and a Saints Day with my mother. The worse is that since I was also named Angela, I am condemned to be a little angel forever. I am Angelita.

We can only speculate as to why the plan to live fulltime in the country was abandoned. Looking at the economic and political chaos of the times we can imagine that they may not have felt secure in the isolation of Los Desengaños. Angela may have had a change of mind once the children came along; what if they were sick; how about when it was time to send them to school. A life without telephone, mail, contact with her friends, was not as romantic as she had envisioned. She may have found that she was not as strong as she thought and hers was not a Pennsylvania homestead with electricity and a paved road to the door. She accepted the split lifestyle that seemed to work for the majority of families of ganaderos in her home province. Adolfo would do the homesteading spending a great deal of the time alone or on the road, and she and the children would live in town and support him from a distance.

It might have been easier to ride out the Depression if they had stayed in the country living off the land, as many did. But they had married at the height of a time so prosperous that Adolfo had reason to expect that he would prosper and things would only get better. As it turned out, the fall came quickly. Steers were selling for $5 if you could find a buyer. It is hard to separate the true stories from the product of Adolfo's humor. One of their favorite depression time stories was this: Angela had found a place near their rented house in San Pablo, in Camagüey, that would buy used clothes. She started selling relics from Adolfo's past, like formal wear, that she knew he would never miss, but the demand was higher for everyday clothing. On this particular day Adolfo took a nap on the couch and when he sat up he felt for his shoes and they were not there "We are having them for dinner", he was informed.

1932 was also notable for the strongest hurricane in living memory to hit the province. The winds came from the South bringing a tidal wave that destroyed the town of Santa Cruz and washed many of its inhabitants out to sea. My uncle Miguel Agramonte was staying at the oceanfront home of his girlfriend's parents. My mother and grandmother, full of both hope and apprehension, met the trains coming from the south bringing survivors. There were reports of bodies of animals, and humans, snared on the branches of trees miles from the coastline.

Of the many people who had taken refuge in that sturdy two story house only Miguel and his girlfriend's younger sister, both strong swimmers, survived. When the ocean water began to rise they went upstairs, then to the roof, and finally found themselves in the water. He remembers struggling in a sea full of floating debris and dark as night when it really was morning. A few days later when my aunt Zoila had a baby girl, tío Miguel asked her to name the baby Georgina, after his lost girlfriend.

When pieces of ceiling plaster started to fall in their rented house in Calle de San Pablo, Adolfo decided that it was time to get out When the winds suddenly stopped, people ran out on the streets thinking it was all over, when somebody shouted, "it's coming back." It was the strange stillness of the eye of the storm. Adolfo took advantage of the temporary calm and moved the family across the street to the home of their neighbors, the Castillo family.

On the north coast area the ocean water was pushed back in places temporarily exposing sea floor never seen before. In Los Desengaños the wind knocked down the algarrobos, carob trees that were standing alone, unprotected, in the middle of the pasture. The windmill was blown away; the house held but was knocked slightly out of kilter so doors and windows never closed properly again.

The Moratorium law that put a temporary hold on foreclosures of rural properties was passed in the brink of time. Regardless of what else Batista did, he saved our finca and my father's dreams. The whole family never lived there full time again as he had planned but we were able to go back for the summer months while we were in school and a few times we even stayed the whole year. My father spent many, perhaps lonely, nights alone in what we considered our family home. I have lived longer in other places, but every creature must have one place that is imprinted as home. To me that is it.

Soon after the hurricane of 1932 the family moved from the damaged house to another rented house outside of town in an area called Garrido. At the time we moved the house belonged to my aunt Pepilla, but somehow she lost it in a business transaction and the new owner deeded it to a charitable organization, an orphanage named Amparo de la Niñez . The rent went to the orphanage but any repair was up to us, the renters. All childhood memories are centered on either that place where we lived for fourteen years, or Los Desengaños.

To this point my story is based on family oral history, hearsay, a few letters, and some guessing. For the next few years it will be based on my recollections of events, places and people I have known. Since we lived in town the biggest part of the year, it seems logical that I would have more memories of the house in Garrido than Los Desengaños, but that is not the case. In Los Desengaños was where memorable things happened. And parts of what was memorable were the moves from one location and way of life to another.

1938. Taller grass and fatter animals

We are preparing for the move to Los Desengaños even before school is out. I am finishing the first grade at Las Teresianas and Lucy is downstairs in the class the nuns call parvulas which is between kindergarten and first grade. Lucy can read very well now, and, of course, so can I, but she reads aloud, all the time and everywhere. When we go downtown she reads all the store signs aloud, which is alright; but some people like to write ugly words on walls and inside the trolley cars and she reads those also and then wants to know what they mean.

We will be sure to take our books with us but today we are buying something just as important: our country shoes. Getting ready for summer always included a visit to Casa Gorrita.

This leather goods shop is not downtown near other commercial places but in the area known as la Caridad. All of Camagüey is a cattle town but La Caridad is more so. The Avenida de la Caridad is a wide avenue on the East side of the river from the antique core of the City. It has been named Avenida de la Libertad since Independence Day when the Cuban officials exercised their clout and freedom from Spain by renaming everything. That's when the City went from Puerto Principe to Camagüey (a native name) which made sense, since there is no longer a reason to honor a Spanish Prince and it had never been a Port. But the old name of this avenue still lingers since the end wraps around the Plaza de la Caridad and the church of that name, where I was baptized.

The trolley car, our usual form of transportation could drop us right under the connected porches that line the avenue but that would be only after circling the whole city. By walking we can take a much shorter route. We walk mostly in the shade across the Casino Campestre, that combination park and botanical garden that is, or should be, the pride of Camagüey. We pass the Greek facade of the Instituto de Segunda Enseñanza, and there we are, walking on the covered porches not feeling one bit guilty that we are trespassing on what is a part of somebody's home. Everybody does it; why walk in the sun when you can walk in the shade. If somebody happens to be sitting outside, Mami says a few words, and moves on.

We were expected at Casa Gorrita. The owners are personal friends and, besides, Papi does lots of business with them, from saddles to harnesses. This is not the place you would expect to find clothing for two little girls, but we are here for one item only: a pair of strong botines, the rough leather boots that will last through the summer. Actually, they are so strong that when Oli outgrows his, they pass down to me, and mine pass down to Lucy who not only finishes off my outgrown shoes, but has the tips cut off hers when she outgrows them so she can wear them a bit longer without cramping her toes. And looks? That is not an issue. We love them for what they represent: the months of discovery and complete freedom ahead. We grabbed our new botines and headed for home to continue packing.

The day of the move whether it is from Camagüey to La Costa (a name that covers Los Desengaños and other lands near the North Coast) or the return trip, always has to start before daylight. Because I am not used to getting up in the dark, I am still in a dreamy state and that gives the whole endeavor a sense of adventure. We still don't wear our botines and home-made coveralls that will be our uniforms once we are there. We girls usually wear dresses in town when we are not in school uniforms. We are allowed to take a few personal things, like books and games. We don't need much to entertain ourselves, which is good. Space is limited since the final leg on the trip will be on horseback. Everything for the whole family has to fit in two yellow canvas bags.

The first leg is by Model T Ford. In Camagüey this conveyance would not be called an automobile, auto, nor carro as it would in other places more or less sharing our language. Here it was a machine, maquina. This maquina belongs to Papi, but he doesn't drive it. Papi always claims that he can drive but being unable to grasp the steering wheel with his right hand is a problem. Considering that his hand is not a problem for anything else, he probably doesn't drive because he doesn't like to. Since he seldom has need for a car, he has some sort of business arrangement with Faustino Velazquez the only black person close to the family. Faustino makes a living hiring himself and the car, sort of a taxi service, although the passengers usually sit in front with him. The deal is that in the infrequent occasions when we need a car, like a trip to the railroad station with our large cargo, Faustino and the Ford would be there for us.

Papi and Oli sat in front with Faustino. Mami, las niñas, as Lucila and I are collectively called, and Mena, the current mother's helper, sat in the back seat. The two yellow canvas bags were strapped to the outside.

The railroad station is another magic place that we children visit on-ly as part of the move from our city life to our Desengaños life. We were ordered to sit on the shiny mahogany benches that wrapped around the pillars and stay put until it was time to board the train. Running around or any kind of rowdy behavior was not even a possibility. We were too enthralled with expectation for that.

As far as I remember (and that goes for almost anything in this narrative) there were only two train stops on the way to Nuevitas: Altagracia, and Minas. Altagracia is within minutes of Camagüey but we waited until Minas, about half way on the ride, for our breakfast of café con leche and empanadillas. I suspect some people make the trip this far just to eat the meat pastries; they are like nothing else. There are vendors running on both sides of the train and even climb aboard when allowed. Since the empanadillas always taste the same—flaky, but not too flaky; savory, but not too savory, we can assume that they are produced by one talented cook somewhere in that small village. This was the only time and place where Mami allowed us to eat street food, I don't know why, because some people eat nothing else and thrive on it. The train stop was long enough for us to eat the empanadillas sitting at a small table near the train and accompanied by café con leche served in a glass. Why they serve boiling hot milk and coffee in a glass instead of a mug with handle, who knows? I guess that is all they had. They are tricky to hold but the whole breakfast tasted better than anything served at home.

Minas was named for the chrome mines that had been its reason for being but had long ceased operating. Like so much it Cuba, it had been a foreign operation, this time Scandinavian, maybe Swedish. Their legacy is great swimming holes at the sites of the open pits and the tall blondes we see in Minas that don't look like the blondes from northern Spain we see elsewhere.

The approach to Nuevitas is worth the trip. You don't realize that we had been climbing but we were, and then, all of a sudden, there is a cut on the hill, and through it, you see the ocean way down below. For a short distance the train travels inside the white walls of this cut thanks to the engineering and business acumen of my great-grandfather, Pedro. And then, we are at the Nuevitas station, right in town and just a block from the waterfront. Across the street from the station there is a row of warehouses and on the opposite side there is an almost vertical bare chalk hillside where you always see people and goats walking on trails carved like shelves against the wall. They must be going somewhere, so there must be something else just out of sight. My cousin Andresito has an import spice business in the warehouse just across from the station and he lives with his wife and child in the upstairs apartment where they can use the flat rooftops of all the warehouses as their observation platform to watch the trains and the movement of this busiest part of the city. It seemed like a perfect living arrangement but it must not have seemed so to his wife, a sociable young woman from Camagüey— who I hear had been queen of the San Juan festival— because a few years later, they picked up and moved to La Habana.

In my memory, Nuevitas is all white. One squints to look at the city on a hillside and at the glitter of the water in the well protected bay. Not only the exposed hill is white, but the gray cobblestones on the street shine white in the sun. The buildings are painted either white or very light colors which in this light is the same as white. The unpainted wood structures along the waterfront have been bleached white. There are no street trees; except on the Paseo Marti, the long park that serves as a main street. My tía Amelia, the only one of the twelve Sanchez Miranda siblings to stay in their hometown, always says that here you must be careful to always dress in spotless clean clothes because the light is so bright that any dirt will show.

I take a perverse pleasure in claiming Nuevitas as my birthplace after my mother went to so much trouble to have me registered as born in Camagüey. But I know nobody here except for my aunt and her family and probably could not find my way to her house if I found myself more than a couple of blocks away.

Tía Amelia, tío Andres and their two youngest daughters, Elsa and Alicia were waiting for us at their front porch, a worn brick platform that was high above the street on the bay side and level with the street on the uphill side. Hills fascinate me since Camagüey and the ranch are perfectly flat. The old house is at the top of the hill in the corner of Maceo and Maximo Gomez. Maceo is the steep street down to the flat part of town just barely above sea level. Maximo Gomez runs along the crest of the hill; they both bear the names of Cuban patriots of the war of independence. They had other names in my grandparents' days, like Calle de la Reina.

It is not my habit to call the spouses of my aunts and uncles anything but their given names, but tío Andres is the exception because he is family himself. In the Spanish tradition, blood relations are strong bonds, but relations by marriage are not considered family, (unless they are related, which in Camagüey they often are). Tío Andres is the only child of my father's aunt Abisais, therefore, he and tia Amelia are first cousins.

My aunt is always delighted to see us; my cousins less so and have many ways of showing it. Fortunately for them, we didn't stay long and they didn't have to put up the whole family. When my father makes the trip alone, he doesn't stay overnight but takes the afternoon launch to Santa Lucia. If he has to overnight in Nuevitas, his home-away-from-home is the

Acera Marti, a hotel on Paseo Marti. Even with the family on this trip, he stayed at the hotel and took Oli along with him. Nothing gives Papi more pleasure than to show off his only son to his friends. I often wonder what the family would have been like with two boys and I the only girl. Mami, Mena (more about her later) and I, stayed with tía Amelia. Andresito's wife, Ana Rosa, insisted in keeping Lucila. To this day, Lucy recalls what a wonderful treat that was. She may have been trying to make me jealous, because staying under the supervision of Alicia and Elsa is no treat.

It mostly comes down to the water issue. The town of Nuevitas has no water system. The residents are on their own for their water needs which are mostly met by rain water collected in cisterns. There may be wells in some areas, but not where my relatives live. Camagüey has water in abundance and so does Los Desengaños. I am not accustomed to being a water miser. Every time I went near the bathroom it caused a commotion. Why do I remember that when I should only remember tía Amelia reading me stories from wonderful old books, food prepared by the women in the family, not by servants, and the daily trip to Cuatro Vientos?

Quatro Vientos is what was called a balneario. Not a beach in the sense of waves breaking on the sand—what sand there is, was brought from somewhere else, probably from the real beaches just outside the bay. It has in its favor only that it is close to town. We walked down the hill and caught the small bus that makes the rounds from town to the balneario. The highlight of the ride is when we go past the slaughterhouse and can look down on the ocean below. We can see the fins of the sharks moving in the bloody water.

We don't have to worry about sharks: the swimming area is enclosed by closely placed pilings which are toped on two sides by a walkway flanked by dressing rooms, both public and private. I had worn my new swimsuit under my dress, so changing was no problem. The problem came at the end of the day when it was time to go home. I was told that wearing wet bathing suits was not permitted on the bus. I had neglected to bring underpants. My mother and the others in our little group didn't think it was a big deal. I had a dress that covered me down to my knees, but I felt all eyes on me as I walked up the hill holding down the hem of my dress.

Crossing the Bay

The bay of Nuevitas changes character with the time of the day. In the early morning it is at its friendliest and so are the people around the docks. These are not the deep-water docks — those are farther west and away from the city — these are the domain of local fishermen. Some of the boats are already out even at this early hour. The sails are mostly dark and with large patches—none of them white like you see in pictures—and are set at the angle that would catch the lightest of breeze. These fishermen know the wind, the fish, the currents and who knows what else that I would never know. Those are things that you don't learn from any books. There are just one or two men sailing each boat headed for the open water outside the bay where the big fish are. They will have to tack several times to get there but this evening they will sail straight in with the wind and with a load of fish.

A family with small children is a novelty on the dock this time of the day. A man, who apparently lives on his boat, had something to show us: baby caimans. Oli got to hold one and could have kept it if only Mami had said yes. Even I knew that it would not make a good pet.

A passenger launch makes a regular trip from the embarcadero of Santa Lucia to Nuevitas. The schedule is designed to accommodate the people of Santa Lucia who can, very conveniently, take the morning boat to town, take care of business or shopping, and take the afternoon boat back. The problem for us is that Mami gets seasick or, more likely, scared on rough water and the Bay of Nuevitas can get pretty rough in the afternoons. That's why Papi has to arrange for a boat just for us for the trip out. On the way back we will come in the regular passenger boat.

The boat has a big, noisy and smelly gasoline engine in the center and benches almost all around. The fun place to be is where I'm not allowed: the top. We can still enjoy the view from anywhere since the sides are open. As we move farther away, Nuevitas looks more like a flat painting with the streets going straight up to a church that is more impressive from a distance than it is in reality. Looking the other way, one can see a solid green line of vegetation with no apparent opening anywhere. There are several men running around the boat doing things but I don't know who is in charge since nobody ever explains things to me. I knew the sail had gone up when the boat leaned just a little to one side. The engine was turned off and things became very quiet and nice. I had the nerve to ask a sailor (if that's what he was) how he knew where to go, and he explained about the Ballenatos.

There are three small islets in the middle of the Bay that with some imagination may look like whales, ballenas, to someone who has never seen one. The tallest one, in the center, is fifty-four meters above sea level and it is called Ballenato del Medio. To one side is Ballenato Grande, and to the other, Ballenato Chiquito. Sailors use them as landmarks to know which way they are going and how far to go. We are heading for the estuary of Santa Lucia because the Ballenatos are forming one continuous line, with no space in between.

That still doesn't explain how they find the estuary. I try to see the entrance from the distance as I had done in every trip and never see it until we are there. What looks like a green line from the distance are really manglares growing on the water edge. The boat pilot knows where he is going; when it looks like we are heading straight for the solid line of mangroves, the boat slows down, and the engine is on again, not with a roaring sound, but a gentle chug, chug. The sail must be down, although I never saw it. And then all of a sudden, there it is: the greenest and calmest water you will ever see. The mood changes, maybe because Mami is no longer concerned with one of us going overboard. We hang out over the side of the boat; we want to look at the little crabs running up and down the mangrove roots as the water covers and uncovers them with the wake of the boat. On some trips we have passed real close to cargo boats going the other way. Santa Lucia is notable for growing the largest plantains anywhere. They grow other things, but plantains are what they are proud of.

The mangroves disappear and we see the landing on our right and other boats moored on the left. There is a clearing with the general store by itself, on one side, and several other open buildings to the other side. Even before we are helped out of the boat and unto the planks, I can see the group of horses from Los Desengaños. There are no other horses like them in these parts. We like to brag about everything connected with Los Desengaños. We think we have taller grass and fatter animals.

The landing is called LaPlaya even if there is no beach here, and the store is La tienda de la Playa. The store owner is a Spaniard as are most store owners. We think of him, and anybody from northern Spain, as Gallego but we don't know if he is from Galicia. He lives in a couple of rooms behind the store and we have to wonder how did he ever find this place, and what is it like here at night when it is only he and the mosquitoes.

Although the estuary looked like no humans had ever left a mark on it that is only as seen from the water, the only way most of us ever see it. But the higher areas in this labyrinth of waterways is the domain of the carboneros or charcoal makers. A few of them are milling around the landing and in the store. They are also newly arrived Spaniards, but they are not here to stay like the store keeper, so nobody even bothers to learn their names. When they finish their charcoal and make enough money or run out of wood, they will move on. But in the meantime, they are friendly, smile a lot, and they must be good customers to the store because I saw a string on alpargatas hanging from the ceiling. Nobody in the farming community of Santa Lucia wears the rope-soled canvas shoes. The carboneros probably have a charcoal oven nearby. I hear that at least one of them has to stay near the oven, a mountain of wood covered with dirt, day and night to put out any flames by adding more dirt, or they will lose all their work. To do that, they must climb on the oven. I hear the work is very dangerous.

Papi is "tío Adolfo" to thirty-seven nephews and nieces, all born before he was married. Some of them we hardly know but Papi keeps track of all of them. He has a strong sense of family, up to and including second cousins. Some ties are stronger than others; that is the case with Cutin who has been living in Havana since his father died. Now he is about twenty-two or three and studying architecture at the University and seems to like horses as much as buildings. He plans to spend his summer vacation with us, as he has done many summers. He and a man from the ranch brought the horses.

We make a stop at the store where Mami goes to the back room to change to the only pants I have ever seen her wear — some wide legged things — and she only puts them on when she has to ride. It takes a while to get organized and it gives us time for cold drinks, the last ones we will have in months. Then we mount for the long ride. Mami doesn't need any help. She is probably as good a rider as anyone, but doesn't say so. She lets Papi choose a gentle horse for her, and the same for Mena. Cutin also chose a gentle mare called Caricortada because Lucy, whom he calls La Chiquitica, is riding with him. I ride with my father. When we were little, we were carried in front of the rider, but now we ride a la zanca, on the croup of the horse. We can ride alone, but not this time. Not enough gentle horses available. In front you can see better but it is more grown up to be on the back. Oli has a small horse of his own. The man from la finca who I don't know because he is new this year, will lead the mules with the load.

Cutin tells how he arrived a few days before, was sick with the gripe and Elva (wife of the encargado) prepared an herb tea for him and he was cured overnight.

The first stretch of road takes us away from the waterfront on whitish fill dirt brought from elsewhere. There is some water on the sides, and crabs move quickly out of the way of the horses. We come to a place that if we go straight with the road, we will end up in the poblado of Santa Lucia. But we are not going there. I have never been to Santa Lucia. It is a much

36

admired farming community where people from many parts have settled. They are usually known by the name of the country of origin. There is El Aleman, who built the only two story thatch-roof house most people had seen; and Asturias, a regular visitor to Los Desengaños.

We turn right on a less travelled trail and, as we move away from the coast the trees are taller and the dirt underneath is darker. There are a few small farm houses visible at the end of side roads, always with chickens and other fowl near the house. Dogs bark but keep their distance. As we ride on, the farms end and there is only woods for what it seems like forever until we come to where both sides of the road are fenced. On our right is Pancho Perez' finca and on our left, ours. Pancho Perez bought that land from tío Julian. He has worked for my father and they still help each other as needed. His wife Esperanza Perez (that she has his same last name is a coincidence. Wives here don't take the husbands' name) is from a Santa Lucia farming family. They have a bunch of wild boys. Pancho Perez stutters and Oli does a good imitation of it but of course Pancho doesn't know about it or it would hurt his feelings. Pancho cannot make a "k" sound. Sounds like this: e alor, parece e va a llover andela.

If we stayed on this road a little longer and then turned right we would be very close to the water again. There is another boat landing there. It is much closer to us than the one at Santa Lucia, but nobody uses it anymore.

We are entering Los Desengaños by the back door. There are woods on the right and the estancia on the left. Papi says that you must always leave some untouched woods or monte because you never know when you are going to need a palo. If I had my way I would leave it all untouched. The estancia is ours but somebody lives here and is completely in charge. They don't even let our horses go inside the enclosure: we have to go around. The estancia is another one of those arrangements they have in almost every finca. If it wasn't for the estancia, the ranch workers would eat nothing but tasajo rice and beans. Even with the estancia, we never had the kind of fresh vegetables that the Chinese sell in Camagüey, like lettuce and tomatoes. Besides plantains, the estansiero supplies the ranch with yucca, boniatos and other starchy vegetables; in return they have a place to live and land to work. Same as the Santa Lucia farmers, they sell their crops through the Cooperativa. That's all I know. They also come to the batey every morning for free milk.

We are almost there. Not only does every finca have a name, but every fenced pasture within the finca has to be known by some kind of name usually derived from something that is there or something that happened there. The first and largest potrero is La Represa, named for a dam, or what is left of a dam that was one of Papi's engineering projects that didn't work out. It is easy to underestimate the arroyo since it is almost dry most of the year; like now. When we cross it, it is nothing but a depression. Not a drop of water. Next we bypass the potrero de la Vaqueria , where the dairy cows are, by going directly to the corrales through a fenced off corridor we know as el callejon. Here in the main corral is where every animal in Los Desengaños can find water any time of the year thanks to our wonderful well and windmill.

From the corral we ride into the bare dirt yard that surrounds the main house. Just a piece of timber staked to the ground separates the yard from the dirt floor in the large common room. This is mainly the home of the encargado or person in charge, Manolo Pelaez and his family, but the main open room, not the enclosed area, is shared with everybody. We walk around this house and through a fenced off chicken yard. Chickens and other fowl are everywhere, but this is where they belong. There are also two small buildings and many fruit trees in this yard. On the other side of the second fence is our house. From this side, and with all the wood shutters closed, the house looks like a blank, grey wall floating at eye level above the ground. All the other buildings in the batey sit right on the ground with either packed dirt or a cement floor, but this one is built on pilings or en pilotaje. We always get the question "Were you expecting the water to rise?" Sometimes we say that it is to keep the pigs out— pigs unlike dogs, cannot climb steps. But that is not a good argument either since the batey is usually out of bound to pigs.

Our house is like no other house since Papi just made a few straight lines on a piece of paper and told a carpenter "Here, build this". He may have liked the feeling of being high off the ground and a two story house would have been too expensive and beyond the expertise of his carpenters. Whatever the reason for that type of construction, it created a perfect play world for children under the house: any adult venturing in this underworld will soon end with a sore back or a bump on the head. We had our own area, same dimensions as the house above but with dirt floor below and wood above, and there we worked on our miniature ranch. Children of truckers play with toy trucks and children of doctors examine dolls, we built a ranch complete with fences and water tanks. The animals were bottles and we know exactly what kind of animal by the kind of bottle. The small round vaccine bottles are calves, there were many of those and we will have more after the beneficeo; we only have found two of the large clay canecas and they are the bulls. The other bottles we dug out of the dump in the recogedor. We are not sure who drank these things, but we know what they were because some had labels; the rounded belly one that we used as cows were from Maltina and the flat ones, our horses, originally contained a syrupy concoctions that we had heard advertised for the promotion of good health.

The underside of the house is also the place where things that nobody wants are dragged to and never looked at again. There are parts of the old cast iron stove and pieces of pipes. Those keep forever, but wooden things like crates are already half eaten by termites. Termites don't eat the posts that hold the house up because they don't like that kind of wood but they are already nibbling on the floor boards above.

That is also the place where Guarina had puppies last year. I was sick at the time with Malaria, which makes you sick only in the afternoon, and was in bed one day when Oli brought me one of the very new puppies to keep me company. I had it hidden under the sheet but Guarina had no trouble finding it and took it back to her hiding place under the house. We had to wait until they were a little older to play with them.

As can be expected in a place built on the site of old ruins there are bricks in abundance. They were used for the ill-fated dam; they were used for the steps going up to the porch and they line a path from those steps to what was meant to be the front gate but is never used as such since our rare visitors usually leave the horses at the batey and walk over.

The roof is thatch in the center and corrugated metal on the porches. The house itself is all wood with the most straight-forward room distribution imaginable: there are three bedrooms—one huge, and two smaller, a small living room and a larger dining room. Since there is no hallway, the bathroom, a regular source of conflict, opens to two bedrooms (Who left this door locked!). When we were little, we all slept in the largest room, all five of us. Now that is our parent's bedroom and Papi's office—just a table in a corner. The other room with access to the bathroom is where Oli and, now, Cutin sleep. All sorts of things are also stored there, mostly under the beds. Lucy and I have the room that everybody walks through. It is very public with two doors, one to the living room and the other to our parents' room, and a large walk-through window that is used more than the doors.

A wide porch wraps around three sides of the house and, with all the windows open and used as doors, the porch takes the place of the missing hallway. At one end there is a room for whoever Mami brings as a helper, and at the other end, but not accessible from the porch, unless you climb through a high window, is the kitchen. There are wood stairs down from the kitchen to the other side of the house. The house has a wonderful unfinished feeling, because it was never finished. All the lumber is exposed; nothing is painted. There are no glass windows; no screens. The room partitions stop half way up and the outside walls don't meet the metal roof so there is enough room for creatures to fly or crawl in. They can and they do. One time that Oli stayed sick in bed with nobody else in the house for many hours, we returned feeling guilty for having left him alone, and he said, "I was not alone," and pointed to a minute owl, the kind we called tu-cu-tu (for their call) that had found a perch on the partition right in front of his bed and had stared at him all day.

The building has no useless ceilings. I especially enjoy looking up at the complex structure of support beams, and, beyond them, the dark recesses topped by the underside of the stems of the palm fronds that make up the roof. Before falling asleep at night, and while there is still some candle light moving about the house, I like to imagine myself walking around on those round beams like a circus performer.

Cutin had the house open for several days before we came, so we were spared the surprises we usually find when we reopen the house. We know that when we are not here, the rats take over. One time we found a trail of toilet paper from the bathroom to Oli's room, and there under the bed there was this neat white nest with baby rats. I never knew what was done with them and knew better than to ask. Another time, rats removed or chewed up the labels from the cans that were left on a shelf in the dining area. For a while the cook didn't know if she was opening canned peaches or pork and beans.

Lucy and I are expected to do a little more housework here than we do in Camagüey. Mainly sweep the wood floors, and run errands between the houses, which we like. Oli goes everywhere with Papi. But not today. Our first day back we stay around the batey getting re-acquainted. Several years ago when Manolo had just moved here with his wife Elva, Lucy went over to introduce herself and the rest of the family. She told them that she was known as la chiquitica malita, the mischievous little one and I was la princesa llorona, the crying princess. It was cute to everybody but to me. Every time they bring it up I almost cry.

Now Elva and Manolo have a boy, Manolito. Elva is the only fat person I know and Manolito is a little fat also, but we like him as he is and call him cachete because of his chubby cheeks. Elva is a good friend to my mother but she and her family will be leaving soon. It will be a big change. She has inherited some property so they will live and work at their own place. There are few workers at a finca like this and they are usually close like a family so next time we come everyone will be new. Except for Dario. He is not related to anybody here and doesn't even know his parents or how he got his blue eyes and kinky black hair. He came from an orphanage in Camagüey and his only loyalty is to Papi. He likes to read and he is an artist. Two of his works are permanently displayed at our house: a tiger, and a blond girl we think looks like the daughter of el aleman. He and Cutin are buddies. Cutin told me that he and Dario entered in a horse race in Santa Lucia— something tío Adolfo would not have approved. Cutin won with a horse named la Peluita. Papi at one time raced his horses at the track in Camagüey, before the fad for tall English race horses, and he still has some of the best, but here he doesn't like to mix work with games.

Mami is very different here; she has to be. In Camagüey, if somebody is hurt, you call a doctor, or if it is serious, you go to the emergency hospital or the Clinica Agramonte. Here, Mami is the doctor. She has a drawer full of strips of fabric from old bed sheets that can be sterilized by ironing them with an iron made hot enough over a charcoal fire — That's the only use of the iron because our clothes are not washed or ironed here but taken somewhere else— Last year Dario had a machete cut across his shin and had to sit across from Mami every day at her post in front of the large dining room window while she examined the cut and changed bandages. That was a common kind of accidents for people that use machetes and don't know how. We children never touch the whole machetes; for our projects we use the handle half of the broken ones. The other half is used for shoe scrapers. Guajiros can do anything with a machete from sharpening a pencil to preparing a green coconut for drinking its water. They never go anywhere without a good sharp machete.

El Ingenio

Siesta time is almost sacred for adults, but not for us. This is the best time of the day to visit the ingenio. In the middle of the afternoon you can feel not so much the heat as the stillness. It is almost like the world has come to a stop. The adults that are not out for the day are indoors at siesta. Even the animals are napping. Under every tree there is a small gathering, horses on their feet, cattle, down, their eyes closed, moving only their jaws and pigs undistinguishable from their bed of mud. Human children are the only creatures not affected by the midday lethargy. If Oli were here he would think of something to do. He is always building something and we help him, but he has gone to La Gertrudis with Papi. Papi's land is in two parts with tío Ernesto's finca in between. La Gertrudis is by far the larger and there is more going on over there, so Papi leaves in the morning most days and comes back with the last light of the day.

We are free to do almost anything, as long as we do it quietly. All Manolito has to say is "Let's go to the ingenio", and we are on our way. There is only one way to go without running into cattle that have the gate open to the corral, and to drinking water. We go through the casa de vaqueria, a large open building where they milk cows in the mornings and at other times it is used for anything they want done to animals. We stop in the back enclosure to pet a few new born calves. They are soft and silky and unimpressed with our presence. We cross a couple of fences and we are in the potrero del ingenio. Adult cattle are never in this pasture. One reason is right by the path we are taking: wild onion. I hear the flavor gets in the milk and you can even taste it in the cheese made from that milk. This pasture is where calves spend the afternoon and evening separated from their mothers. A group of curious ones follow us from a distance; when we stop, they stop, but never get any closer. We start again, and they move again.

We can already see one of the towers. Most visitors come to see the towers (which are really chimneys), or to eat anoncillos from the trees that have grown around the towers, or just to see the parrots that feed on the anoncillos. But that is not what keeps bringing us back. What we are interested in are the tunnels.

The path takes us right to the first and tallest tower. They are both completely different. The base of the farthest tower is like a little room. You can go in and look all the way up, but always looking out for wasps. This one is divided in two and the openings at the bottom are no larger than a home fireplace. We stop there just long enough to see if the owl is still there. It is. It looks down on us as we examine some of the newer "eggs." I don't know what else to call them: they are about the size and shape of guinea hen eggs and each "egg" has the remains of a meal, a mouse complete with head bone. All crushed, digested and compacted. Still attached to that tower is a wall that has been kept upright by the roots of a tree growing flat on its side. Aside from the towers and a small roofless room attached to the second tower, that's the only wall left standing. There are several tall posts, blackened by fire, left at odd angles here and there and chunks of bricks everywhere. There is a square well head a few steps to the right, fenced off for safety. That's all you see. Where are the tunnels?

The entrances to some of the tunnels are not hidden; the reason more people haven't found them is that there is no reason to go there. If you are going from the first tower to the second, you go on a level path to the left, not in the depression to the right, full of grass and rubble. But that's where we go. You do have to crawl for a moment to go in, but once inside, even adults could walk around without bending. There is a row of tunnels here, but the last one we found was going in a different direction. Oli was walking around one day and discovered a loose brick under the tall grass. He lifted it and instead of a dark hole, there was light underneath. We all looked around until we found the entrance to this new tunnel going off in a different direction. Funny how dirt builds up, grass and trees grow where once there was something, until there is nothing there anymore. Just a few markers, here and there like the towers, as a reminder of what was.

*

There is a reason I chose to describe Los Desengaños as it was in the summer of 1938 as the point of reference to use for the changes to come. The reason is a photograph. It must have been taken with Cutin's camera, although he is in the group picture. There are not many photos of that time since Papi's old accordion-type camera had ceased to work before my days and it was only kept as a relic of days past. The one photo dated 1938 shows the largest group of cousins ever assembled outside of a wedding or a funeral. Besides the five of us and Cutin, there are four of tío Ernesto's six grown children and their mother; the future husband of one of them (who is related to my mother) and the two women cousins from Nuevitas, who must have been visiting with them at La Amelia. In the back with Papi and two nephews is Pedro Gallo, from neighboring La Rosalia —the only one wearing a hat which marks him as a genuine guajiro— and, being carried on a pole, Pedro Gallo's masterpiece: a perfectly roasted pig. The pig dates the photograph to 2nd of August. The one date when a pig was always roasted in Los Desengaños to celebrate the day of Our Lady of the Angels, the Saint's day of Angelas. As far as I know there is no Santa Angela. On rare pious days at Las Teresianas I thought of trying for it, but my religious convictions were shaky at best.

Nothing like a photograph to keep a story teller honest. I always say that we only wore overalls and botines at the finca. That's what Oli is wearing in the photo, but Lucy and I are in dresses and with huge bows on our heads. It was all in Mami's honor, but she sits to one side and almost out of the picture.

It was around the time of that photo that Oli conducted an experiment that almost cost him his life. In town, dinner was at seven, no exceptions, but in Los Desengaños dinner was whenever Papi came home, and that depended. Work at the ranch is not always routine. Papi with the help of a few men were always moving cattle from here to there or there to here until it was too dark to see what they were doing and then they headed for the batey, and let the poor cows settle for the night. He had spent the day in Las Gertrudis as often happened since most of the cattle were there. If the family had been in town Papi would have supper and spend the night in Las Gertrudis and resume work tomorrow. But since we are here, and Oli is with him, he would be coming home for the evening. They had ridden out right after breakfast and we were not expecting them back as long as there was daylight left. Late afternoon was the best time of the summer day for work or play and we make good use of it.

That afternoon, all of us left behind had already bathed and changed and were more or less gathered in the large open room of the house we simply call la otra casa. Elva had already done all advance dinner preparation and was sitting with Mami. Mena, whose job was to do the cooking and other things, like sit with Mami and listen to radio novelas, had already set the table at our own house and prepared everything for dinner except fried tasajo and bananas which she will do while the men showered. After dinner she would go to la otra casa and flirt with the two single men.

We were not expecting the riders for a while and were surprised when the dogs jumped up with wagging tails and barking joyfully. They knew the horses well. But what we saw was different from the usual. Instead of riding side by side engaged in the cheerful talk usual in the cool of the late afternoon that follows a hot work day, Papi was in front in his big palomino named Rubi, and he was guiding Oli's horse. Oli was just hanging on and bundled up in Papi's big olive rain cape, even if there was no sign of rain. He was looking down under his straw hat and holding to the saddle with both hands. Not a word from anybody. In a moment we all ran to the horses. Lucy and I opening the gate, Manolito, the cook, the dogs... a man that had been walking back from the shower ran with a towel still draped on his shoulder and his hair wet. He held the horses. Papi said just two words, "piñon lechero." and dismounted. Then everybody started talking. I had no idea what it was all about. Oli made no move to dismount until Papi went to help him, and then he smoothly slid down till his feet touched the ground. Papi could easily have carried him but he just put his arm around Oli's shoulder and guided him. As they passed close to me Oli gave me a weak little smile and said, "China, it's nothing." He smelled of vomit.

Of course, Mami, our self-appointed doctor, took over. She always seemed to know what to do or at least acted like she did which was enough to make everyone feel better. When there are no professional medics within reach you don't question the credentials of the person willing to take charge in an emergency. She treats anything from rashes to poisoning with equal confidence.

I don't know what she gave Oli that night. He probably would have survived regardless since he had already thrown up everything he had in him and had already received some unknown treatment at La Gertrudis. Dinner that night was a hurried affair with only Lucy and me at the round table, and no fried plantains. Our parents were taking turns at Oli's side. I think they stayed with him all night. Half asleep I heard movement around the bare wood floors and saw the flickering of lamps been carried about. But, although a little scared I slept. Nothing really bad happens here. By break-fast it was all back to normal. The five of us around the table; bowls of corn flakes on the tablecloth, a pitcher with newly separated and very thick cream. . . .

Oli was a little paler, but nothing striking, and he was his usual hap-py self. He wanted to tell me and Lucy the whole story — our parents obviously knew it already, but he was stopped again and again. We children were discouraged from having long conversations at the table. We were there just to eat and the cook was always waiting to clear the dishes and go do whatever she did with the rest of her time. What I heard only made me more curious. Oli, with great pride, "Mello was just as sick as I was." Why was he glad that his friend was sick? And then, "Now we know that piñon lechero doesn't kill. Papi. "Don't be so sure, if we hadn't. . ." Mami, "Not at the table." Not until we left the table and sat on the porch did I find out why Oli had purposely eaten something that is supposed to kill.

The encargado of Las Gertrudis is a man named Jose Maria Alonzo, who has a large family including Ermelio, a boy about Oli's age whom we knew as Mello. Last year Mello had spent the school year in town with us, an experiment that was not entirely successful and was not repeated this year. The idea was that since they were best friends here they could continue the friendship in town. Here their activities were close to the land, animals and plants. On that they were on equal footing; if anything, Mello was the most knowledgeable. In town there was too much difference in their schooling; they were not in the same class, not even in the same school. But when June came and everyone was back where they belonged, Oli and Mello are again a good pair.

That day after lunch, Papi and Jose Maria stayed at the table talking ranch business. Nobody was going to ride out again that afternoon; if they were, Oli would have followed his father. Instead, he joined Mello and his younger brothers and sisters and went for an aimless walk. On the side of the path they were following, nuts fallen from a tree were scattered on the ground. Oli wondered if they could be edible. He was getting ready to eat one when Mello told him that if he ate one, he must eat another one. One was poison, two were not. Oli argued that if one was poison, two would be even more poisonous. Since Ermelio and his siblings lived there full time, they felt that they could teach Oli a few things, This time they tried to convince him that those nuts, from a tree called piñon lechero could be eaten safely only if you ate an even number. If you ate odd numbers it would kill you.

Ours was a family firmly rooted in scientific facts. We discussed and questioned everything. Oli set out to disprove this ridiculous theory and teach the other children a lesson. "Just because everybody says something, you don't have to believe it."

We never did find out how many piñones were eaten by which team. Apparently it took a while for the effect to take place, because they went on eating with the younger children cheering them on. The adults at the ranch house didn't know what was happening until a little girl ran up announcing "Oli and Mello are going to die." Apparently they had lost count and didn't know if they had eaten even or odd number of nuts. But, if anybody is interested, we now know that par or none, it doesn't matter. Everyone was equally sick.

Visitors

We had few visitors, but some of those tended to stay a long time. Another cousin from Habana, Walter, visited several times, once staying for about a year. He was just a year older than Cutin, but not a student. He is half English; I suppose he was trying to decide what to do with his life. He also found a friend in Dario who introduced both of them to the community of Santa Lucia. Life in Los Desengaños would have been impossibly lonely for city young men without him. Dario was himself still in the process of adjusting.

Visitors who stayed just for one meal and one night's rest were the guardia jurados also known simply as the pareja, and Tecla, the Sirian travelling saleswoman. The only restriction Papi put on those visitors was that they leave their horses in a pasture next to the batey, el recogedor. Ranchers lived in fear of the spread of an invasive plant known as marabou for its beautiful fluffy pink flowers. Horses that have been who knows where will carry the seeds to our pastures. So, whether it was the soldiers' tall army horses or Tecla's short pack horses, they stayed segregated from ours. The pair of uniformed soldiers was always welcomed. In their quiet way they kept an eye on things. Cutin tells that the first time they met, somewhere near San Miguel, they recognized his horse as being "one of don Adolfo's." He had no trouble explaining himself since they had already heard that there was a nephew visiting from la Habana.

And thanks to Tecla one could live here without ever going near a store. Tecla rode on top of the load on one horse and led the other. Everybody helped in unloading the containers from the horses, but only Tecla opened and displayed their contents. Most of the items were by order, so we knew who, down the road, was getting a new shirt. I thought she was an old woman, but maybe she wasn't. She had blondish hair rolled into a knot, a thin face, bad teeth, and smoked. She wore men's trousers and a skirt on top of them. And she was constantly writing in her little book: taking orders; keeping track of what was owed…Besides ready to wear clothes, she sold fabric, threads, and buttons to women who chose to make her own. Perfume, scissors… you name it, and it was in one of those cases. She may have to ride all day to visit maybe five households, but obviously she managed to make a living.

I don't want to clutter my narrative with too many characters, many of whom just walked in and out of our lives. Everyone was important in their own way, but some will, out of necessity, be left out. Take our criadas: in earlier days they hardly qualified as servants since they were paid next to nothing but still some were a big help to my mother. Here it is unthinkable that a woman could take care of children and do housework too. There is always a young relative or daughter of a friend, willing to live in and help. Mami had quite a collection: from Emilia, the daughter of a ranch worker who went with us to Camagüey mainly to go to school and see the outside world. She didn't do much more than play with us. There was Manuela, part oriental, who taught herself to be a great cook. Almost every evening she would announce a plato sorpresa. We looked forward to her meals but she was soon married and snatched away. And there was Mena. She was sent to us from the orphanage Amparo de la Niñez when she turned eighteen. Her father had been a peon de ganado, sort of a free-lance cowboy a profession found in towns like Camagüey, surrounded by cattle ranches. They own their horse and saddle and can be hired for short jobs, like a cattle drive through town to the rail yard. Mena's father had been known for jumping from horse to train, and back. Maybe as a result of that or some other stunt, he died young. I also heard that he died of tuberculosis. Mena's mother was very much alive, but she had remarried, had younger children, and had no use for Mena.

Mena must be very attractive to men because she finds a boyfriend wherever we go, even if we are there for just a few days. She is not attractive to us children: for one thing, she is mean to my cat Figaro, a pet that stays with the caretaker in our house in Camagüey. We also have an Airdale that never comes with us, Mami always had hangers-on willing to look after the house and pets. Mena has lived with us longer than most but to me she is not part of the family. I think Mami likes Mena, but not as a friend like Elva. Mena is a compulsive liar; she can't help herself. Mami and Elva laugh together and compare Mena's latest tales when she is not around like the time she told Elva that Mami has false teeth. The social rules are different in Los Desengaños than in Camagüey. In Los Desengaños Mena, or any criada we happened to have with us, sit with Mami in the living room in the afternoon to listen to soap operas on the radio. In Camagüey criadas just bring her coffee and leave.

There is someone else from those days that I must mention: Carlos Cazola Peña. There is a reason to remember his name so well, even to his second surname, when I hardly remember his face and so many others have been forgotten. Carlos couldn't read or write; he wasn't interested in learning either. He wasn't going to waste time learning the alphabet or reciting the cartilla (the indispensable little book of the home-schooled) He just wanted to sign his name. Papi always paid with checks and maybe Carlos didn't trust anybody else to sign for him. Whatever the reason, teaching him was a group project. He filled pages in a copybook with just his name. Whoever was around, including the children, instructed and corrected him, but he particularly liked Mena guiding his hand. Carlos used to go visit a girlfriend somewhere and ride back at night. Riding back in pitch darkness, he gave himself courage by singing as loud as he could. In the silence of the night, we could hear him while he was still in the camino real, finding his way home on the public road that was no more than a couple of parallel ruts made by carretas or by two riders riding side by side.

Late in the summer Cutin left to go back to the University. Papi also was gone for about a week. He has to work so hard because his ranch is not all in one place. Here he has to ride an hour just to get to La Gertrudis and once there he rides all day before heading back. On top of that he has to do business in Camagüey and take care of El Destino, even farther South. I always see him with his well-worn alforjas, or saddlebags over his shoulder where he keeps underwear and a bottle of quinine capsules. When he came back he brought the vaccines so they can finish the beneficeo before the rains start.

Papi works all the time and Mami doesn't work at all. But she is the only person around here who walks. She could have asked for a horse but it would not be the same. Maybe because it would take planning or maybe it was just more fun this way. We only rode horses when we went with Papi. With Mami, we walked. If we feigned tiredness she would just say "Get a horse." We found a suitable stick and galloped away full of energy again. She can walk all the way to the estancia with us in tow. There she does what she loves most: give advice. She is the expert on anything that has to do with babies: clean baby bottles; cure rashes… The family at the estancia has a girl about my age with the strange name of Maria Las Puyas, or just Puyas for short, and several younger boys. The mother is a pathetic figure; so mosquito bitten that she looks mangy and she doesn't know how to do anything. Mami tries to help her. Everybody in that family has rashes and runny noses. You would think that with a sister almost my age I would not need another playmate, but I like to be with Puyas. She and her brothers can tell some funny stories. One day Mami finally let me spend the day there and when they took me back home in the evening Mami went through my hair looking for lice. She said she found one.

Mami also likes to visit the fruit trees she had planted earlier and look for ripening fruit. She has several kinds of mangoes, caimito, red and yellow mamey, ciruelas, and many others. She eats more fruit than anyone. The only fruit I like is guayaba and those were not planted by anyone. They grow mostly in the area we call El Guayabal. Everybody loves guavas, from horses to birds. I also like jobos, or pretend to like them just to be different, because nobody else does. There are the small, yellow fruit from trees that are so tall and straight that you can't climb them. You have to compete with the pigs to pick the fruit off the ground.

Next to visiting the ingenio our favorite thing to do is climb on the algarrobas. Many carob trees fell down during the 1932 hurricane. About ten of them stayed alive and kept growing but now with a horizontal trunk and some of the roots up in the air, sometimes with one long one pointing toward the sky like a finger. There must be enough roots still in the ground to keep the tree alive and healthy. It was clear which way the wind had blown since all the downed trees were arranged in the same direction: with the tops toward our left when looking from the house. They could have been cut after the storm and made into firewood or charcoal, but, maybe because there were more urgent tasks at the time, they were left where they fell. A brilliant decision to do nothing.

Most of those trees are within sight of the house. The only perils we face when walking through the tall grass to reach them are cows and ticks. Grownups can walk through the pastures and cows don't even look up, but they like to chase little people, and dogs. As for the ticks, there is not much you can do until you take your clothes off in the evening when they have had time to attach themselves. Sometimes you touch a branch or a blade of grass full of tiny newly hatched ticks and they climb on you and you don't even see them. Papi says that one of the favorite places for the ticks to attach themselves was around the waist because he wore a belt; they climbed up the legs and when they reach the belt they can't go any further. Since we didn't wear belts and we played in the grass, we could find them anywhere on the body. You feel around with your finger and if it can be moved back and forth as on a hinge, it is a tick and not a scab.

The canopy of the downed trees is lower to the ground than regular trees so the cows can reach up and eat the tasty seed pods. Some branches drag on the ground where pigs can rub against them. Even the large branches, that in normal trees are so difficult to reach, here are accessible to less than intrepid tree-climbers like me. Each tree has a different character. It takes different level of skill to climb to where the branches divide from the main trunk. One thing they all had in common was the large black ants we call muerde huye, because they bite and run, don't hang on like other ants. You always have to be on the lookout for them because they drop on you from the higher branches. We like to pretend that the trees are houses and each branch is a room. I like playing house best; sit on a branch and make up stories about the people that live in that house/tree. Lucy likes to compete to see who can run down the hump from the branches to the tree truck. Not crawling, but on our feet. She always wins.

That was the summer when I broke my right elbow by falling off the porch. I managed to turn that minor setback into a major watershed in my life. This is my version of how it happened. Lucy's is considerably different. The deep porch on three sides of the house was probably larger than the house itself and certainly more used. That it never had a railing was not thought of as being a hazard. On the contrary; it made it very convenient to be able to jump off from anywhere and Oli can even pull himself up. I will call the side toward the pastures the North side because the ocean is that way, but then, I remember the morning sun on that side, so, let's say northeast. That is where the five of us sit in the dark every evening. The adults sit on the two rockers that are permanently on that side; the rest of us may bring more seats from the other, longer side, sit on the hammock that is always tied between the two corner posts, or sit on the floor. You'd think that there is enough floor space for all, but that fateful evening, two sisters wanted the same spot, so they could lean on a post. I ended up brusquely on my side on the ground below. It was only a four or five foot drop and I had jumped there many times before, but this time I was caught by surprise, had no time to react, and hit my elbow hard.

I don't think of myself as a wimp, on the contrary, I dream of doing glorious deeds— pulling people out of burning buildings, that type of thing — but I do have a way of shedding tears. Not wailing, just crying quietly. Papi can tell me to cry, and I cry on cue. What he doesn't know is that it hurts my feelings that he would ask me to do such thing, and that makes me cry. This time there was a reason; as it turned out, I had fractured my elbow, but it wasn't obvious. It was a lengthwise break. I didn't stop crying for days. We couldn't leave yet since there was much work going on so everybody tried to make it better. Of course, there was no ice. Papi was all for massage, which made it worse. The pain didn't stop until we finally went back to Camagüey and my skinny arm was wrapped in a plaster cast from fingertips to shoulder.

I played my injury for all its worth. Since I am right handed and pretty helpless with my left hand, I stayed home from school much longer than it would seem necessary. My parents didn't object since not much importance was placed on our education. When the plaster cast was finally removed from my arm and I tried going back to Las Teresianas, the nuns decided that I had missed too much school and couldn't catch up with my classmates. Considering the antagonistic relationship they have with my parents, they are not about to do us any favors. People that like the nuns refer to them as Madres Teresianas. At home they are Monjas Teresianas. I was taken out of school again, tutored at home, attended Pinson, a co-ed school in la Zambrana, walking distance from our home in Garrido, for just a few days, and spent days at home doing nothing. That's how, when I entered the third grade in Las Teresianas at the beginning of the next school year, I ended up in the same class with my little sister. Nobody can take us for twins; but we both live with the same challenge; always trying to be treated as a whole person instead of half of a pair. That was even harder to do now that we were in the same class.

The nuns in Las Teresianas are obsessed with neat rows, be it desks, pencils or girls. Before and after classes, every time we go anywhere or any time they feel like it, we have to form a line. We can't just form a line any which way; it has to be strictly by height, shortest one first. The smallest girl in the class proudly walks to the front (I almost said "runs" which is never allowed) and stands patiently while the others assemble behind her. Since I am older than most and tall for my age, I am always the tallest and therefore the last in line. How I wished that just once, someone would walk behind me.

1943. Two places called home. Camaguey and La Finca

Several times we tried spending most of the year at Los Desengaños, not just the school breaks. After all, Mami had a career in education before she married, so she should have no trouble teaching her own children. We brought our school books and tried turning the dining room into a class-room. The house has no glass windows and the large wood shutters that take almost the whole outside wall of the room had to be left open or we were in the dark. That gave us a front-seat view of the whole batey, pigs, dogs, horses and even the animals in the corral. The distractions were unbearable. Oli would say "there goes Manolo, wonder where he is going?" and we all got up to take a look. As much as Papi wanted us with him, it just didn't work if we were to be schooled.

So home to us had to be alternated between Los Desengaños and the rented house in Camagüey where we lived during the school year. The address in Camagüey is Calle 3 numero 256, Garrido. I know the exact address only because it is printed on the top left corner on my father's stationary which he used long after we moved from that house. It sounds like a street address, but in reality the house is in the middle of a marabou wasteland.

The builder or promoter of the few houses built here and there in what was supposed to be a suburban neighborhood of Camagüey was ahead of its time. Camagüeyanos were not ready for suburban living. But for us, it was perfect. Papi could keep a horse in the horse barn in the back and ride it to El Destino without going through town.

Another convenience of the location is the tranvia or trolley car that stops right at our door. Papi takes the tranvia to go into town to the club Liceo where he plays dominoes and gripes with other cattlemen about the weather and government price restrictions. At one point he changed his in town attire from white drill suit, black bow tie and flat brimmed straw hat to guayabera, with no tie or hat. He also put away permanently his baston since he never needed it and it is no longer in fashion.

What was meant to be a street is a washed-out gully, which doesn't matter since we don't have a car, but we have that wonderful tranvia, and the rails to test our balancing skills. Half a block away there is the paved street Cornelio Porro with a clinic (where Oli was born and where young women have their appendix out because it is in vogue) and a tiny café across the street, known simply as the Kiosko de Manolo. That is important because when Papi has to come to town while we are at the ranch, he eats there. And when we arrive in town and there is no food or cook in the house, we eat there. Or rather, they bring the food to us, carrying several platters in a parade down the trolley rail track.

We have neighbors across what passes for a street, but no houses on either side or behind us. The house has iron bars on the windows as most houses do, but since my father is away most of the time and my mother never became used to being alone (children and a teenage servant don't count), she inspects door locks every evening including the metal bar across the back door. We don't know if she is afraid of burglars — the inherited silver has already disappeared—or of kidnappers. Papi, of course, kids her about it. He says that since the Lindbergh baby's crime every mother guards her children as if they were worth ransom.

If we have to live in town, Garrido is not a bad alternative to Los Desengaños. We don't need a park. There is an old unused cemented tennis court where we learned to roller skate and a cleared area good for flying kites. And the best thing of all, good playmates, many of them children of my parent's friends. We are permitted to visit and play at their homes after school and on weekends, as long as we are at the dinner table at seven o'clock sharp.

I have no idea at what point the family fortunes changed. The house in Garrido was cheap and our way of life didn't seem to change. During the lean years when my father was trying to build a cattle ranch with borrowed money and that combined with the Great Depression which had hit Cuba hard my mother embraced frugality with passion and it became a way of life. We children knew better than to expect any non-essentials. Every sliver of soap was saved; no pencil was too small. She was always after the criadas who she thought were wasteful. But now small luxuries were not out of sight: we were taken to the movies to see Snow White, and regularly bought Gorrion and Rataplan (weekly comics); Papi subscribed to The New York Times and the Saturday Evening Post; Mami bought Vanidades.

The moves back and forth between Camagüey and Los Desengaños continued to be an adventure. The one time we tried to go the land route on the Ford we made it thanks to Faustino's ingenuity but it wasn't easy. Papi had made this trip on horseback several times and this was the route taken by cattle drives, but a wheeled vehicle other than an ox cart had a challenge even in the dry season when the river beds were dry. Several times we stood around our little car while Papi and Faustino deliberated as to what to do next. The best route was not on public roads, but through several private ranches, so we had to open many gates and pay many short visits. Faustino didn't wait around for the rainy season. He retraced his route immediately and, when we returned, we did it the usual way: crossing the bay. It would be years before we went by land again.

We have all new people in Los Desengaños now. It has taken a while to find a new encargado. This is not just an employee. He and Papi have to work very closely; almost read each other's mind. Miguel even has the same last name, Sanchez, but we are not related, as far as we know. I don't know how Papi found him or who recommended him. Miguel came from the cattle country of Sibanicu, to the South, and brought with him his two brothers, because he also needed people he could trust. He has a wife named Coral, and a two year old son, Miguelito. Coral may have been the reason he was willing to move, because her family is from San Miguel, an hour's ride from here. Later Coral's three brothers came to work with us also.

Joseito Cuesta is a different story. He is not related to the others and he had no experience with cattle. He grew up in the farming community of Santa Lucia and was destined to be a farmer and a carretero like his father, whom we knew as Asturias. There is a carreta and at least one team of oxen in Los Desengaños, but not an experienced carretero. When Papi needs a hauling job, he goes for help to the farmers in Santa Lucia who help as neighbors and as a source of extra income. Asturias came often with his own carreta and brought as his helper his younger son, Silverio. They both had the looks typical of the region in Northwest Spain where, as the name indicates, they originated. Silverio was playful and a great storyteller, although, I suspect, he didn't take his work as seriously as his father would have liked.

Just one time, Asturias brought his older son, Joseito, as his helper. Joseito was a teenager like us but he already had all the schooling he would ever have and was expected to act as an adult. Asturias must have counted on Joseito to carry on with his work, just as Papi counted on Oli, but it was not to be. While Joseito worked with his oxen for several days at the ranch, he had time to look around and liked what he saw: the white cattle, the green pastures, and the horses. Papi had the firm belief that food should not be wasted in any but the best animals and at Los Desengaños, from the chickens to the bulls, they were the best available. One day, Joseito walked over to don Adolfo and told him quietly, "I want to stay here."

It is customary for the encargado to have the final say on hiring. There is a good reason for that. This is not the kind of workplace where a worker does his job and goes home at the end of the day. Aside from the encargado and his family, there are no more than two or three men working and living here. They eat together, sit around together in the evenings, and divide the work amongst them. Saying that they are a family is not enough. They are much closer than most families.

Our larger ranches, Las Gertrudis and El Destino, are more typical cattle ranches. In the province of Camagüey most ranches keep at least a few barnyard animals and may milk a few cows for local consumption, but Los Desengaños is more a combination cattle and dairy farm. We also have pigs and chickens. All that as a result of the original plan for the family to live here full time. The dairy part in particular, involves lots of work. Papi claims that the monthly check he gets for selling the cream to Guarina, a factory in Camagüey that makes cheese, butter and other dairy products (and belongs to a relative), is the one income he can count on. He may have used those arguments in convincing Miguel that a farmer like Joseito was a perfect fit. It was, and it didn't take long for all of us to wonder how we ever managed without him.

Echoes from a distant war

We didn't need the constant reminders on the radio that there was a World War on, The Camagüey airport had been taken over by the U.S. Air force and there were men in uniform highly visible around town. Some of the young women, just a few years older than I, had certainly taken notice. The local young men didn't seem to resent the competition; the war propaganda was so strong that at least one local man that I know of went away and enlisted to fight in a war that only indirectly touched us. Everybody was trying to learn English. If there were war-time shortages I didn't notice, but then, I was not the one buying for the family or the business.

In 1943 we finally left Las Teresianas where I had been suffering, off and on, since first grade. Our parents, while always interested in our health, manners, and moral upbringing, were not too overly concerned with our formal education. Pulling us out of school in the middle of the school year was a common occurrence. At one time a teacher was hired to tutor Lucy and me at home for a few months. Her name was Ester Brunnet. I am not sure of the reason but it had something to do with our family schedule of moving back and forth didn't coincide with the normal school year. We mostly sat at the dining room table and talked. Las Teresianas, with their emphasis on religion was a bad fit. We went there because it was the place where the daughters of my parent's friends went. Several of our cousins were there as boarders at one time or another, but the nuns showed a marked preference for girls that showed some religious fervor or at least followed the mandates of the church. My sister and I never had the First Communion ceremony and were photographed looking saintly in a white dress. Papi didn't allow us to go to Confession (it was alright for Oli), Mami didn't provide us with the long white stockings that were part of the uniform, and a myriad of other requests from the nuns that went unfulfilled. We were always bringing home little notes that went unanswered. We were also cajoled into contributing to causes of someone else's choice. The result of this lack of compliance was that we were always bypassed for honors regardless of the academic subject. Every week honors were bestowed in the form of bandas, ribbons worn by the honored students across the chest like bandoliers. A certain color for good behavior, another color for good scholarship. The red one was the most honored of all. I, in my secret world, thought of myself as a good student. Maybe I was, maybe I wasn't. I never had bandas to prove it.

Lucy was lucky enough to distinguish herself, but not in the classroom. Aside from walking on the streets of Camagüey in religious processions, the whole student body (but not the nuns) had to be represented on patriotic occasions at parades. All the schools, public and private, had to be present or be subject to a fine. Not only the nuns complied, but they used it to the schools advantage to show the world our superiority. Our physical education class was not fun and games; it was calisthenics and for that they had engaged a layman, Ernesto Silva, old friend of my mother. He organized a marching group and chose Lucy to lead it. She marched proudly at the front of her platoon on many parades. Delighted, Mami even bought her white gloves and the gala uniform.

Oli had been attending the Escuelas Pias when he took the entrance exam for Segunda Enseñanza. He had never taken school very seriously so we thought that he had not done well when he came home early claiming proudly that he was the first to finish. But he did get good enough marks to pass on the first try. The exam is given a second time at the end of the summer giving a second chance to students that fail the first time. It is much better to pass the first time, before the summer vacation; otherwise one spends the summer studying. The plans are for him to go to boarding school in the United States just as soon as the war is over, and eventually to

Lehigh like his father. There are no plans for Lucy and I beyond the eighth grade, if that much.

Papi has never stopped considering the United States his second country, although he does not approve of the war, is secretly sympathetic of the Germans and never liked FDR. For many years he couldn't take the time, or afford, to travel, but he kept in touch with his friends from Lehigh and especially with his fraternity brothers. Soon they will be able to have more contact than Christmas cards.

When we go through Nuevitas on the way to the fincas, the U.S. military presence is even stronger. The conversation is all about the German U Boats that have sank several merchant ships as they left the port, and just outside the entrance to the bay, that we call La Boca. The purpose of the airmen in Camagüey is to hunt down the submarines. Apparently, in this area, submarines are very visible from the air because the clear water and white sand bottom of the North Coast. The tales we hear of the sinking and rescue efforts, usually involving sharks, are both gruesome and heroic. But we see sailors throwing a football at Cuatro Vientos happy and unaffected with the danger waiting outside.

The crossing of the bay by small boat was not any different than any previous crossing, but now I kept my eyes on the distant water. The changing colors of the waves made me fancy seeing submarines. I wondered what we should do if one would surface next to us. I felt more pity for them than fear; so far from home, just doing what they were told to do. As far as I know, no submarine was ever spotted inside the bay.

At the embarcadero there are horses waiting for all of us. There is no riding behind or in front of the adults anymore. We are trusted with good horses: I get Mabulita who until recently was considered too spirited for "the girls." Papi rides one of his usual overweigh horses and Oli, already the tallest in the family, rides the smallest but prettiest horse: a mottled Arabian named Sonico. We are all happy to see Joseito and Ramon, who brought the horses, but we are not in the habit of great shows of affection. We don't even shake hands.

On the way out of the embarcadero we pass a passenger bus parked in its own open shed. The people of Santa Lucia now have their own bus service between the farming village and the boat landing. It is the only motorized vehicle to regularly use this road and in a way it is captive. They probably had to wait for a particularly dry spell to bring it here. Some small trucks make the land trip at times, and Faustino has made it in the Ford to

Los Desengaños a few times. Neighbors are always improving the road on their own because the government has no money for caminos vecinales.

We are not only bringing a cook, but she is bringing her whole family. Her name is Juana Pisonero and she has a teen age daughter, Irma, and a boy just a little younger named Hector. We have noticed that Juana has a problem pronouncing certain hard consonants, like R and K. It seems to me that she could have chosen different names for her children. As she says them, their names are Idma and Hedto. I was told that that's because she is Puerto Rican and that is the way they talk.

Papi has only been gone for a few days; just long enough to go to Camagüey, turn around and bring the family. He rides in front with Joseito who is reporting what few events, mostly mishaps, have taken place in his absence.

This time we are going to enter the finca by the main gate, not through the estancia. It is a longer route but we won't have to open so many gates. We ride to the point where this road makes a 90 degree turn to the left. If we had turned right on the even less travelled road, we would reach La Teja, at one time the finca of Rogelio Zayas Bazan governor of the province of Camagüey and now belongs to his son, also a politician. Doesn't seem like a good place for meeting people but maybe politicians like to hide away once in a while. That land has access to the bay by its own estuary and, according to old maps, it was all part of the original Desengaños and the landing was called Embarcadero Los Desengaños.

The road we are on is a camino real, which is wide enough from fence to fence, but in practice it is only a narrow trail. A type of thorny bromeliads we call mayas have been planted by our neighbors across the road to reinforce their poorly maintained fences. The plants keep extending until they have become a hazard. But they serve their purpose; no animal can walk through this thicket. I have to admit that there is a great contrast between what we see to our right and Los Desengaños to our left. The soils must be similar, but our side is planted in guinea grass with many trees to shade the cattle in hot weather. On the other side, there doesn't seem to be much for cattle to eat beyond the thorny fence. No wonder they try to get out.

Before we get to the new entrance double gate, Papi's handiwork and not even painted yet, we hear a welcoming sound. It is picked up and repeated like an echo from all directions. We go through the gate and over the two-arch brick bridge from the sugar mill days all the time listening to what sounds like "Fuego, fuego…."

Animals

Years ago, our old cook, don Blas, had a problem with the peacocks, the call that most of us interpreted as "Fuego!" he heard as "Viejo!" taunting him. Wonder what English speakers hear. Anyway, it is loud and clear. In most country homes it is the dogs that give the alarm when visitors approach, but by the time the dogs bark, riders are almost within sight of the compound. The peacock's domain extends several miles in all directions and since they ignore human boundaries, they can sound the alarm from adjacent lands. The animals breed as freely as guinea hens and we have no idea how many adults there are, probably in the hundreds, but curiously, they have not reverted to the wild. We don't feed them—except what other animals share with them. Their favorite food is palmiche, the nut of the royal palm, which they eat off the ground, just like the pigs, but, unlike the pigs, they also can fly to the palm top and eat off the raceme. I suspect that there are some individuals that never leave the batey, but it is hard to tell. There was a male in the habit of cautiously walking on our porch, but all males look alike and all females look alike. I have been able to distinguish individual pigs, chickens and ducks and made pets of them, but not peacocks. If there is a difference, like a broken feather, it is only temporary. As much as their looks, we admired their regal ways. No wonder they are called pavo real, or royal turkey. The males can walk with such dignity, keeping the long tail high and out of the mud. Even the drab female walks with grace as she introduces her chicks around the batey. It is impressive to see them fly in to spend the night on the high algarrobo in the recogedor. And, yes, they are good eating.

Why they do so well in Los Desengaños is a mystery. We have given away many pairs to other ranchers, and years later, they have no more than the original pair, if that much. On the other hand, domestic geese don't like it here. We had a male (white) and three females (partly grey) for years. One year one of the females managed to raise a young gosling, and that year the old goose died. Our turkeys, the same way, they barely managed to hold their own, but the Plymouth Rock chickens did well, although hardly in a commercial scale, considering how little care they received. My favorites were the ducks. I insist that they are the superior intellect of the feathered world. They recognize people, are good parents, can swim and fly. And there is nothing prettier than a flotilla of a dozen yellow and black fluffy ducklings following their mother in the laguna, our little pond in the guayabal, a short walk from the house.

Friendships with farm animals never have a happy ending, but still we persisted. I even had a pet pig named Chencha. Returning after a few months in Camagüey, I looked at a sea of identical black pigs. I called out "Chencha!" There was a little movement, a grunt, and one of the pigs came running toward me. That was just too much. I didn't pursue the friendship because she would be shipped with the rest of them in the near future. Similar experiences we had with calves again and again. Dogs made safer pets. We have never had a cat here that I can remember. Wonder why. We have a cat in town, but he stays there. They say that cats are more attached to the house than to people. They don't like to move. Maybe I am more like a cat than a dog.

As expected, there are three or four dogs at each ranch; always one female and the others male. They are used to work with pigs as well as cattle and the men insist that dogs work best as a team if there is one female; just one, no more. To avoid the hassle of frequent litters of puppies, the female may spend some time living in a barbacoa, a loft accessible only by a ladder. We have several barbacoas . The one over the pig house is used for feed storage. The large one over the casa de caballos is where the single men sleep in hammocks. In spite of all the precautions we do have a litter of puppies once in a while. That breed of dogs may not have a name but they are all identical. They come in two colors: black with white markings and yellow with white markings. And the markings are always the same: collar, tip of tail, paws, and part of the face and collar. Papi never rides anywhere without a favorite dog following his horse.

With every move back to town there are close-to-tears farewells at the embarcadero when one or more dogs try to jump in the boat with us. There was a lucky one that found a place in both of our worlds. He was a terrier named Duque that was given to Oli when he went along when Papi visited his cousin Bernabe. As there is a lack of foxes in Cuba, the breed here is known as rat terriers. In the case of Duque, it should have been chicken terrier. Little Duque turned out to be a demon. In Camagüey, Oli and his friends proudly told how he had fought and killed a mongoose. Yes, mongoose had prospered in the equally foreign marabou thickets around our home in Garrido. When Duque arrived in Los Desengaños he didn't find foxes or mongooses, but he found chickens. He eventually learned to leave them alone, but not until the population was greatly reduced.

Now for the smallest creatures. We have the usual flies, mosquitoes and ticks, but what this region near the coast is notable for are the jejenes. They look like gnats, except that they bite. When mosquitoes come, we sleep under mosquito nets, and that's that, but jejenes require different measures. They come (from where, I wouldn't know) at dusk, and are gone by the time it is completely dark. The trick is to keep the house closed tight for a couple of hours each evening to avoid coming to a houseful of invisible biters. Screens could not have kept them out, they are so small. Screens could keep out the rich variety of flying creatures that regularly visit us, but I can see why putting them up was never even considered. They would take away the wonderful feeling of being out in the open.

Jejenes seem to bother some people more than others. I feel them bite my bare arm, and with a finger, smear the soft black spot, about the size of a flea. Unlike a flea, the jejen doesn't jump away; and unlike mosquitoes, they don't have to be slapped hard, just rubbed off.

The trouble is that some people, like Mami, become very agitated when they feel the invisible bite. They start scratching, rubbing things on themselves, and talking about going back to Camagüey.

We have something that is even smaller than a jejen, the nigua. Not many people in Cuba are familiar with them, and we had them only in the dry season since they can't survive in mud; they love dry dust and bare feet, be it pigs, dogs or children. Their English name is jigger fleas, and they also have a Latin name: Tunga penetrans. That last name tells it all: they penetrate under the skin and you don't see them or notice them until you feel the itch. When you look closely, there is a little black spot, usually under your toe or by the toenail. You can dig it out right away with a needle, but we prefer to wait a day or so when it starts to form an egg sack which we called cayaya. Then the needle can pull it out in one piece without that much digging, leaving a neat round hole. The poor dogs have no needles and make a mess of their paws by trying to pull them out with their teeth so we spend lots of time doing it for them. As for the pigs, they solve that and many other problems, like screw worms, by digging themselves in the mud.

I wasn't planning to mention the screw worms since I find them so revolting but we have them and they are a problem. They are the reason there is a pot of creosote, or alquitran, with a dauber handy on a post in the casa de vaqueria, and as soon as Miguel, or anyone else, spots any break in the skin of an animal no matter how small, they paint it with creosote to keep away the screw fly. That goes also for the belly button of newborn calves. The screwworm is the larva of a fly larger than the house fly and with a greenish iridescent body. They are always looking for an open wound where they can firmly glue their cluster of grain-like eggs. All animals seem to know that and fear the approach of those flies where they ignore the other, more abundant, flies. The eggs develop into flesh eating worms that turn a tiny cut into a gruesome hole. Strangely, the worms eat flesh, but not other tissues, like tendons, so they don't cripple or kill a large healthy animal. They want them alive so they can feast for a long time. They do kill newborn calves; sometimes we even find the worms in the calf's mouth. Apparently the flies are attracted to the mother's milk as well as to blood, or those may be larvae from house flies. Before leaving the subject of screw worms, I am going to reveal a well guarded family secret but without naming names. Papi likes to poke fun at a particular relative who he considers stuck up, the worse possible trait as far as he is concerned. One time when he was visiting he noticed something on her little boy's head. It was hard and white. Sure enough, it was a cluster of eggs. She swore it could not be. We don't talk about it anymore.

A typical day

The day in Los Desengaños begins at four in the morning, whether you get up or not, because that's when Papi gets up and he doesn't even pretend to do it quietly. That would be a wasted effort since in this house every footstep resounds on the bare wood floors and travels through the unfinished wood partitions. He may even speak to me as he walks on the porch past my window because he knows I am awake. He says that I am like an owl because I may look asleep but I am usually awake. The rest of us stay in bed a couple of hours longer but never after sunrise. He seems to think that staying in bed in daylight, when one could be doing something useful, is sort of sinful. "Sun nearly caught you in bed," he would warn. As part of that same rule, one had to get fully dressed upon rising. No robes; no house slippers. He doesn't pamper himself and doesn't let us do it either. When in Los Desengaños, there is a reason for rising even earlier than usual. That's when the milking chores begin and even if he does not do them himself, staying in bed while others work for him may have been against his code.

There had been a carbide central lightning system that turned the night into day in the whole batey, or so I was told, but that self destroyed years ago. The remnants of that failed project are still around: a tank, posts and twisted tubing here and there. We now use individual carbide lamps and also kerosene and candles. We also know how to move around in the dark.

In the dark, Papi goes to the other house which we always refer to as la otra casa. There are so many buildings, mostly small, scattered around the batey that we use an exact name for them so there is no mistake. Our house is the casa de la familia, and the other, larger, house is where everybody gathers. The enclosed room to one side is the private room of the encargado. It has cement floor, a step above the main room. There is another enclosed room that is used for storage, and the large open area with dirt floor is dining room and community hall. The kitchen is right next to it, but it is a separate building. Kitchens are supposed to be in a building of their own because of the danger of fire catching one guano roof and spreading to the rest of the batey. Except that here the two buildings are touching, and at our house the kitchen is part of the same building.

Dirt floors are really easy to live with and not as dirty as some people think. After they are in use for years they become as hard as cement and can be swept with a broom like any floor. A little sprinkle of water keeps any dust down. There is something friendly about a dirt floor; for one thing, you don't have to wipe your shoes or keep animals out. People must like them because, even when all the other rooms have cement floors, the large gathering place at every ranch has dirt floor. In La Gertrudis somebody came up with the idea of using burn tractor oil on the floor; I guess because they didn't know what else to do with the spent oil. Anyway, it was a mess.

The shower is a separate room, open to the sky; that and the outhouse have wood planks for a floor. The outhouse, of course, is some distance away. The chickens, the pigs, the horses and the carts, all have their own thatch roofed place and each place has a name.

In the early morning the men have coffee, but nothing else until they are finished with the morning routine. It begins with using the caballo de la guardia, an old horse whose job ends before everybody else's begins. He spends the night in the corral and is used to bring in the dairy cows and other horses, and then he is finished and is released for the rest of the day. By the time I get there the milking has started. The two men that do the actual milking keep a small stool hanging from the belt. They bring the calves in, one at a time. The calf runs to his mother bypassing all the other similar cows, takes a few hungry gulps of mother's milk and then is tied to one side while the rest of the milk goes into a pail. The cow must reserve some or produce more, because all the calves seem well fed. Mother and calf are released together to the pasture until the afternoon when they are separated again. Moving around on foot in a corral full of large Cebu cows trying to get to their calves takes nerve. The older animals are used to all this and cooperate, but you have to be on the lookout for the recien paridas, or new mothers, that have not yet developed trust in their handlers. The cows have been selected out of the larger herd as the best for milking although

Cebu mixes are not really dairy cattle. It takes a lot of effort to collect the amount of milk that just a few cows of a dairy breed would give, but, on the other hand, they are good beef cattle and that is the main business here.

Papi brings a pot of milk for our household making sure it is rich milk from a cow with older calf, and we have breakfast together sitting at our round dining table. Another pot of milk is boiled so it will last through the day without spoiling. It doesn't taste like the cold, fresh milk we drink in Camagüey, but you get used to it. We now have an icebox brought from our house in Camagüey when we replaced it there with an electric refrigerator. The icebox is not very useful because it cools only at irregular times when a block of ice is brought from the store coated in sawdust and carried in a dripping gunny sack. It is used more for a once in a while treat than for keeping food fresh. And not even for that. We have found that we like our well water best just as it comes from the tap. We don't understand it when visitors say that the water tastes salty. It is not salty at all. It is more like bicarbonate of soda. Cooling it with ice seems to intensify that taste. And it does make glasses look cloudy. Papi's glass is never washed because he says he can taste the soap, so it stands in its place looking, well, dirty.

The milking takes a good part of the morning because after the cows and calf are gone somebody has no clean-up. And then comes the other operation in the building called la lecheria . There is still a wall with shelves from the abandoned cheese making operation, but now the place belongs to the descremadora, or centrifuge separator. This amazing machine is cranked by hand to separate the cream from the skim milk. It is not hard to do, but it takes patience. The skim milk goes directly through an opening in the outside partition into a canoa on the other side where pigs are waiting. They must like it by the sounds they make while waiting. What we really treasure is the cream. Somebody has to go to the embarcadero every day with the cantaras, milk cans full of cream, loaded on a mule, or on the mule powered cart called guarandinga. We had a mule named Blasina, (after a cook named don Blas) that could follow the road to the embarcadero and back without a guide, although we didn't test that. The cream somehow made its long journey to the factory and we not only received checks for it, but we can pick up slightly misshaped Gruyere cheese at the factory as a bonus.

After breakfast, Papi, Oli and one or two others take off for Las Gertrudis to help with the beneficeo that has started over there. We won't see them again until late this afternoon. Some days, Lucy or I join them, but never both. When Mami suggested that we go, Papi decided that one should be enough. There is a new house and corrales being built in an area of Las Gertrudis closer to us. It has been given the name of Los Angeles and, appropriately, a man named Angel Nuñez will be living there with his family as caretakers. As the woods come down in that area, there is more and more pasture and more cattle to look after. That will also be a break in the long ride from here to Las Gertrudis. In Las Gertrudis the person in charge is another of Coral's brothers, Ernesto Diaz.

This, and most ranches, manages with so few employees because large jobs are contracted out. The employees do the routine work and fill in the rest of the time with repair jobs and caring for animals, but when there is something big, like a new fence, an outside crew comes in. For the once a year beneficeo where all the new animals are branded, vaccinated, dehorned and counted, all the able men from all the ranches participate. Some that are especially good at roping, like Miguel's brother Eusebio, look forward to this opportunity to show off.

Nothing special is going to happen here today. In mid afternoon, and marking the end of siesta time, the two men who had stayed behind ride out to bring the dairy cows in and separate them from the calves that had been with them since milking time this morning. That is not a difficult job, but it requires two men. Most of the cows know what is expected of them. The men know them well, by name and by habits. The bulls are all pure Cebu, also known as Brahmas, and the cows are getting close to being pure bred, but there is always a difference in look. That the men know them here where there are about fifty that they milk everyday may not be extraordinary, but in Las Gertrudis where there are many hundreds and don't get milked, at least some of them are also known by name.

After the cows go back to their pasture, Lucy and I try to make friends with some of the calves by enticing them with seed pods from the algarrobas. Most of the calves are white with grey shading; but a few are red and, rarer, spotted. They are frisky as colts; they kick the air as they are moved across the corral and to their own potrero. When we feed them they rub their forehead against our hand shaking the head in a mock charge.

Poor Irma, she almost pulled out her hair on her first day here. She has long bleached blond hair and somebody neglected to tell her not to wash it with well water. We were standing around in the afternoon when she ran out of the bathroom crying. She couldn't untangle her wet hair; it was a frizzy mass. There are so many things that we have to be sure to tell visitors, and warning them about the water is one. They notice the taste the first time they drink and complain about it, even if we think the taste is fine. The problem is when you add soap to it. We forget that people from town just don't know how things are done here. Irma learned quickly. She is so nice, and looked so distraught, that somebody went to the little well by the brook and brought her a bucket of soft water so she could wash her hair again. I hope she doesn't drink from that water. We don't think it comes out of the ground like that at the deep well, but seeps from the muddy water hole next to it, popular with pigs. From now on she will wait to wash her hair in the rain, like I do, or go to the little well herself. Washing hair in the rain is best but you need a good heavy rain; then we stand on the edge of the porch and stick our head out under the pouring water.

Papi likes to take a nap whenever he can. In warm weather he uses the hammock we have strung across a corner of the porch. As soon as he gets up, and quickly before he takes off again, one or more of us children rushes to make his lemonade. There are several lemon trees around the batey, one of them right next to our kitchen, but for the one special lemonade we prefer the one in the pasture because it is fun to run for it and Papi can watch from the porch. It requires going through the fence, running through the tall grass to reach the small tree. We take just one perfect lemon—these lemons don't turn yellow, just a slightly lighter shade of green, so you have to know when they are ready.

The recipe is simple: juice from that one lemon, a spoonful of sugar, and our special well water. (Once when we had a block of ice in our little icebox we tried putting ice in the glass. None of us liked the taste.) Papi always emptied the glass without taking a breath and with us standing in front of him watching and waiting for approval. Then he always said "That is the best lemonade in the world." Then we rinse his glass, careful not to wash it with yellow soap like all the others, and put it back in its place. I said we don't notice war shortages, but good soap is something I hear about. Also, there is no barb wire to repair fences or to string new ones.

One day Irma and I were walking along the fence in the potrero del ingenio, which is used only for calves, when we noticed a break in the fence. She was concerned that large animals could get through—since we had to come this way again on the way back and she was not comfortable around cows, so we went and repaired it ourselves. We used what we could find, from rusty pieces of wire to twigs, and went on feeling proud of ourselves. When one of the men came across our repair work there was lots of teasing going around blaming the work on one another, until Irma and I confessed.

Mami, invariably, takes a shower at three in the afternoon, drinks coffee while listening to a soap opera, and goes to the other house to visit with Coral for the rest of the afternoon.

Coral had a second child; a little girl named Maricusa. Now she and Mami have a lot to talk about. Mami is more interested in babies than in food. It is good that Coral's cooking meets with the men's approval because cooks have been fired for too much or too little salt on the rice. What they call el punto. Buen punto, meaning: just right. When meals are always the same, rice, beans, tasajo, and fried plantains, the food must be just right. Also, to be considered a good cook, one must use lots of lard so the food "goes down smoothly." I have seen men pour melted lard over the rice. Coral can make extras like pumpkin fritters and milk and eggs desserts, but that is not what she is judged on.

Sometimes we go for months without fresh beef and sometimes we have it even for breakfast. When the tasajo is running out — or when an animal is hurt and must be butchered— we can have every cut of beef, but only for a day or two before it is all salted and made into tasajo or it will spoil. It is usually old cows that provide our meat here. If it bothers Miguel to kill an animal that he has known, he doesn't show it. That is the way it is in a farm: one day the chicken, pig or cow is running around and the next day it is dinner. The first meals after the cow is butchered we have liver and onions, brain fritters, kidney in its own gravy . . . the parts that are not made into tasajo. But before that, somebody has gone to the store for a hundred pound sack of salt, and to tell the neighbors that there is fresh beef.

Aside from the dining table and benches, the most important item in this common room is the radio. It sits high on a shelf, powered by a car battery. For a while it used wind power from a small wind mill on top of the house, but that didn't last. A vulture flew into it and that was the end of the bird and the generator. We went back to the car battery. There is a table under the radio shelf that sees various uses, like writing or playing domi-noes. There is a palanganero –a water basin for hand washing with a pail hanging by it and set on an outside corner so the used water can be emptied right there. And there are taburetes, chairs with raw leather back and seat. They are all around the room, and mainly next to the posts, so they can be used leaning back with two legs off the ground.

We are very proud of our water system. Our well has never let us down, but the windmill, although rarely, will sometimes come to a complete standstill. The water tanks are there so we will have water for quite a while after the wind stops. Today, the directional blade with the letters A. R.

Sanchez points proudly to the right as there is a steady breeze from the North. Lucy and I have been left in charge of switching the water from the large tank in the corral to the two elevated tanks that store water for the batey and our house. The cattle come first, of course. We keep an eye on the marker outside the round cattle water tank that is attached to the float inside the tank. When it reaches the full mark we go to the well head to do the simple, but important, task of pulling down a lever. Mami doesn't like the idea of us climbing on the well, so she comes with us and stands by. I don't know what she plans to do if one of us falls in.

Dinner time is whenever Papi shows up. Coral has dinner ready and the same with our cook, but they are used to this wait. As soon as riders are announced, both cooks will go to their kitchens, but there is no hurry. Workers always shower before dinner, even in the winter. The well water is about the same temperature all the time: cool. Unless you are the first one to the shower, in which case you get the water that had warmed in the metal pipe coming from the tank. While they get ready, the cooks will do the last minute frying. Everything else is kept warm over a few pieces of charcoal covered in ashes. Coral gets a small salary for cooking for the single men, one of them, Ramon, is her brother. Some farm wives also do laundry, but here the laundry is taken to another housewife in another finca, or rather an estancia within the finca La Rosalia, across the camino real. The few pieces Coral washes and hangs over the barb wire fence must be full of holes, because there are threads stuck to the barbs.

When the jejenes begin to bite, we are sent to close the shutters in our house. That helps some. Jejenes don't seem to like the complete darkness. They are very particular; don't like wind either. We open the house before dinner and are not bothered again.

Another chore that is expected of us is preparing the carbine lamp for the evening. This, of course, is best done before it gets dark. The spent ashes from the night before we empty on the entrance brick lined walk, retrieve any surviving pellets and add new ones from the closely sealed storage. Papi, still the chemist, has explained to us that the pellets are Calcium Carbonate that when mixed with water gives out a combustible gas and leaves behind the ashes, which are really caustic lime, or calcium hydroxide. That's why the lamp is made ready, but not put together until we are ready to light it. This lamp only goes in the dining room, and later, in the kitchen. It may be lots of trouble to get ready, but the light is as bright as any electric light. For moving around the house we use candles in white enamel candle holders with a finger ring. The light of the moving candle, changing recesses from dark to orange and dark again is one of my favorite sights.

After dinner, the carbine lamp is taken to the kitchen. We don't take any light out on the porch but move by what little daylight there is left or by our familiarity with the place. We always sit on the side facing the potrero where, on a clear night, we can still see the light shapes of the grazing dairy cows. This is Papi's favorite sight. He never tires of looking at his animals.

Once we are settled down, we talk quietly or play word games. Lately we have been playing Twenty Questions. We have perfected the game way beyond the usual questions of: Animal, vegetable or mineral? Or, is it larger than a shoebox? The sequence of questions is important; we try never to waste a question. We usually go for something intangible, like "Fear"; it takes more skill to narrow down than tangible things like "the dining room table." In the dark, we can see the red glow of Papi's cigar. He is hardly ever without a cigar, but he only smokes it when he is relaxed like now. At other times, he just bites on it. When they are working cattle he often bites through it and it drops to the ground. It is a source of joking. Miguel and most of the men, not Joseito, smoke cigarettes which are probably more expensive than Papi's bandless cigars bought in bulk from a small manufacturer. I don't know when or for what reason Papi added the cigar to his image but now it would be difficult to erase it. In the dry season, like right now, anybody who smokes does it with great care. Papi doesn't light at all when he is on the move, and Miguel carries a tin can ashtray wired to his saddle.

None of us likes the smoke, but we have learned to protect ourselves from it. The breeze here is usually from the Northeast, so we sit accordingly. I sit on the floor with my back against a post; always my favorite place. If we could make time stop, this will be a good spot: the five of us sitting on the porch.

Most nights are uneventful, except for Mami's nightmares, but we are used to them. She starts moaning softly and we start discussing when it is time to intervene. We carry conversations from five different beds in three separate rooms as comfortably as if we were all together. When the moaning grows louder, as it always does, Papi throws a pillow at her, she mumbles a few words, and goes to sleep. If she knows what is in her nightmares, she has never told us, and she never says any discernable words.

I kept the family up one memorable night because of a scorpion that fell on me from the rafters and stung me on contact. If you have never been stung by one, I can only describe it as an electric shock that keeps on shocking. Candles were lit; bedding was shaken, and no scorpion. As soon as everybody went back to bed, it stung again. That scene was repeated several times until the scorpion was found, I can't remember where. All I know is that I spent most of the night on a crouching position on the edge of the bed. We see scorpions often and are always on the look-out for them, but seldom get stung. We know not to put on shoes without shaking them out first and never to stick our hand under anything without checking. Captive scorpions are a source of amusement for some; supposedly they sting themselves when angry, but I avoid them.

And then we had the excitement of the nights of the wild dogs we call jibaros. For a long time I refused to believe that wild dogs existed until a couple were pointed out to me, way in the distance, at Las Gertrudis. They are just feral domestic dogs, smaller but similar to our ranch dogs and somehow had managed to survive by staying out of the way of their more powerful kin. Since the only time they were mentioned was like "I killed a jibaro today" it is remarkable that they lived at all. They were no big deal until this year when a few had ganged together and started killing piglets within squealing distance of the batey of Los Desengaños. At first we were not sure where to place the blame but when all our dogs were accounted for barking from the comfort of the house and we ruled out dogs left behind by deer hunters — we hate hunters and would have liked to blame them, but the consensus around the large room of the main house was that these were not hunting dogs. Taking a clue from the American West, Papi offered a bounty. $5 per dead dog.

Our independent minded pigs have over four hundred acres of fenced pasture area where they are free to roam. The fence should have kept out the wild dogs, but it didn't. Most pigs sleep near the houses which give them a choice place at the breakfast trough. But there must be some advantage to sleeping at the almost-dry brook away from the houses, because that is the favorite overnight home of some breeding sows. The dogs wait until hours after dark and then the commotion begins. The sows at first managed to fight them back but the dogs got bolder. Our only weapon was going to be our 22 caliber single shot rifle. Papi has his revolver but he decided to stay out of it other than offer the bounty and a whole set of instructions to keep them (mostly Oli and Joseito) from shooting each other.

We shouted from our beds "They are here!" as if anybody could have missed the racket. It took several nights and only one dog was killed, but the others didn't come back. I never saw the dead dog, or the dead piglets. Trying to protect us from the sight of violence or anything ugly was not easy, living always near the life and death of animals, but Mami saw it as her duty to shield us.

The next evening we were back at our favorite spot. It may be a long time until anything as exciting as the dog hunt comes along, but you never know. We can spend an hour sitting in the dark, sometimes talking, sometimes just thinking. We don't even leave any light in the house because the fear of fire is always present. When it is decided that it is time to go to bed, all we carry to the bathroom is a candle in the enamel candle holder, and to the bedroom not even that. Who needs light to change into pajamas and crawl into bed. The conversation continues for a while across the distance between beds and through the single layer partitions.

I don't know why Mami won't live here permanently. She is so happy and alive when she is here. It must remind her of her childhood in Palma Hueca. To her a few months in Los Desengaños are like a temporary retreat into her past, but she won't accept it as her permanent home. The excuse for having another home in Camagüey was that we had to go to school. But we could be boarders, like my cousins and many of our friends whose parents live out of the city. Come to think of it, that doesn't seem much better. We all like it here; but to me, it is more than like. I belong here and every time we start getting ready to move back to town I show it the only way I know how: I cry.

Papi has dedicated his life to his ranches. La Gertrudis, with over a hundred caballerias is by far the largest. El Destino, a long way from here, keeps him on the road. It has the richest soil so there is where the young animals are taken to finish them for the beef market. To keep abreast of the cattle market he has to spend time with other cattlemen, with buyers, with suppliers, and with a whole red of people who touch his business in any way. So much and so many people depend on him making the right decisions. He could not do that sitting here watching his cows graze. The time spent here in Los Desengaños is the payoff for all the hard work. He shows his feelings more than my mother. With Papi you don't have to guess; he loves the time spent here with the family, he is happy and he shows it.

Oli would be happy anywhere. He is enthusiastic about whatever he is doing and he is always doing something or planning something. He cannot understand why I should be unhappy just because we are shutting down this house and hoping somebody will care for the animals we have made pets of. He is always giving me advice: "China, don't look back. Look ahead." That's easy for him to say. From the house in Camagüey he is closer

72

to El Destino, and to him that is his special place. Here there is the advantage that he has Lucy and me to help with his projects, but he is always making comparisons between things here and at El Destino: everything is better there, from the food to the horses. I know why he likes El Destino better. When he is there he is treated almost as a grown up; here he is a child and part of the family. He may find a way to make El Destino his home and live there fulltime, but, more likely, he will follow his father's example and be on the move all the time. Only, life will be easier for him; Papi has already done the hard work.

I think Lucy likes it here as much as I do, but she has good friends in school and is looking forward to going back. Anyway, she never cries. If she is unhappy she goes to bed. She used to have a special blanket named *chafa* that provided her comfort, but it has disappeared. As hard as our parents tried to turn us into one we are very different in looks and personality. When we are not called "the girls" we are called *AngelitayLucy* the words run together into a single word. We dress alike; are given identical presents and when we were little, we rode on the same horse, one behind the other, alternating places, even when there were lots of horses available. She may not show her feelings; she may not cry when leaving Los Desengaños, but we do have something in common: we love this place like no other.

To me, this is the only place to be. As we start to get up to go inside to bed, I tell myself, "Someday I will live here, and never have to leave again"

The return trip in the fall is still exciting even for those who are not looking forward to going back. By the time Papi calls out that it is time to get up, I am awake even if it is in the middle of the night. He can't say, as he sometimes do "Let there be light", because it is a couple of hours before sunrise. Everything has been packed the day before. We will have some café-con-leche at the playa store, but the adults had plain coffee at the other house which Miguel made while the others are getting the animals ready, horses for everybody and a mule for the canvas sacks.

We saw the sunrise on the straight clay road to the embarcadero, the last leg of the ride. On the return trips we don't have the store and the boat to ourselves. The small bus from Santa Lucia was almost full—and there are a few that came by horse like we did.

It takes time to get everybody settled on the boat benches. Everybody has parcels, although not as large as our canvas bags since they are just going for the day. There is a woman already nursing a baby; Mami, of course, sits next to her and immediately starts to give advice.

1943. Two places called home. Camaguey and La Finca

I wish we were going just for a few days, but we, the family, won't be back until next summer.

Woods to Inferno to pasture. Making the place bigger

Lucy and I together never ride with Papi because he has a strict rule: only one of us at the time can go out with him. We have to take turns; I am not sure why. Either he cannot stand the two of us together, or, and more likely, he wants each one to feel important and special. We already have too much of being treated as one. The rides are usually all day affairs, and we know better than to cause trouble or complain about anything since tagging along is considered a privilege. And sometimes, as we grow older, we are even asked to do something useful.

Cattle are always being moved from here to there; sometimes just one or two animals, sometimes every last animal in the pasture. And for that, extra riders are needed and even one of us girls can be useful. Just last week I rode with Papi and every available man from La Gertrudis. I was invited to come along and expected to help. I am sure they don't move cattle just for the fun of it. There must have been a reason, but I was not told what we were doing or where we were going.

I could see that every animal in the large area known as Los Angeles was being herded toward the corner where the road and the old railroad right-of-way meet; the point we call *Cuatro caminos*, (although there are only three). There is a gate there. Everything was done in slow motion; no shouting, no running. Our mix of Cebu and *criollo* can be excitable and the last thing we want to do is make them run because every ounce they burn is money lost.

Since I was the closest to the gate, and doubtless, the least useful, Papi signaled to me to move ahead and open the gate. Everything was done slowly and relaxed like. I dismounted at the gate; opened and pulled it to one side and sat quietly back on the horse. My job well done, I thought, I waited, blocking the road on that side. Then I looked up. The front of the herd was almost to the gate, and where they go, the others will follow. And in the distance I saw Papi and everyone else wildly signaling to me. I had assumed that they wanted the cattle to move right on the road, toward Los Desengaños. It turned out that they needed to go left.

It wasn't a major disaster, but all day I kept explaining my error by saying "Nobody talks to me."

Papi does talk to me. We even have our own word for those long talks: we call it "*philosofear.*"   It is a verb we made from the word philosophy. But the best place for those talks is on the front porch, not when he has decisions to make.

Soon it was my turn again to ride with Papi; just the two of us followed by a large dog named Birama. Papi leads the way in silence as is most often the case; not that we have nothing to say, but we will save the talking for when we can ride side by side on twin trails through pasture. Not here; this was newly cleared land and it was slow going with the horses gingerly high-stepping over the tangle of charred branches that *carboneros* will soon be collecting. My mind is never idle, and seldom engaged in everyday practical matters, just spinning tales never to be told. One of my fantasies is that I am alone with somebody, far from any help, and that person is hurt and I, heroically, save him. I never had to put my heroism to a test and, fortunately, today I didn't either. Papi's horse suddenly tripped right in front of me. Papi went down, horse and all, and came up, horse and all without even saying a word. I guess he couldn't without dropping the cigar. I don't remember him ever cussing or even making any exclamation sounds. That could have been the purpose of that unlit cigar. The incident was not even discussed.

The word we use for a place like that is *tumba* from the verb *tumbar,* to fell, cut down; coincidentally, *tumba* also means tomb. A sad reminder of what this clear-cut former woods has become to all the creatures that formerly made their home here. Any valuable timber was first removed, dragged by teams of oxen to the main road and then loaded on trucks to the lumber mill. What was left was burned on site with the results we were now inspecting. The woods in what we used to call El Monte de Los Angeles is being carved piece by piece into Finca Los Angeles. This was probably second growth woods, since timber operations took place here in my grandfather's days, and probably earlier, but it is still sad to me. Papi promises to keep some as El Monte de Angelita.

This year's drought has been one of the worse. But then, we say that every year, forgetting last year's waiting for the rains. We never lose cattle to the drought, but it takes lots of planning and moving them around. Tío

Ernesto, next door, has lost some. Papi calls the afternoon wind viento mata vacas , because it may push already weakened cows over the edge, and he keeps looking at the sky for signs of the rains getting closer. Half jokingly he tells men not to take rain gear because it would "scare away the rain" and he promises, "It is getting closer." The dark clouds are up there, blowing across the sky with the cow-killer wind, afternoon after afternoon. At Los Desengaños, our well never goes dry; it is the only water we can always count on. Without that well there would be no Los Desengaños. But the creek under our bridge is only a dry ditch. The only visible water is in the center of the reservoir that was dug when our now broken up dam was built. Cattle can still drink there but to get to the water, first they have to wade through thick mud of their own making. For some reason they never drink from the bank but take a few steps into the water and the clay soil is soon trampled into mud, The laguna in the guayabal has just a few spots with clear water toward the center and cracked dry mud around the edges. The ducks still fly to it. Sometimes we have seen a couple of pink Spoonbills there, but not regularly, and not now.

The river in Las Gertrudis is still running; it even has good clean water holes here and there good enough for swimming. Oli is the only one in the family to enjoy them. He is a good swimmer but I'm not. The couple of days once a year in Cuatro Vientos are not enough for me to gain confidence. We joke that Oli learned to swim by correspondence course when we know where he learned. There is a filthy branch of the river Saramaguacan near our house in Camagüey. Of course, we are not allowed to go near it, and, of course, every boy in the neighborhood learned to swim there. When in Las Gertrudis, he swims in the clean river at every opportunity with his friend Ermelio and his brothers. I know Mello because he went to Camagüey with us for a whole school year but boys and girls are discouraged from playing together at our home so I never got to know him well. We play with Oli, but not with his friends.

Workers are not sitting idly waiting for the promised rain. They take advantage of the dry weather to get some work done. Besides moving cattle around, they inspect fences; look for hidden newborn calves, and for anything in need of repair. The most visible tool is the machete because it doesn't fit in a tool bag. And because they are never without it, I believe, more out of habit than need. There is a sharpening stone in every batey and it is used often. Machetes are very useful but only if you know how to handle them. I hear complains about the quality of the newer ones. It seems that the best came from Germany before the war, with the not very Germanic brand of Gallo. A machete is great for cutting brush, but these men don't do much of that. Most often a crew of destajeros is brought in to clear the maniagua, the all encompassing word we use for all unwanted vegetation, now made more visible because the good grass has been eaten until it is less than a foot high. That is low for guinea grass after the rains it will be as high as my head.

Guinea grass pastures are treated more like crops. They are cleared, cultivated, and allowed to rest, recover, and maybe even re-seeded. That's why the finca is divided into fenced pastures and the cattle are moved around as needed to care for the grass.

A crew of destajeros is already at Los Desengaños.   They know that this is the time to chapear, before the rains begin and puts a damper to all work. The drought makes their job easier. The crew leader has been negotiating with Miguel and Papi. By his sing-song accent and his Indian looks it is easy to place him as an oriental, from the next province to the East. The three of them look like friends visiting sitting on reclining taburetes at the main house. The crew leader is confident that he will get his contract. He has done this before, and his crew is already in the field some distance from the house. They don't come in unless invited.

Papi gets up; goes to our house and comes back with a piece of paper which he hands to the crew leader who accepts it with a smile. It is just a paper with a few hand written words and a signature; it is a vale which the crew leader will take to the store for supplies. The crew now has a job for the next couple of months and they move fast so by nightfall, they will have a roof over their heads.

They don't have to start from scratch. There are still remnants of the shelter they built last year. The type of construction is called vara en tierra which means that the rafters go right to the ground. All they need is a machete and some woods nearby with guano palms. I know that thatch roofs can be made from grasses, reeds, or other kinds of available vegetation but ours we call guano roofs and are made from palmetto fronds. Farther south and away from the coast palmettos are not available on site so sometimes thatch roofs are made from royal palm fronds. It works but the roofs don't look as good; they look untidy. It is almost like the palmetto fronds were designed by nature for the purpose of building roofs. If built with care they look neat from the outside and the inside. Like so many traditional crafts, the work is usually done by a team working together with at least one person knowing what to do. You start at the bottom letting the fronds hang over the edge and spacing the wood stems carefully because that's what will be visible from the inside. The stems are tied, or even nailed, to the structure underneath. Each succeeding layer overlaps the last until they reach the top ridge. Then the stems are trimmed and covered with yaguas (the frond sheath of, the royal palm) The destajeros don't bother with those niceties for their temporary shelter; they will leave the stems sticking up in the air. The roof will not be completely water tight, but nobody is counting on rain before their job is finished and they move on.

If a pasture is really in bad shape, if there seems to be more brambles than grass, it is burned instead of cleared with machetes. First, they clear a fire break, or guardaraya, literally, guard line and then the fires are started upwind, using our indispensable palmetto fronds to ignite the pasture. And, strangely, palmetto fronds are also used to stamp out the fire when needed. In the city they may put a fire out with water, but here, at the fire line, we wouldn't dream of using out precious water for anything but drinking. I am never invited to go help at a fire; I suppose I would if it was close to the house and help was badly needed. It seems that I hear of more fires getting out of control than otherwise. Whether the burning goes as planned or not, Oli and all those involved in the burning come home with singed arm hair and even eyebrows. The heat turns the hair into little balls that can be rubbed off. Some people find fires exciting. To me they are destructive and the stuff of nightmares.

Almost twenty years after our house was built, painting it has finally made it to the top of the list of things that needed to be done. Papi bought drums of green and grey paint and those became our official colors: not only our house, but our other buildings and structures of all kinds became grey with leaf green stripes. The much improved road to San Miguel makes it possible to bring supplies by land instead of the much longer water route through Nuevitas. Amongst other things, we acquired a gasoline powered generator. A small separate house was built for the generator and it is my job to put gas in it every evening and start it. We always have had good running water, a flushing toilet, (with a latrine as back up, wind does die on occasion) and now we have some electric lights. We still don't have a refrigerator; just the useless icebox. And we still cook over wood charcoal.

With much effort and expense the road to San Miguel is fit for trucks most of the year. The area called the derramaderos because that's where the river San Isidro spills (or derrama) during the rainy season is still a challenge. But the road, as it is, is making a big different in life here and even in the area of Santa Lucia.

A truckload of milled lumber was unloaded in our yard and Papi spends every available moment making gates. He set up sawhorses right next to the house and found that Lucy and I can be very useful. He does all the cutting with a hand saw and we have learned to use a hand drill and to fasten the bolts that hold the boards together. But our biggest contribution, aside from bringing boards and glasses of water, is just sitting. Papi reassures us of the importance of the job of holding down the boards he is working on by sitting on them.

Gate by gate, the barb wire gates known as rastrillos are being replaced. Some of those were just tied with a rope or a piece of wire and were not too hard to open, but the mean ones are the rastrillos de garrote. The garrote, also known as tolete is a strong wood rod, or just a branch, two or three feet long that hold the gate (just a loose expanse of wire fence) closed under tension. When not used, the garrote hangs harmlessly on the gate post. To close the gate you hook one end of the garrote to a loop on the wire fence and, pulling hard on it, hook the other end behind the post. To open the gate, you release either end, careful not to let go of the garrote. If you are not careful and lose hold of it, it can hit you on the jaw and knock you out. But we didn't consider that a drawback; the reason for replacing, at least the most used ones, is that you have to dismount to open them.

As to be expected, this type of rastrillo can provide us with many anecdotes. One combines with it another of our favorite targets: the visitor from the city, this time all the way from distant La Habana. I'm sure there are millions of jokes told in the big city about "simple" guajiros so it is only fair to laugh at anybody having trouble when outside of their familiar territory. This story is told by Oli who was showing a distant cousin around. This visitor was warned about the treacherous gates, so he dismounted, studied it before releasing the tension, he held on to the garrote as he was warned to do so it would not fly out of control and hit him; he dragged the wire gate open while holding on to the garrote; walked through, and pulling with all his strength, managed to close it again. Only, he left his horse on the other side.

A Beef with Havana

The long drought of '43 and '44 had political consequences. The central government in its infinite wisdom has decided beef is a staple food; it is the birthright of every Cuban to eat steak twice a day. That steak has to be boneless, trimmed of all fat, freshly butchered that day, and available for no more than forty cents a pound. Normally, we in Camagüey were happy to oblige and the train loads of cattle kept moving west. But after a long drought grass was scarce and the cattle were barely surviving, let alone putting on weight.

The lack of understanding between the residents of the capital city and those from what they call "the interior" runs deep. The people on the streets of La Habana have the ear of Batista's government and the sympathy of the press. The cattle people are being depicted as greedy, holding back cattle in the hope of getting higher prices from the poor beef-starved people of La Habana. One of the most ridiculous charges claims that cattle were been hidden in the caves of Cubitas (in the mountains of the same name in the central part of Camaguey)—ignoring that beef cattle is one of those commodities that must be sold the moment it is ready, or you lose money every day. Fresh beef is classified as essential food and it is the job of the government to see that it is always available and at the price set by them. The government threatened to send the army to the ranches to confiscate cattle and take it to the capital if the owners didn't comply with the orders to start shipping animals.

It was in that heated atmosphere that my father and another Sanchez cattleman, Bebe, son of his cousin Bernabe were arrested, not as individuals, but as representing the National Cattlemen Association. In the legal squabble that followed, Judge Miguel Agramonte (who nobody seemed to notice was my father's brother in law) judged that the government has no right to force the cattlemen to sell. The prisoners (who in truth were not taken to jail but detained in a club house) were released, and the citizens of Habana had to eat chicken or pork for a while longer. As expected, the rains came, grass was eaten, and soon cattle trains with thousand pound steers arrived in the capital again. The typical consumers in Cuba like their beef lean, boneless and cheap, but they have no idea of what a drought can do to grass fed animals.

After the crisis was over, at least for that year, the cattle people organized a demonstration as a show of unity, by bringing every available rider to the streets of Camagüey. They repeated it for several consecutive years and it was known as "La Manifestacion Ganadera". Thousands of well-behaved guajiros rode through the streets carrying flags. My mother was in the food committee that fed them at the old hippodrome. The menu included large bakery trays of pastry with sausages baked in it. If they provided their own Hatuey, it was mostly after the parade was over. It was exciting but not disorderly. In a photo of the manifestasion taken on the Avenida de la Libertad (still locally known as La Caridad) , a wide, straight street unlike the narrow twisted ones that characterize Camagüey, and where the character of the parade can best be appreciated, Judge Agramonte can be seen riding on the front line of the cavalcade The effort would have been more effective if we could have taken it to Habana, but, contrary to what they think in the big city, ranching is work; nobody can stay away from a ranch for days. I wonder if they even heard about the parade in the capital. Papi said that he hoped his friends up north didn't hear that he had been arrested. "In the United States only criminals go to jail," he said.

We like to think of Camaguey as a small town, but it isn't. There are no large impressive buildings, and other than La Caridad and La Vigia, another avenue on the other side of the tracks, the streets are narrow and twisted. But officially, it is home to over one hundred and ten thousand people most of who were born here and would not think of going anywhere else.

In 1944, at the start of the seventh grade, we transferred to El Porvenir. Lucy's best friend since second grade, Marta, followed. It was a small coed school, different from all others, and the creation of the Larrauri sisters. Originally there had been three sisters involved, but I only knew two, Rita, who was the nominal director of the school and a constant presence, and Ernestina, to whom the school was one of her two jobs; in the mornings she was also a professor at the Escuela Normal de Maestros, the teachers college where our mother had once taught. Since they knew my mother, and not my father, while we were at El Porvenir we were often referred to by my mother's family name as the Agramontes, ignoring my father's last name.

The Larrauri sisters had fashioned everything about their school following their ideas and completely ignoring the conventional ways, or government regulations. To begin with, the school day is only half a day. While Las Teresianas collects the students by bus in the morning, delivers them home for lunch and makes the rounds again in the afternoon, making for a long day spent mostly on the road, we show up for school at El Porvenir at eleven, nice and fresh after an early lunch at home. Compared to those at Las Teresianas, the uniforms are comfortable and practical: no long sleeves, stockings (which we didn't wear anyway) and the dark blue skirt does not have to be kept spotless as the white ones. They don't have to be as long either. The school break in the middle of the afternoon is for a merienda of a snack brought from home, or ice cream bought from the Japanese vendor that comes to the school door — who we call El Chino. The school, of course, has no buses. We arrive by public transportation and usually walk home after school. There is no homework, just reading assignments, and if that is not enough, Friday is known as Viernes Literarios where students "volunteer" to perform for the entertainment of the rest of the school. There have been poetry readings, singing, and even an infamous tap dancing performance (I won't name the participants). After school, some of us started taking guitar lessons nearby from Catalina Guerra. I showed no talent and quickly gave up, but Lucy, Marta, and other friends performed, playing the guitar and singing at formal recitals given by the Academia Tarraga, the name of Catalina's the guitar school.

Other days we walk, sometimes even in the rain, to the Club Atletico, that is on our way home. We have, formed an after school basketball team coached by some of the best players from the Club team. All this a far cry from what our ex classmates are doing at Las Teresianas. And, oh yes, no more parades. The Larrauri sisters pay the fines rather than have their students show off for the public.

The master plan (Papi's) called for Oli to go to a good preparatory school in the United States for a couple of years to be sure to be accepted at Lehigh. War or no war, it was going to happen. Fortunately for all involved, the war was winding down in the summer of 1944 as plans were made on the porch of Los Desengaños worlds away from all conflicts. Papi's friends had been canvassing the school scene for him and somebody had recommended Blair Academy, in Blairstown, New Jersey. Correspondence began; Papi has always been a great letter writer, as are many of his generation. He can type fast too, using two index fingers. Plans were made for the two of them to travel in the fall of 1945. In the summer, the news of the use of atomic bombs left no doubt that the war was over in the Pacific also. That war may have been remote to us but the newsreels and radio reports made it close. Now, because of wartime shortages in the U.S. the school asked that Oli bring, amongst other things, his own soap.

Our family has a reputation of being tight with money. In a joking manner it has reached me many times. I don't consider it demeaning, on the contrary, it gives me a sense of superiority that we don't need what we don't have. We are extremely lucky to have the land that provides all the pleasure that we would ever want. I was going to say, "And it is free", but it isn't. Papi had taken a huge personal debt to keep some of the inherited land and make it productive after being abandoned for a generation. To pay back that debt we all learned to be frugal, and liked it. Papi likes to say with pride that he doesn't need more than a pair of shoes (not counting boots) since he only has a pair of feet. Mami just loves being poor. The truth is that for years every spare penny went back into the ranch. Now we are starting to take some of the income from the ranch for personal use. Papi resumed contact with his friends up north and talks about attending the yearly homecoming class reunions. They have purchased a vacant lot just around the corner from our rented house in Garrido on the Avenida Cornelio Porro, and started making plans to have a house built there.

As far as I can see, Mami's life didn't change with the family's change in fortune. She never was part of the card playing or fashionable charities groups. Where other women around her have their favorite dress makers, are always going for fittings and talk about fabrics and flattering colors, she buys her clothes readymade in two yearly visits to El Encanto, at the start of summer and winter. The saleswoman is Mami's friend and probably expects her and is ready for the event. Lucy and I, of course, come along and sit in awe as Mami is told how great she looks in dresses that she would never wear but tries on to please her friend. She finally chooses a couple and takes them home. She is a perfect size, so no alterations are required. From there we walk just around the corner to my abuela's house. She regularly visits a few friends and a lot of relatives usually with her daughters in tow .We take the trolley or walk.

We have been taking English lessons from a northern expatriate we know simply as Mister. Papi never speaks English to us but he does sing in English. The three of us learned to sing the Lehigh Alma Mater and other college songs as well as the official song of his fraternity, his much loved D.U. (Delta Upsilon). I suppose he just wanted Oli to learn them but we girls learned them as well. He also sang songs from his youth. There is one in particular that must have had special meaning. I never heard it anywhere else. On quiet moments on the porch, he would take the cigar out of his mouth and sing softly:

"The hours I spent with you dear heart,
Are like a string of pearls to me,
I count them each and every one apart.
My Rosary, my Rosary."

Early in September Lucy and I were picked up in Faustino's old Ford in front of the El Porvenir for the ride to the airport to see the travelers off. Papi was beyond happy to finally have the opportunity to introduce his son to the scenes of his youth he has been talking about for years. Mami should have gone also, but school has already started for us, girls, and Mami will not leave us; she has never been out of Cuba, but I guess this is a special trip and only for Papi and his son.

Faraway places. Going away to school

Oli didn't come home for Christmas that first school year away. It was decided that it would be better if he didn't take a break so soon. He spent his vacation at a farmhouse near Baltimore, the home of one of Papi's fraternity brothers, who sent a 45 rpm record so we could hear his voice. We were so proud when we first heard him say "OK" to his host.

Sending his sixteen year old only son away was planned, but Papi felt his absence. To him it was imperative to give his son some of the opportunities he had. It wasn't so much an education as the opportunity to experience the people and the places that we had been hearing about all our lives. Still, the first trip back to the United States after an absence of about twenty years was a strange experience for a man who had lived in two worlds, today's Cuba and the U.S. of pre WW I. He and his school friends had never lost touch and getting together again they picked up where they left off and had a chance to compare the changes that had taken place over the years. Some of them silly, Papi objected to a girl being called a "gal." To his friends, he had been frozen in time.

After seeing that there was something on the other side of the water, Oli could, hopefully, decide that he still wants to be a guajiro. But now he can be a more worldly and educated guajiro, like his father. While waiting for his son to come home to stay, Papi has to rely more than ever on Miguel in Los Desengaños and Coral's brother, Ernesto, who has been put in charge of La Gertrudis now that Jose Maria and his brood are gone. Papi is having a masonry house built there so he can stay where most of the action is, instead of going back to Los Desengaños every evening even when the family is away, as he has been doing. He doesn't say so, but it must be sad for him to be alone here. Even I get a spaced-out feeling in the batey of Los Desengaños, late in the afternoon when there is no one around. I have never been alone in Las Gertrudis, and probably nobody has.

The man in El Destino is Pedro Carbajal. He married late and has no children of his own. He adores Oli and to Oli he is second only to his own father—if that. He taught Oli how to ride on a pony named Tomeguin. El Destino is not on another world like the ranches near the north coast. You have neighbors who visit. It is close enough to Camagüey that you can ride to town and be back for supper, or the other way around. We have a horse stall in the back of our house in Garrido and it is used often.

When Oli arrived home after a full year up north he didn't look much different except a little taller and with a lighter complexion, but his dog Duque didn't recognize him. To us the main difference was that he had lost his tan, but to a dog he smelled different after being fumigated with the airplane before landing. He must have been a little disappointed that his dog didn't greet him, just stared at him and went and sat in a corner. Duque eyed him from across the porch for a long time. Everybody was talking as we were getting reacquainted when something clicked in Duque's little brain. He bolted from across the room and on to Oli's lap in a wild display of affection.

In 1946 Lucy and I graduated from eighth grade at El Porvenir — together, of course. We donned long white gowns and, lipstick! And had our portraits taken professionally. I cannot leave out this one honor since I had not been considered a top scholar until we transferred to El Porvenir: at the graduation ceremony at the Teatro Popular, and in front of a full house, I was proclaimed first in the graduating class.

The Larrauri sisters were outraged that Mami, an educator herself, was willing to let two of their prize students stay home and do nothing. It is difficult to pass judgment on people and situations too close to home, but the fact is that in the Sanchez-Miranda household all but one of the six brothers graduated from college while no one of the six sisters even considered attending. As far as I know they were tutored at home, if that. We cannot reason that it was only the ways of the times, because many women of their situation accomplished more than getting a husband. Lucy and I were too young to go husband hunting yet as a fulltime occupation. We filled the time as best we could as our classmates went away to prep schools, in the U.S. or Havana, entered the Instituto, or any of the several secondary schools specializing in commerce, teaching, domestic arts, etc. We studied English upstairs of the Royal Bank of Canada, with Nuna Connolly, daughter of Papi's long time friend and former business partner. More guitar lessons with Catalina Guerra (wasted on me) and Lucy even went back to Las Teresianas for something.

Finally, Mami couldn't stand us any longer and talks began about what to do with "the girls." The most logical place where to continue our education would be the local Instituto de Segunda Enseñanza — where my mother had studied a generation earlier, had excelled and recalled with fond memories — but it was co-ed and therefore, out of the question. El Porvenir is co-ed also but apparently my parents felt they had to keep us away from boys at this stage. The best girl's boarding schools in Havana were run by nuns; Papi had had enough of them. He remembered a girl's school in Bethlehem, Pennsylvania, known in his days as Fem Sem. It is now Moravian Seminary for Girls. One of his best friends is a trustee, and Papi has enough friends left around Bethlehem to keep their eyes on us. So Moravian it will be.

It was around that time that we had an unexplainable, major change in Los Desengaños, and in the farms and ranches in the whole area around it. The housewives picked up and left leaving behind bewildered husbands and abandoned children. But it caused less of a commotion that you would expect. The story of why it happened was repeated everywhere you went which of course doesn't make it true, but that is all I have to go by. It is hard to understand unless you are a follower of the novelas. I am not going to translate it to radio soap opera, because the novela is different. As far as I can ascertain, the soap opera goes on and on and never gets anywhere. The novela is fast moving, especially when it gets to the end. Those that have the time to listen every afternoon can't wait for the outcome. And that includes men as well as women.

When the woman on the radio left her husband and went into the world to seek her fortune, nobody thought it outrageous that Coral, and others like her would do the same. Coral left two young children and an incredibly accepting Miguel. Esperanza, in the neighboring homestead, had teenage boys that could fend for themselves and more resources. Those and the others had one thing in common if the radio theory is true they felt trapped in their world.

To me Los Desengaños is heaven and I always thought I would be happy living here all year. But what if I had to? To me the door was always open but to Coral it was shut. Mami couldn't take it years ago. But to her there was a proper way out and she took it. Coral may have loved this place as much as we did, but standing there in the company of children and animals day after day waiting for the arrival of the men so she could serve dinner and wash dishes, she may have asked herself some questions, and the radio novella answered them.

Of course, the story could be completely different for each woman and just a coincidence that three or four of them left at the same time. They were not in touch with one another. Had no telephones and seldom, if ever visited. Coral could have left with a lover. If Miguel knew the truth he must have told Papi. But there is a code of silence between them and I knew better than to ask. Papi is open with his thoughts. He doesn't hide much, but he can keep somebody else's secret. The hole left in the batey by the departure of Coral was soon filled. A young man with a limp, known as El Cojo (of course) was hired as the casero, a combination cook and caretaker who would feed the chickens and see that the water tanks are filled. The hole left in the life of Miguel was harder to fill. Or was it? The next time I saw them, the children seemed happy and well cared for. I think Joseito had been doing much of the day to day child care even before Coral left.

We have a name for Miguel, behind his back. El Reyesito after a cartoon character of a little king that was as wide as he was tall. Miguel is not fat, but he has very broad shoulders and short legs. On horseback the resemblance is not noticeable, but on foot he has a regal way of walking with his chest out and his shoulders thrown back, He has always looked the same, and still does. The men dress pretty much the same: long sleeve shirts, regardless of the weather, loose fitting pants of drab green or gray, or whatever Tecla brought them, tucked into high laced paratrooper boots. The machete belt is a common accessory, but it is usually left with the saddle unless there is a need for it. Now Oli introduced a new fashion: blue jeans. He also at times tried wearing white tee shirts as outerwear that may have been just the thing in New Jersey, but it is new and different here. Papi said that it is like going around in underwear.

The summer went on as if nothing had happened. We all enjoyed having small children around. It was as if Miguelito and Maricusa were everyone's children, and nobody talked about their mother. Came August and Mami had the honor of pointing the finger of death at the pig that would be butchered earlier than his peers and become a lechon asado on her Saints Day. The others will have to put on weight before going to the slaughter house; the chosen one had to be leaner and just the right size. For today's purpose they want one under a hundred pounds. It was her choice but Miguel and even Papi had veto power. Her first few picks were always deemed as too big. "They look much bigger on the pole than on the ground" explained Miguel.

Pigs of all sizes were not hard to find. They have the run of the whole thirteen caballerias of Los Desengaños with the exception of la estancia. The perimeter fences are pig-proof and the other fences are not; they go under the wires like we do. Everywhere you look you see the gray bodies, sometimes with one half caked in dry mud, moving around purposely making the rounds of palms and other trees with edible fruit. They all have the same notch in the ear to show that they have been counted and vaccinated and the same rectangular body shape of a good breed. Joseito and Oli were tagging along with a couple of dogs and the moment a pig met with everybody's approval they grabbed it. The pig that just a moment ago was walking along nonchalantly was now squealing for his life while his former companions kept their distance.

There are two things that Mami has always protected us from watching: the killing of animals and mating (especially horses). Both bans impossible to enforce, but she tried. She has finally given up, but still she prohibits discussing animal sex life around the table. As for killing, if we want to eat them, they have to be killed. Seems hypocritical to look the other way and let Miguel do the unpleasant work. But that is exactly what I do. I stood around the corner of the house looking the other way, and when I looked back the pig was dead. It had a neat knife wound by its front left leg. It had been stunted with a blow to the head first, so the stab to the heart was quick and accurate. There are so many things that guajiros do so well that they don't teach in school.

The next step turned the dirty grey puerco into a clean, white lechon, something more at home in a butcher shop than running around in the field. Now we can stop thinking of it as a living thing, and think of the feast ahead. It was placed on a simple set up that has seen many pigs: a sheet of roofing metal on an outdoor table. The hair and dark outermost layer of skin were scrapped away using boiling water and a piece of broken machete. They take great care of every detail, the ears, tail… because this is a special occasion pig. It takes time. Next, Miguel gets his best knife and plays the surgeon. The liver is sent to the kitchen on a plate and the rest of the entrails go into a bucket. It will be dumped in the recogedor where the dogs and the other pigs will share them (pigs will eat anything, even other pigs). One year we had as a cook a country woman from northern Spain. She was critical of how wasteful we were in this land of plenty. She said that back home they find use for every part of the hog, but the squeal. The final touch was a rub with a brick and a rinse, inside and out. Joseito and Miguel worked together, but Miguel did all the talking, mostly to entertain the audience. We have many "remember when" of incidents that are best forgotten.

By the time they are finished for the evening, the pig has a pole through it, coming out the mouth and the rear end. The legs are stretched front and back and wired to the pole. A large nail is hammered through its snout to be sure it doesn't turn on the pole. In that ignoble position, the pig and the pole spend the night leaning against the wall. The trench is made ready in the area between the two houses called the gallinero even if there are no more gallinas (chickens) there than anywhere else. Now the rest is the job of Pedro Gallo, our neighbor and official pig roaster.

Pedro Gallo is a sheepherder. He is an old man who knows how to roast a perfect lechon asado and in that capacity he was summoned to Los Desengaños. I don't know if he gets paid. I supposed he does in a very discreet manner because he is basically a friend doing something for fun and as a favor. He lives in La Rosalia with his sheep and I suppose he is a poor man.

It isn't my habit to get up before daylight (not even on my Saints Day) so by the time I went to the dining room look-out the fire was on and several figures were standing near it speculating on its merits. I joined them. Papi's face was pink because of the fire and his eyes twinkled as they often do. He said, "if only it was winter and we had some chestnuts." I had never seen a chestnut, but I knew what he was talking about. Pedro Gallo didn't. We went back to the house for breakfast.

The five of us eat together at the round table, three meals a day if possible. The table is always set with tablecloth and silverware properly arranged but it is a little wobbly if not properly balanced because termites have been nibbling at the four slanted legs that keep the pedestal upright. We sit down together and rise together. But we don't say grace. We are not a religious family although we go through the paces when required. Breakfast today is typical, dry cereal with bananas and cream followed by café con leche with galletas. We never have bread because it doesn't keep. The crackers keep about forever in the ten gallon can they come in. I am the only one that drinks milk without coffee. Because at one time I said I don't like coffee and now I can't back out. Our breakfast is not always this simple. On the rare occasions that we have fresh meat, Papi likes a small fried steak. If there is something special the night before, like arroz con pollo, the leftovers are sometimes saved and reheated for breakfast, but at other times they go to the dogs.

After the porch, the dining room is the place where we spend more time. There are markings on the doorframe showing how tall we were at different ages. At one time I was almost as tall as Oli and much taller than Lucy. Now Lucy and I are about the same and Oli is much taller. We are not going to measure us anymore. We are almost finished growing.

We left the table on time to watch the pole with the pig placed on the forked supports at both ends of the fire pit. We watched for a while until we lost interest. Pedro Gallo will be here most of the day attending that fire and raising and lowering the pole as needed. He sits near the pit on the north side. The breeze here, near the north coast, is steady from the northeast and cooler than farther inland. It blows softly and predictably, unless there is a storm coming, in which case it changes direction. The breeze determines the placement of the buildings around the batey. It is not coincidence that the pigpens and casa de vaqueria are to the south.

Several items on today's menu are only served with lechon asado. We don't have them at any other time. One is garlic sauce, served on the side. Papi hates the taste of garlic. He traces his dislike to a day he took a short cut through the kitchen of the otra casa and saw a small dish with what he thought were almonds and popped a handful in his mouth. They were peeled garlic cloves. Since he won't eat garlic, it is not added to the food, but served on the side as a sauce as a compromise. It is only garlic fried in olive oil, with salt and lemon juice added, and it is placed by Mami's plate. Another sauce made with chunks of the pig's liver is called mondongo. This is another compromise because the real mondongo is made from tripe. That is served on top of the casabe. The flat, round casabe was the staple food of our native ancestors and that may be the reason we all love it even if it is almost completely tasteless. It can be served toasted or soft and soggy under the mondongo. It is becoming harder to find. The yuca root or tapioca from which it is made is planted and eaten everywhere but the casabe is not that popular. I guess few people know how to make the flat cakes anymore.

One more part of our special dinner — I'm not counting rice and fried bananas, which are always present— is red wine. One bottle (only) of vino tinto Marquez de Riscal has been brought from La Playa. That is enough for one small glass for the parents and maybe a watered down glass for us. There was no corkscrew around so I was allowed to open it a special way: by tapping the bottom against the soft dirt. If all that shaking was bad for the wine, we didn't notice. We had always been served small amounts of diluted wine since small children. There is no fear of becoming addicted since it is not available most of the time.

All through the morning Pedro Gallo stayed near his roasting pig, occasionally making changes to the fire or turning the pole. The men didn't take the day off — in a ranch there are no days off— but stayed near the batey doing small repair jobs. And making plans for the next day. In the hottest part of the day, Papi went to the hutch in the dining room where he kept a bottle of aguardiente. He poured a small glass and gave it to me to take to Pedro Gallo. It took me forever to go down the steps and the short distance without spilling it. Pedro Gallo threw the rum in his mouth and handed the glass back to me in one smooth movement. Obviously he was expecting it.

In some places they baste the pig as it roasts. Here we prefer roast pork to taste like roast pork. No distracting flavors. As the smell got stronger, we came closer to the pit, and after boring hours alone, Pedro Gallo was finally the center of attention, or rather, his pig. Now the question is, "is it done?" It smells done. It is golden all over. Oli asks if he may break off an ear. He does, and reports that it is perfect. But that is not enough; the whole pig has to be so well done that it will fall apart, and only Pedro Gallo can decide. Joseito and a helper bring a freshly cut yagua, and flatten it on the table. They sharpen their knives and machetes.

Pedro Gallo gives the body of the pig a push and the leg joints fall apart leaving the feet wired to the pole. That is it. It is done. Now it is carried very carefully to the yagua; they pull out the nail and the whole thing slides off the pole. It is chopped with the machetes, skin, bones and all. The chopping has to stop often while everybody grabs pieces of skin or meat. By the time they get it to the table, the best part is over.

Boarding School

On the way through Nuevitas we had taken the first step to legally enter the U.S. as students. Papi was already an expert with the paperwork having done it for Oli two years earlier. With girls (of any age) there was an additional piece of paper: a certificate from the Camagüey police that we had no criminal record as prostitutes. The rest was the same: chest x-rays to prove we had no tuberculosis, somebody able to pay expenses and proof of enrollment in the school. As in any official form, every question must be answered no matter how ridiculous. On the line "occupation" the clerk had filled in Actividades propias de su sexo. Papi used that to tease us, on and off, forever. We saved a trip to Havana because there is Consulate Service in Nuevitas. Not a busy office. My grandfather had held the same post of Consulate Agent as a sideline, almost a century before.

Oli graduated from Blair Academy after two years. The main reason for going was to prepare him for Lehigh — it would have been a shocker if he was not accepted, but, of course, he was. He tried to please his father and even had his picture taken in football uniform, but there is a limit to filial loyalty. Lacrosse was no longer popular as a men's team sport and Blair probably didn't have a team. Oli's medals were in javelin throw. A surprise. He didn't travel with the rest of the family in September of 1947. He had reported early to Lehigh.

The trip was a new experience not only for Lucy and me, but for Mami also. We flew in a Pan Am flight that stopped at the Camagüey airport on the way to Miami from somewhere in South America. We were given Chiclets to clear the pressure in our ears but still I couldn't hear for hours after landing. The rest of the family was not bothered by it. In Miami we rode in a taxi through almost rural outskirts to the city itself and to the Miami Colonial Hotel on Biscayne Boulevard. Next morning we took another taxi for the short distance to the downtown train station where we took the Silver Meteor to Philadelphia. I was equally impressed with the dining car and with the passing countryside. The white tablecloth, neatly placed silverware and distinguished looking waiter were in sharp contrast with the houses we saw near the tracks. Those were not much different from small town or country houses in Cuba, metal roof and open porch with steps in front. But there were no thatch roofs here and the people we saw sitting on the porches were mostly Negroes.

In Philadelphia there was much visiting with Papi's friends and their families, with everybody trying to understand and be understood across the language barrier. Papi is not good at translating. When he goes into his English speaking persona even his looks change and it is almost as if he no longer understood Spanish. Mami solved the language problem by smiling a lot and then Papi had to translate things like "they say that you have beautiful teeth." It was easier for Lucy and me. Adults don't really expect much of somebody else's teenagers. Whatever we did or said, it was fine. Then Papi took us to a very large department store and went back to his friends while Mami and the two of us shopped for hours for the things we were asked to bring to school. We have to bring everything, even sheets and towels. We bought winter coats but not too many clothes since we will be wearing uniforms most of the time. Mami also bought things for herself, including a silly hat with a feather that hung down in front of her eyes like a fishing rod. I had never seen her wearing any kind of hat.

We took a train again; this time to Bethlehem. What a gloomy town. It is a steel mill town and the sky is permanently gray. And to think that Papi yearned for it in clean, beautiful Cuba. But the people are incredibly nice. Not only at the school, where they had to be, but everywhere we went. My parents left us at the school and spent the night just up the street at the Hotel Bethlehem. In the morning they were leaving for New York and would be back in a few days for a final good by until we go home for the summer. We were the first to arrive. A big mistake. That night was like the famous noche triste in Mexican history. I kept looking out of my bedroom windows to the windows in the hotel wondering which one was my parent's room. Papi joked later that Mami spent the night mooing like the cows when their calves are taken away.

The Moravian buildings are supposed to be very old and historic. One of those places where Washington slept, or could have. They didn't look that old to me and I wasn't much impressed with the history. But when the other girls began to arrive, things changed. At first, all we could do was watch as the incoming girls were joyfully reunited with friends from last school year. We had instructions not to speak Spanish to each other so we just stood there looking dumb. There was one other Cuban girl, from Havana, who apparently had the same instructions. It didn't take long to sort ourselves out and figure out who would make good friends and who wouldn't. My assigned roommate was a sophisticated (I thought) girl from New York City but the one that was to become my first friend was in the next room. Margie was Arabian and had lived in Lebanon, among other places. She spoke French before English. Now she spoke English like a native. At home in New York, her family spoke several languages, but Spanish was not one of them. Still, she was accustomed to hearing imperfect English spoken with different accents. She understood me perfectly when others didn't, or pretended not to. She became my interpreter.

At first, Lucy and I were placed in several English classes in an ef-fort to catch up. We didn't get a chance to shine until we were in some courses for our level (10th grade) like Math and Science. We were surprised to discover that we had learned in El Porvenir material that was not taught here until much later. We had skipped the 9th grade which didn't prove to be any problem. The 10th grade Plane Geometry we had studied in the 7th grade. English class was a different story. The first time I was told to write a sonnet I just sat there in shock. The teacher might as well have asked me to fly like a bird.

The best part of the school was not the classrooms and other parts of the buildings. It was in the back and hidden from the street. Between the buildings and a canal and some wooded areas was the playing field. Lucy and I took to Field Hockey as if we had played all our lives. We also did well in Track and Field. We had been running all our lives and, as for jumping, Oli had built a high jump bar at Los Desengaños and we had been practic-ing all of last summer. In the field nobody cares if you have a funny accent. In truth, this school was small enough to give everyone a chance to shine at something.

Oli was now a freshman at Lehigh, on the South Mountain just on the other side of the river. The first time he came to visit it caused a sensation at Moravian. To me he was just my brother. I had never realized that he was seen as very good looking. Every girl in the school found a reason to come by the Blue Parlor. My roommate suddenly became friendly.

Everything at Moravian reflected the wishes and the taste of the principal, Miss Haupert. I had trouble with her name— people heard it as Miss Hopper— but not with the woman. In a way she was like my father, but without the humor, the twinkle in the eyes. The resemblance was only in that she avoided what she considered the soft life. She didn't pamper herself or allowed us to be pampered. Since the bedrooms and classrooms were under the same roof, she thought that we should take a walk before breakfast to compensate for not having to walk to school. And that meant in any weather. I don't remember any mornings when the weather was fair. It was windy, raining or cold. Usually all of the above. We were sent out regardless of weather, checked at the door to make sure nobody stayed behind. We walked around for at least a couple of city blocks, sometimes looking in the windows of the hotel and watching the guests comfortably eating breakfast, and we discovered that the double entrance to a furniture store could provide us with protection from the howling wind. This was not the school for spoiled girls: we made our beds, cleaned our rooms and mended our clothes on Saturdays.... The heat was turned off at night and we slept with open windows in all weather.

Everybody that grows up without it remembers their first snow. Bethlehem, the Christmas City, looks like a postcard under the new fallen snow: the churches; the distant mountains; the street trees… I was impressed at the sight but only in a detached way, this was not mine. All the girls, most of whom had seen snow every winter of their lives, had to run outside and play in the snow just like us who were seeing it for the first time. But within minutes the streets turn to grey mush. We ran inside, cold and wet. There is a traditional tree lighting ceremony before students go home for the holidays. A giant tree is placed in the intersection of the bridges and some dignitary has the honor of pulling a switch from the steps of the Moravian Church at the foot of the Hill to Hill bridge. This year we had a bonus attraction. The tree went up in flames when the lights were turned on. It was rumored that the proximity to an engineering school had something to do with the "accident."

Being Catholic in a Protestant school was no problem at all. Papi is not a practicing catholic at home, but in the States he is. One of the many instructions and warnings we had received was to always proclaim our religion. "Here they don't care what is your religion, as long as you have one." It was not so much being hypocritical, as fitting in. We attended the daily chapel and vespers and loved singing hymns. Specially the Christmas ones. On Sundays, the few catholic girls in the school walked to the Catholic Church on 4th Street on the South side of town. That was quite the treat and some non-Catholics sometimes obtained permission to join us. We crossed the river on the Church Street Bridge, an old plank bridge that in my father's days was called the "Penny Bridge" because pedestrians paid a penny to cross it. Except for the day of their traditional Lehigh-Lafayette game when students crossed chanting "we pay no toll tonight." That and so many other stories were told in what here seems like from another world: talking in the evenings on our open, balcony-like porch looking at the dark shapes of the algarrobas trees and the cattle moving like ghosts in the darkness.

There is one sure cure for homesickness; writing letters home. You would think that receiving letters was the cure, but it isn't. Writing is even better. I shared what I saw and by doing that brought my parents into my new temporary life. Some of Papi's friends visited us at the school and we visited them. I suppose they reported on how we were doing. News from Camagüey came every week in two letters in one envelope addressed to all three of us. Papi's letter was typed and Mami's was in her florid handwriting, identical to her sister's and that of everybody of her age group. In one of those letters she reported that my uncle Miguel Agramonte, the judge who had ruled in favor of the cattlemen, died of kidney failure. The Asociacion Ganadera gave his widow a house as a show of gratitude.

Oli was living at the D.U. fraternity house, not coincidentally the same my father had belonged to, but had not pledged. One evening when I called to share with him the content of the latest letters, as we often did, the man (at Lehigh you don't say boy) who answered the phone told me that Oli could not come to the phone because they were in the middle of a bridge tournament. It took me a while to grasp that Oli was their bridge champion, or at least part of their best team. We had never played cards at home; Parcheesi, dominoes, even chess, but never bridge. If we had a deck of cards at home it would be of the old Spanish kind. I guess he was a fast learner.

We arrived back at the Aeropuerto Internacional Ignacio Agramonte in June. We are lucky to have a good airfield close to home, courtesy of the U.S. Air force wartime effort, so we don't have to travel through Havana.

The terminal is mostly informal, but we had to go through a side room where an unfortunate custom agent had to rummage through suitcases full of dirty clothes, before we could hug our parents and head for the old house in Garrido. The new family home, nearby at Cornelio Porro 54, was being built as funds became available. Papi was not going to borrow money again. The builder, because of personal friendship, and because he had other projects to keep his crew occupied, was agreeable to the plan. When we arrived in Camagüey for the summer of '48 the construction had stopped. The house was a grey concrete structure resembling more a fortification than a future home. If it is ever finished, no hurricane is going to blow this house over.

We stayed in Camagüey long enough to enjoy the festivities of San Juan, not religious as the name would suggest, but carnival-like. Originally the time was chosen to coincide with the dry season and the sale of cattle. A festival a few months later would have been in the rain. There are parties at all the clubs Here there are clubs for all tastes, interests and, yes, social position. Although at the club level social and economic standing go together. If there is money, a friend to introduce you, and no enemies to "black ball" you, eventually, one goes to any club (except Maceo that only accepts blacks). But to have a good time in San Juan you don't have to belong. The best parties are street parties. There are some blocks that are closed off for the five days between San Juan and San Pedro (June 24-29) and there is dancing every night. The chaperone system that is in force during the Christmas-New Year party season is more relaxed during San Juan. As long as we are with a group of known friends, we can go almost everywhere. For those on wheels, the main attraction is the Paseo. There are decorated floats with a selected "Queen", of course, and many assorted vehicles. You go around and around a designated circuit in the center of the old city: the length of Cisneros to the bridge and the other way on Independencia, Maceo, Avellaneda, all the way to the railroad station and return on Republica to Padre Valencia and to Cisneros again. That covers most of the city, which is not a long distance but takes a while during the festivities. If somebody wanted to go somewhere in a hurry they would be better off walking.

Once San Juan was over, we headed for the coast. There was no time to waste. It was the end of June and time for the annual beneficeo. We would not have wanted to miss the yearly branding. Oli is one of the main participants, but Lucy and I help also, but from outside the corral. Papi does all the vaccinating himself. This year there will be one fewer procedure done thanks to the peculiarities of the Havana meat market: they don't want steers; buyers want bulls because they claim steers are too fat. The buyer with the money rules, so we will let these male calves grow into bulls. But bulls are harder to handle and more dangerous. Some of the animals worked today are already yearlings that were too young to brand this time last year. A Brahma yearling is a handful. There is a lot of laughing and teasing as men are thrown around but nobody gets hurt. Besides the muñeco on the rump the females are getting a number "8" on the shoulder. If they are kept for breeding it will be useful to know their age, if not, no harm done.

The beneficeo in La Gertrudis is not nearly as much fun, but a lot more efficient. There is now a chute where the animal is trapped and held tight while attacked from all sides. Branding, dehorning, vaccinating is all done without roping and throwing the animal to the ground, and it is all over before it knows what hit it. This same crew will do ten times the number done here in about the same time and without anybody rolling in the manure.

We still travelled the long way from Camagüey to Los Desengaños by crossing the bay by boat, but it is increasingly easier to go by land. A packed earth and gravel road, or terraplen to San Miguel was built by neighbors (mostly us). The area called the Derramaderos is still impassable to vehicles as soon as the river swells. Papi now owns an old truck and a Caterpillar bulldozer, both bought second-hand. Oli is our main mechanic and seems to be good at it. He is beginning to think that he would rather be a mechanic than a mechanical engineer. But, dutifully, he is going back to Lehigh.

We also went back to school in the fall. This time we had to go through La Habana. It seemed that the regulations have been changed and the little consulate in Nuevitas doesn't handle student visas anymore. Please notice that I use Habana and Havana interchangeably. The name of the city is Habana but for some reason, outside of Cuba people insist on calling it Havana. My father has three sisters and their families there but I remember visiting them only once before. He has good relationship with his sisters — and with all his relatives—but only goes to Havana on short business trips and then stays at Hotel Lincoln, right in town. Many Cubans in the provinces, or el interior as they say in Havana, that can afford to do so, go to doctors, shop and follow the happenings in the capital in sports, politics, and even in the society pages of the Diario de la Marina, but we choose to ignore them. It is a form of reverse snobbery to say that we don't need the capital city. But for traveling to the U.S. we do now, and, I hate to admit it, but we enjoyed the short stay. My cousin was most proud of and wanted to show off the modern stores. The escalator at Sears I remembered from the previous visit when we found it most entertaining, but now we had seen others in Philadelphia. What they still have in Havana that nobody else can equal is the Malecon, their ocean front wall, the entrance to the harbor with ships so close you feel you could touch them, and the view of the Morro Castle on the other side.

At Moravian, this year we are amongst the old timers arriving to the joy of friends. My English was not, and probably will never be, perfect, but I am not worrying about it anymore. We are now on a higher floor; more steps to climb. I have two roommates, both of them seniors, but I still have another year to go. One of my roommates is a dedicated musician. That is all she lives for, and since I know nothing about classical music, we have nothing to talk about. This is a music centered school. The whole area is. About every other girl can play the piano. What little I remembered from my most basic music lessons is useless here. They never heard of do re mi, they use a letter system that I can't figure out. I don't have to worry about that because I am not taking music lessons, but there are so many other little differences to figure out, like the dates with the month first, and the weeks beginning with Sunday instead of Monday.

My other roommate became a close friend, along with Margie. Shirley and I had something in common, being a long way from home. Actually, Shirley has no home. Her mother is dead and her father is an army officer stationed in Tokyo and has recently remarried. There is another girl with parents in Lebanon, but most of them come from the New York, New Jersey area and go home often. Many have divorced parents, so they have two homes. And some, especially the day students, are here instead of in public schools because the family is of the Moravian religion. I don't spend time with Lucy, she has her own set of friends, but we are in the same classes and both play hockey. Other sports also, but hockey is my favorite.

There is a required course named "Problems of American Democracy." It always surprises me that here they use America meaning the United States, and don't include us. Anyway, the course is about U.S. government. It is presidential election year and the students talk about the candidates constantly. Everyone is sure that Thomas Dewey will win. I suppose that they just mimic what their parents think. We all stayed up half the night listening to election result and they were shocked in the morning to learn that Harry Truman was re-elected. That shows that the people around me don't always represent the sentiments of a country at large. It reminded me when a few years ago in Camagüey our friends were sure that Batista was going to be re-elected. Children, including my friends and I chanted:

Batista president, Pedraza coronel

y Grau de limpiabotas en la puerta del cuartel.

As it turned out, Batista was not re-elected, but moved to Daytona Beach, Florida. I have no idea who Pedraza was, but I know that Grau was not polishing boots at the gate to the army post, but was elected president of Cuba. I should have learned to listen for voices coming from beyond my circle of friends, who sometimes just echo one another, and in the case of Moravian girls, their parents.

I try to answer questions about Cuba, but it is so easy to be misunderstood. They know so little about anything outside the United States, and are always so ready to accept that other places are primitive that you have to be careful what you say. For instance, if I say that I can't call my father because there is no telephone where he is, they will assume that there are no telephones in Cuba. Our Civics teacher has been to Havana on a cruise ship and considers herself an expert on all things Cuban. But in general, the girls at Moravian are inquisitive and probably more open minded than most. They discuss religion and morals by the hour. One of the favorite topics, especially amongst the Jewish girls, is whether being Jewish, is a religion, a race, or, as some argue, just a choice.

None of us went home for Christmas. Lucy went to New Jersey with her friend Jean. Oli went somewhere with friends, and Shirley and I took a train to Columbus, Ohio to spend the holidays at nearby Fort Hayes, a military base. Her father had just returned from serving with the occupation force in Japan. Shirley still has to learn to share her adored father with his new wife. As it turned out, we had a great time. We learned to eat with chop sticks and I left with a great recipe for Sweet-sour Pork. But the best part was being almost the only young women in an army post full of young men even if we didn't actually date any of them. Just walking around was enough. One surprise to me was that there were German prisoners this long after the war. They moved around freely and did jobs like stoking furnaces, but they were prisoners, or so I was told.

Both Lucy and I went to our first school dance at the Hotel Bethlehem. Up to now we were with the group that served punch and tried to look like we were enjoying it. Now somebody found us blind dates and we went looking for dresses. I bought the typical ruffled pastel color taffeta, but Lucy bought an out of the ordinary striped golden and green color formal. Maybe it was that dress, or maybe that her date was a popular Lehigh

Junior, or maybe that Lucy had been beautiful all along and we had never noticed, but she was a sensation. Unfortunately, the glamour didn't stick and the next day she was herself again in a faded uniform with frayed hem.

We came home for the summer knowing that I would be the only one of us three going back in the fall. We had a surprise waiting for us in Camagüey. From the airport we didn't head for our old house but went right to the newly finished one. They had rushed the construction to have it ready for us and there are still finishing touches being worked out. The house is sparsely furnished, but for the first time in my life I have a bedroom to myself. To humor my father, they have put in a working fireplace. So there will be no doubt whose house it is, the intertwined initials A.S. (which could stand for Adolfo Sanchez or for Sanchez Agramonte) are built into the terrazzo floor by the front door. A house warming party was already been planned. As it turned out, it rained that day. There is still no lawn around the house and the guests tracked in mud to the point that it was as muddy inside as out. The stairs made with especially milled lumber had to be refinished, but I suppose everyone had a good time even my mother; this is really her house, nobody else's.

Oli immediately bought a Jeep. Going back and forth to Los Desengaños is no big deal now. From now on, Oli will be moving around as much as Papi because he will be in charge of El Destino. His friend and mentor Pedrito Carbajal, who had been the encargado for years, have died. In a touching gesture he left, in writing, his horse and saddle to Oli. Until now, El Destino was used to finish cattle for market. Oli has to continue that, but he also wants to put together a pure bred Brahma herd to sell as breeders. Papi may have made a mistake but it will take years to know for sure: In an effort to improve the dairy herd in Los Desengaños he had bought two Brown Swiss bulls to cross with his mostly Brahmas cows. Their calves look puny to us compared to the others, but he has been assured that they will make good dairy cows.

We came by car to Los Desengaños. As simple as that. Now anybody can get in a vehicle anywhere in Cuba and end up at our front gate. In a way, it is a disturbing feeling. More than ever we have to worry about things like hunters. The men have tied down a couple of droopy-eared hunting dogs that had chased a deer right into the corral. Our dogs stopped them but now we don't know what to do with them. Nobody here liked hunting or guns — in somebody else's hands, because Papi has always kept a revolver by his bed, and Oli used to have a 22 caliber rifle which all three of us have used for target practice, and (I'm ashamed to admit it) have shot woodpeckers and parrots. Our excuse was that they ate fruit, as if it mattered. There are fruit trees all over, some planted, some native. Most of the fruit falls to the ground and is eaten by pigs.

Joseito is courting a girl in San Miguel. She is the younger sister of the now-forgotten Coral. That makes her the aunt of Miguel's children, which seems like a good arrangement for everyone involved. Her three brothers also work with us; the oldest, Ernesto is the encargado at La Gertrudis, the youngest one, Ramon works right here. The third one's name is Benancio but for some unexplained reason he is known as Bataclan and he is mostly at Las Gertrudis. Joseito's girlfriend is named Carolina. We all hope that she will be happier here than Coral was because, even with the road passable most of the time, she still will be living here in isolation. No friends will be stopping by to visit. There may be some trucks on the road, but Joseito still rides his horse to San Miguel. He no longer has to ride through mud the consistency of peanut butter, wade through dark waters and take detours, but it is still a long ride.

Moravian Seminary for Girls moved during the summer of '49 from the historic buildings on Church Street, in Bethlehem to Green Pond, a country estate given to the school. The setting is different but the character of the school remains the same since Miss Haupert is still in charge. Turning a mansion and outlying buildings into a boarding school was a gigantic job and, I suspect, done on a minimal budget. Miss Haupert solved the problem by putting us all to work, and making us feel pride in doing it. One of the first jobs was to get the outdoor swimming pool ready, which we were interested in doing before the weather turned too cold to use it. It had been filled with leaves, perhaps for years telling by the state of decay. We shoveled that mess into wheelbarrows and pushed them up and out of the pool on a ramp. Somehow I can't imagine girls from Las Teresianas doing this. The school "inherited" some of the help that had been living in the estate. We now have a not so solemn ex-butler who picked me up at the station in an old wooden station wagon. I never learned where the fortune that had built Green Pond had come from. In Camagüey you would have expected a sugar mill next to it. But here it was: tennis court, horse barn, servant's quarters.... with no means of income nearby. Maybe the money came from Bethlehem Steel and the owners kept their distance from the dirty mill.

I shared a two bedroom one bath suite, right over the front door of the mansion, with five other seniors. Lucy's friend Jean and her pal Susie were my roommates; Marge and two others were on the other side of the bathroom. The set up, although not primitive at all, reminded me of Los Desengaños with a much disputed bathroom between two bedrooms. We took every opportunity to explore this and other buildings. Most of the valuable furniture had wisely been removed but there was a trove of treasures to be found in attics and cellars. One cabinet was packed with Chinese lanterns. We could picture an elegant summer party taking place, perhaps in the rose garden — which we had discovered after pulling out a jungle of weeds.

With so much to do and think about, and with friends that I had known for two years, I didn't feel the absence of Lucy and Oli. But the happiest day of the year was probably the one when I was playing hockey and looked to the sidelines, and Oli was standing there. At first I thought that I had to be mistaken. But he was looking at me with his huge smile and the hands placed on his hips. He just visited that one day and went back as casually as he had come, but there was a touch of sadness surrounding him as if he wished he could stay at Lehigh with his classmates. Nothing worse that wanting to be in two places at once.

Almost from the beginning of the senior year, girls began to talk about their plans for college and discuss the merits of different ones: Jean wanted a Junior college close to her home in New Jersey; the best students planned to apply to the prestigious women's colleges. I never had had any plans beyond finishing here the equivalent of a secondary education, but I got caught in the mood. When Miss Haupert corralled me in her tiny office under the stairs, our knees almost touching, she said she had just the college for me. "What you want…"was the way she put it. And, of course, that was not what I wanted. She was recommending a small women's college in North Carolina. I had been protected and cared for all my life and she was trying to give me more of the same. . I told her I wanted to apply to a large co-ed University. I had no idea what was what and what were the requirements. At a school dance I had talked to two boys from Blair Academy who were planning to go to Brown University in Providence Rhode Island. The classes there were co-ed, but the women's part was Pembroke College. That seemed to satisfy all concerned. I applied, not even realizing that it was one of the top liberal arts school in the country and I was planning to major in Biology. In spite of my less than brilliant record, I was accepted. Maybe they were looking for diversity or maybe they needed a hockey player. I was captain of the Purple Team.

Papi did not like the idea, but he would never say no. He just pointed out that he didn't know anybody in Providence; that having me here in Bethlehem did not feel so far because he knew the area. Here he had friends to look after me; over there I would be completely on my own. I never had the nerve to tell him that that was the idea. The cost never crossed my mind and he never mentioned it. In a ranch there is a never ending need for money, and schools away from home are expensive.

A few of us took the bus to Allentown to have our photos taken professionally for the Yearbook. The photographer insisted that we don't wear any makeup. In the photo I look younger than the eighteen I was and the looks echoed the Longfellow quotation the members of the Yearbook staff had chosen to place under my photo:

So mild so merciful, so strong so good
So patient, peaceful, loyal, loving, pure

That is not the way I would have chosen to describe myself. Sounded meek, but then, we never see ourselves as others see us. That's another quotation.

Jean had expressed the wish to visit Cuba after graduation and Papi sent her a nice letter inviting her. Her parents came to the graduation ceremony, picked up both of us and our belongings and drove us to the station in Philadelphia to take a train to Miami. For me it was another trip; for Jean, it was the adventure of her life, up to that point. It was fun travelling with Jean and seeing things from a different point of view. We flew to Havana since, on her first trip overseas, she should see a world known city before going to our quaint Camagüey. I have several cousins in Havana, but when it comes to greeting outsiders, especially English speaking ones, Winnie is the star. In the one day we were there, she took us to their club, the Biltmore, toured both modern and colonial La Habana, and ended the day with dinner at her home in Miramar. Winnie's husband, Gabriel, told Jean that she was lucky to see Camagüey from the inside. "That is not a town for tourists," he said, "If you don't know anybody in the inside, you can walk up and down any street and see nothing but blank walls."

Jean saw a lot more than blank walls. Our friends were eager to try their English on her and she really didn't have to say much. Being little, blond and cute was all that was needed. For the many young men of Camagüey, who have made a sport of wooing, this was a great opportunity to practice their skills without lasting complications, since the object of their attention would be leaving in a month. She had no trouble getting an invitation to the dance at El Liceo when I didn't even have a blind date. As soon as the San Juan round of Club dances, comparsas, and street parties were over, we headed for Los Desengaños. Lucy is driving now, which makes us all more mobile. But before we left, we were standing around the side porch of our home in Cornelio Porro, when my father who was inside listening to the radio, put his head out the window and said, "Jean, your country is at war again." The Korean War had started; we didn't make much of it.

Several of the girls at Moravian, including Jean, had taken riding lessons. They often talked about horses, although I never saw one in all my time up north. They used terms unknown to me, and obviously considered riding a sport not, like us, a way of getting from here to there, or an important tool to our work. Jean was fascinated at the site of horses all over town, although she felt sorry for some of them that were too thin and looked like they may have been overworked. Once she arrived in Los Desengaños and saw a pasture full of beautiful horses, she was beside herself. But when we went riding, she was disappointed.

We rode as a group, sometimes for hours, as somebody, usually Ernesto or Miguel, pointed animals out to Papi. We rode at a comfortable pace, and never changed it unless there was a need to do so. Jean was bored and tired. Finally, she found a way to put her horse "through paces." She would fall behind, and then canter and gallop to catch up with the group. Everybody thought it was a peculiar thing to do. At home she is an outdoor person and camper, but our finca is still too primitive to outsiders. Los Desengaños is just not the place for a short visit. Even with the horses Jean probably enjoyed Camagüey more than Los Desengaños. After much practice, she learned to sing "Cocaleca" a silly song popular that summer, and discovered Cuban coffee was best in small quantities.

I know that Papi had hoped that I would change my mind about going to Pembroke, but he still helped me make arrangements for the trip. Many times he pointed out that he didn't know anybody in Providence, as if that was a requirement for me to go there. I was almost nineteen and felt that it was time to do something on my own. In some ways, we were very independent; we all had our own bank account since childhood, when Lucy and I delivered fresh eggs to neighbors in Garrido. It was all very business-like: The eggs were brought to us from El Destino, individually wrapped in newspaper; we took orders, collected money, and paid for the chicken feed. While he had promoted self reliance when we were children, now as teenagers he was not looking forward to a day when we would be leaving him. I think his underlying fear was that I would marry and stay in the U.S. Or simply, that I would marry anybody someday. Mami's fear was probably that I would not marry and hang around forever.

Arriving alone at Providence knowing nobody was exhilarating. But also, most of what I remember about Pembroke was being lost and confused. The living arrangement was easy: a freshman women's dorm called Angell House. That was fine. But the classes were all over the huge urban campus. There was one class I never found. My assigned advisor was a German professor named Herr Schnerr (or something like it) when I finally found his cubicle in a basement somewhere, I could hardly understand him. He wanted to see me because my first English paper was not up to Brown's standards. I knew that. The world history classes consisted on lectures by a prominent historian in a huge auditorium. We sat in alphabetical order: Salinger, Sanchez, Sanderson . . . and took notes. I signed up for "Art Appreciation" for the simple reason that I like art and learned that it was considered the easiest way to add an "A" to your average. The whole Brown football squad was my classmates. I actually learned something and did well in Biology which I intended as my major, and, best of all, I was one of three freshmen who trained with the varsity field hockey team, all of us from Angell House.

For the Thanksgiving break I took a train to somewhere in New Jersey where Jean and her parents met me. As it turned out it would be far from a typical Thanksgiving gathering. Hurricanes winds began to blow as soon as we arrive in Long Valley. The wind blew stronger and stronger as the day went on. As in any hurricane, the power soon went out. During the eye of the storm Jean and I ran outside and, trying to save a tree that was showing signs of toppling over, we tied it to the house. When I looked back, I saw Jean's mother at the window frantically waving her arms: "Don't, don't"! Where in Cuba a hurricane means wind and rain, here there is an added factor, cold. With no electricity, the four of us spend the night wrapped in blankets around the fireplace. In the morning we surveyed the damage. It was a mess: flooded basement, branches and power lines everywhere, but nothing that couldn't be fixed in a few days. Only, I had to get back to Providence.

The return trip was really the final blow to my career at Pembroke. The trains were not running. Planes were full. We rode through the night on frozen roads littered with broken branches. Finally, my friends put me on a bus in New York and sleepy and tired, I arrived by taxi at Angell House in the early morning. Somebody more determined may have made it to classes that day, but I couldn't move. I was already on probation and this didn't help. The semester finals will not be until after the Christmas vacation. With a superhuman effort, I could possibly recover. But there was something else. The war was heating up, and Papi was worried, remembering the previous war, that travelling would become difficult.

I left my footlocker packed so it could be shipped to me if I didn't return, said goodbye to a few friends, and headed for home.

A time for change

Just as many remember what they were doing when they heard of the attack on Pearl Harbor, I remember where I was standing in March 1952 when a radio program was interrupted to announce that Batista had simply taken over the government of Cuba. Papi called from downstairs and everyone that was anywhere in the house at the time froze, as if playing the children's game "statues", and listened. The information was delivered in a tone designed to show calm. Yet it produced in me the opposite effect. It was an almost physical sensation of being in danger. After the initial shock, I took it as a personal affront. For years I have proudly proclaimed to my friends up north that here we lived in a democracy, that, if not perfect, at least it had several smooth transitions of power without the revolutions and bloodshed that journalists risk their lives to report to the world. And, adding insult to injury and not always incorrectly, they portray generals as comedy characters, and Latin American countries as "banana republics."

Since 1940, and mostly to Batista's credit, we had a constitutional democracy. In 1948, while I was away, Grau gave way to Prio in a civilized election and turnover of power, and now there was a three way race for the next election. Since nothing out of the ordinary was happening in Camagüey we had no reason to think that it was not the same in the capital. But apparently, we should have been paying attention.

If we discussed politics or politicians at all it was as a form of entertainment, much like we discussed baseball and the merits of the various players. In the case of baseball players, even if most of us never saw them, they were our heroes and we followed their careers even if the professional teams were all either in the capital or somewhere to the west of us, and so were the scheming politicians. If we followed national politics at all, it was only at the time of elections. All that came to an abrupt end in the early morning of the 10th of March, just two months before general elections were scheduled to take place.

Apparently much had been happening in the political world of Havana which here in Camagüey we try to ignore as much as possible. We do pay attention to the high drama, like the suicide of the self appointed anti-corruption champion, and probably madman, Chibas — a distant relative. Every Sunday evening we listened as he accused every government official of thievery and gangsterism. On August 1951 he had made one of his explosive talks announcing that that would be the last knock on the door of our consciences (ultimo aldabonazo) and then proceeded to shoot himself while on the radio. He had been expected to be the presidential candidate of the Ortodoxo Party. Now his cousin Roberto Agramonte took his place. For the Partido Autentico, the candidate was Carlos Hevia, an engineer considered to be honest. The third candidate was no one else than ex-president Batista.

The Golpe had started in the early morning hours when Batista and a few co-conspirators simply drove into Campamento Columbia, a large army complex outside Havana, and took over, arresting the few officers that didn't cooperate. Not a shot was fired. We didn't get word of what was happening until that afternoon, which is not surprising since President Prio, in the presidential Palace, didn't know either. But by 1 PM Radio Havana made the first announcement of what was happening, and by 4 o'clock Batista made his manifesto declaring that he was taking over to save the country because he had learned that Prio was planning to stay in power regardless of the outcome of the elections. Sort of like robbing a bank to keep thieves from robbing it.

The drastic change in the central government didn't immediately have any effect around my circles of friends and family. Probably not one of us approved of what happened but as long as we felt secure we accepted it. What else could we do? Business in Camagüey went on as usual and at Los Desengaños the Golpe barely deserved a few derogatory comments. But to me, on that day Batista changed from a white hat (well, maybe grey) to a dark hat.

By that time I had been home for a year. The biggest change from earlier times is mobility. Lucy is driving and I also have my license, although when we are together in town she is usually at the wheel. Papi still doesn't drive much but he has a driver named Antonio Portal, known as Papito, so he doesn't depend on his children, all busy on their own way. The seventy-plus kilometers from Camagüey to Los Desengaños seem to have considerably shortened. Instead of closing one house and moving to the other for months at a time, we now live in both. Mami enjoys her home in Cornelio Porro, close to her friends. She does a lot of visiting, almost daily, mostly to my grandmother, but also to assorted aunts and uncles, most of them on my father's side of the family. When we were younger, she took the children with her to make sure we grew up knowing the family. She prefers to use public transportation, even now that she has a car and driver at her disposal, because it gives her a chance to talk to strangers, a specialty of hers. But our beloved tranvias are gone. They were replaced by buses. When Papi is in town he sees his brothers Armando and Ernesto at El Liceo. I don't think tío Joaquin, who doesn't own a single cow, is a member, and tío Julian is too busy with a ranch, his job as director of the Hospital de Emergencias, and a private medical practice, to sit down and play dominoes.

My only aunt living in Camagüey, tía Pepilla, has dinner with us every Sunday. She also makes regular rounds visiting relatives, but in her case, all on foot. Pilla, as she is better known, is a part of the scenery in town. She visits tío Ernesto's house, or quinta off the Carretera Central, just west of town. To do that she has to cross the bridge and the Casino Campestre Park in all kinds of weather. Always carrying and umbrella and wearing sensible laced up shoes with medium heels. She makes that walk daily because the oldest daughter, Clemencita, is the favorite niece, but she never eats anywhere except at her home and ours. To come to our house she does take public transportation or somebody goes to get her. She has peculiar eating rules, like counting to ten before swallowing each bite, never drinking iced water, and much more, following the advice of a food guru of the time, and she doesn't seem to mind the teasing she takes from her youngest brother.

Once I was in Camagüey to stay, I did a half-hearted search for a job. I actually had a job interview but I did not have much to offer an employer. Then I was offered the perfect job with the best possible employer: my father. Papi had always done his own bookkeeping, his own way, and he took pleasure in balancing accounts to the centavo. (Nothing would have made him happier than finding The Royal Bank of Canada in error.) But when he put some of his assets into a family held corporation, Compañia Ganadera El Muñeco, S.A. he had to let a professional set up his bookkeeping system and that took all the fun out of it. I enrolled in an accounting correspondence course with a company, International Correspondence School, which I found through an ad in a magazine. I faithfully completed and mailed in all the lessons, and I may have learned something about double entry bookkeeping, but mostly I followed Papi's instructions. He still works at his roll-top desk when in town and a table in the bedroom when at Los Desengaños and, for what I hear, he keeps better track of his business than most ranchers do. I don't think we pay taxes. If we do, it must not be a big deal.

I have another sort of job and only when we are in town: I teach English in an informal way and only on a one-on-one basis. My most memorable student is Juan Jose, a boy so hyperactive that he never sits down, but answers questions while climbing the window bars, crawling on the floor, and things like that. I wonder if he learns anything.

I finally made up my mind to drive which makes me, not necessarily more independent since I don't have my own car, but more useful. Oli had taught me to drive his Jeep at the ranch but he needs it all the time, so I have to take turns with the car. I started going to Los Desengaños with Papi for a couple of days at a time and for that I not only have to drive but also do the cooking for the two of us. The most crucial part of the meal and the one that an inexperienced cook has trouble mastering is always the rice. So is with me, no one will let me forget my experience with rice. Cooking over charcoal fire you don't only have to think about the food, but about the fire. One day, I managed to get just the right kind of fire going and placed my pot with rice on it. Then went away and forgot it. When we came back, the rice had boiled over and put out the fire. The rice was cooked just right. Papi always says that I have invented the automatic rice machine. As always, whatever his children do is good.

Playa and King Ranch coming

Two big changes are coming to the area around Los Desengaños. I hesitate to call them threats to our way of life, but I will not say "progress" either, although some think they are. One is north of us. The white sand beaches of the North coast were not a secret, but until a developer managed to open a clay road from Santa Lucia to the ocean, only the few who went by boat had enjoyed them. Soon the whole world will want to see them, and to get there they will be traveling on a road that skirts two sides of Los Desengaños, making a right angle at the corner near the estancia; a road that up to this time has only been used, and maintained, by us and our neighbors .

The other change is coming from the other direction. South of us and near the community of San Miguel there was an untouched wooded area belonging to the Central Manati. We had always called it Los Derrama-deros (the overflow area) and assumed it would always be there. Who would want to farm, or live, in a place that is under water during the rainy season? But the word got around soon enough: They are clearing Los Derramade-ros. Every guajiro in San Miguel and beyond has managed to take a peak. According to the witnesses, instead of cutting the trees one by one with axes, they have these huge tractors with a chain in between them and they uproot everything on their path. There is considerable argument if the strangers speak English, Spanish, or both. Joseito — now married to Carolina and living in their separate little house but still joining the gathering in the main house — had actually seen the strangers and talked to them. He described a very tall one that rides slowly in a Jeep inspecting the work, with his foot outside dragging on the ground. (We assumed he was not driving) He said his name was Seth.

It didn't take long for Papi to meet the strangers in Camagüey and learn the whole story. As it happened, we knew about the King Ranch of Texas because we had been reading the novel Giant serialized in the Saturday Evening Post. They have leased the land from Manati, planning to make it into a cattle ranch and call it El Cafetal. — there is a popular song, Mi Cafetal that may have been the inspiration for the name, but there is no coffee grown in this area; coffee is grown in mountains, not swamps — their plan is to introduce their own breed of cattle, of which they are very proud, called Santa Gertrudis. When they found out that Papi has a ranch named La Gertrudis they offered, half in jest, to buy it. To which Papi replied "El que vende tierra, come tierra." (This makes more sense- in Spanish because tierra can mean both land and dirt). He who sells land eats dirt.

The owners of the King Ranch, the Klebergs, (who bore no resemblance to Rock Hudson and Elizabeth Taylor who played them in the movie Giant), are there off and on, but the manager of the project, Lowell Tash and his wife, teenage daughter and younger son, moved in as soon as the house was finished and became well known not only around here, but in Camagüey. He and Papi have become good friends even if he kids Papi for having pigs, calling him a hog farmer, and Papi retaliates by calling Tash the lumber jack, since their profits so far have all come from the lumber they sell.

The Cafetal does bring occasional visitors to chat with Papi on his favorite spot on the porch, but it does not bring any extra traffic past our gate. The work going on at the Playa does make a difference for us and for the people in the farming community of Santa Lucia. I always remember many summers ago when we borrowed a beach house in what was then called La Boca, a name for the area outside the entrance to the harbor of Nuevitas that extended from the lighthouse, Faro Maternillo, east for uninterrupted kilometers. To people who like clear water and white sand, that beach must have been incredibly beautiful. But when I visited there as a child, it was not even a fishing community. Then it could only be reached from the water. There were maybe half a dozen houses, all built with an open area downstairs and living quarters upstairs. One of them belonging to the practico, an expert that could board a ship and help them navigate the entrance to the bay. I also remember the Salinas where sea water is allowed to evaporate in shallow flats, turning shades of pink before only the salt is left. And that was it: sea and sand. Obeying my mother who was afraid that we could fall off the pier, we children fished through the holes in the latrine, conveniently perched at the end of a pier to keep it from contaminating the precious well water I suppose. But we swam not too far from that pier in water so clear that it looked shallow when it wasn't and we walked on the sand looking for signs of buried pirate treasury. Soon anybody with wheels will be looking on these, no longer empty, views.

As soon as the sand dunes and brush were divided into plots, Mami bought a lot, back from the water and came up with plans to build a cabin. The plan had no bedroom, just a bath, kitchen and an open area. It would be a place to change and enjoy a day at the beach and return to Los Desengaños for the night. Then she bought a larger lot on the water's edge, just in case… Mami likes the beach. Papi will not say so, but I know he considers it a waste of time. It is difficult to assess your own parents: they are what they are. But going by the opinions of others, and my own observations, Papi can laugh and have a good time in a small gathering of friends, but he doesn't mind being alone. As the years go by, he loves his finca more and more. He doesn't need or want anything else. He didn't go with us when we rented a summer house in San Jacinto, near Nuevitas, which we shared with Corina, tío Miguel's widow and her children, or even the couple of summers we went to Varadero.

Only Mami, Lucy and I went to Varadero. The first year, to a guest house called Casa La Rosa that was popular with guests like us, from the Interior. Next year we upgraded to the Hotel Internacional. That was the closest I ever came to associating with Havana people of our age. I shouldn't say associating, it was mostly watching from a distance and, with our small group of provincial friends, joke about what we perceived as the shallowness of their conversations. We even learned to mimic the exchange between two society girls. They mostly ignored us. But some of them were quite talented because they put on a stage show at the hotel that looked like something from Broadway. In it some of them danced a not too modest Can Can.

Now that we have a beach of our own, Oli has taken to fishing with passion. An admirer of Jacques Cousteau, he was one of the first, if not the first, in our area to order an AquaLung and a spear gun. He was not going to wait for the fish to bite, he was going after them. He and two friends together bought a small motorboat and somehow found the time to explore the reefs outside the sand beach. He is almost poetic in describing the sensation of moving silently through a world that was previously out of our reach. He let me try his AquaLung once in the swimming pool at the Country Club and I found it unwieldy, with a single huge tank that would not stay centered on my back. But I did have the opportunity to appreciate the beauty of the reef if only for short spurts. I bought a simple snorkel attached to a mask that has an uncomplicated way of closing with a ping pong ball when I go underwater. I use it mostly to float face down and spy on creatures moving around the sea grass. I could have reached over and grabbed a lobster, but it seemed a shame to disturb anything.

I must include the story of Florencio even if it sounds like fiction, which it isn't. The opening of a road to the beach didn't immediately affect him because his home is east of where the road reaches the ocean, and separated from the newly popular area by a shallow stream that has formed a point breaking the monotony of the straight beach. We trespassed on his domain after we had been to the Playa several times and he was most welcoming. He must have had a few visitors by then and had time to polish his story. Before hearing the story I had to notice items that you would not expect in a fisherman's shack: a cot with cushions, battery radio, tools, and many framed photos on the walls. All of those, gifts from the men whose lives he had saved a decade ago. The German subs had been picking off merchant ships at will as they left the harbor. Florencio had heard several explosions, but that particular night, it was real close, just on the other side of the reef. He knew that reef so well that he had no trouble finding a path to the open water and then, guided by the shouts and the moonlight he plucked survivors out of the water and ferried them to his shack. I don't remember how many sailors or how many days they stayed with him or how they managed to find their way back. But they were with Florencio long enough to establish a friendship that, by the looks of the photos and presents, have lasted all these years.

We are not concerned with trespassers at Los Desengaños — other than hunters. For years, visitors were so rare that almost anybody was welcomed. Even with the road to the beach, there are never any problems with trespassers because what they are after we are happy to let them have, as long as no gates are left open. We call the little fruit "anoncillos", although they are mostly known as "mamoncillos." The trees are around the area of the ruins of the old sugar mill. The fruit ripens in the summer and, in the past, it had provided mostly food for the bands of green parrots that feast on them. For those unfamiliar with anoncillos, think of a green pigeon egg. When you crack the shell with your teeth, what's inside is a pit covered with a thin layer of edible pulp. Hardly worth the trouble of hiking a few kilometers, climbing under and over barb wire fences, reaching up on the trees, all the time trying not to get the attention of the dogs sleeping in the batey. Or they could drive in the main gate, go to the house and ask permission, which some do.

For some strange reason, anoncillos are part of the summer beach fun tradition. They are more entertainment than food. People eat them — if you can call it that—while wading in the ocean. Maybe the salt enhances the flavor.

*

Mami is not only the guardian of the family morals and health, but she tries to shield us from anything that is mean or ugly, and that includes the popular weekly, Bohemia, where those who crave violence go for their "fix." While Batista's illegal government has been recognized and even welcomed by the outside world and by those within Cuba who don't care who is in the presidential palace as long as there is peace, in reality the whole island has never been completely at peace since the takeover. There is always some revolutionary group, of which there are many, that confronts the Havana police or the police abuses them. We try not to notice. But in 1953 even Camagüey had to take notice of the reports of a group of about a hundred armed men (and two women) that assaulted Cuartel Moncada, an army hospital and barrack near Santíago in Oriente Province. The plan may have been to take over the military installation and from there expand into a revolution that would topple the government, but that is hard to believe. It is more likely that it was meant to put Batista's soldiers on the defensive, and that they accomplished. For a dictatorship, Cuba has an incredibly free press. Anything can and does go into print, true or not. Bohemia did its part in portraying the defending garrison as the bad guys and the invaders as the victims. Photos of dead bodies filled the pages of the magazine. That fiasco took place on the 26 of July 1953 and that date was used as the name of the movement yet to be formed. The leaders were not captured at the time, but soon were tracked down and arrested. That's when I first heard the name Fidel Castro.

Fidel (we Cubans prefer to use first names not just for friends, but for enemies) had been causing trouble in Havana for years, but until Moncada, he was one of many. As much as we tried to ignore problems that

didn't touch us directly, we in Cuba had lived with a background of disturbances, mostly in the capital. Shootings, bombs, and the threat of bombs,
were everyday occurrences. There were several groups including one that
had the University of Havana closed for long periods of time. Some were
ideologists upset by the loss of democracy; others would have found an
excuse to fight any kind of government. The different groups didn't exactly
unite after the 26th of July, they were too different for a united front against
Batista, but then Fidel became, by far, the best known of the revolutionary
leaders.

Fidel's trial, like anything in Cuba, provided mass entertainment for
a while. He was allowed to defend himself with a speech that ended "History will absolve me." With those words and the innumerable letters and
pamphlets that came out while he was imprisoned in the Isla de Pinos
prison, he became better known to the general public than he ever was
while he was free. Batista had, from the start, promised elections for Nov.
1953. After much political maneuvering, the general elections took place in
1st Nov. 1954. I stood in line with the rest of the family at a voting place in
Garrido a short walk from our home. It was the one and only time I voted
in Cuba. Batista was almost unopposed because at the last moment Grau
tried to boycott the election and told supporters not to vote for him. He got
one sixth of the votes anyway. Other races were closely contested but I
don't remember any names.

The number of soldiers in uniform has been greatly increasing over
the years, even before Batista took over. Where there was only a pair of
guardia jurados in the past, like in Santa Lucia, there is a garrison now. In
the city of Camagüey there always was a cuartel and a military hospital next
to it, but now the character of the army, or at least our perception of it, has
changed. They have been put on the defensive, and, also, the new enlisted
men may have chosen the military for the wrong reasons. My mother's
employee, what we called her cachanchan, or unskilled helper, was a young
man named Joaquin. He did some gardening, mopped the terrazzo floors
downstairs and that was about all he was capable of doing. The summer that
our school friend, Jean, spent with us she said that she was afraid of him
because he was always looking at her. In truth, that is not as bad as it
sounds. Compared to our friends to the north, we in Cuba look at others
openly. Nobody takes offense or feel threatened by it. But in this case it had
been different. Joaquin was taking a Charles Atlas body building course. We
saw the weights and other equipment in his room behind the garage, which
he kept locked but we could look in the window. He transformed from a

skinny kid into a muscular body topped by a child's head and then he declared that he was quitting his job and joining the army. When asked why, he said he wanted to be a soldier "para dar plano." A very disturbing thought. Dar plano is to hit somebody with the flat side of a machete. Of course, soldiers don't carry machetes, but the whole idea implies corporal abuse. I never knew if in fact he joined the army.

Once Batista felt secure as president by election and things seemed to be going well, he thought that he could afford to be magnanimous. He declared a general amnesty. Exiled politicians were welcomed back, and political prisoners were released. In May 1955 Fidel, his brother Raul, and eighteen other prisoners walked out of prison after less than two years. He spent two months going around making speeches, and then left for Mexico.

I had to mention all those historical events as a background but in fact they were down the list in importance as to their effect on our lives. More important: Joseito and Carolina had a son. He will be called Adolfito and my parents are the godparents. Lucy took great interest in Miguel's children's education. They had been staying with relatives in San Miguel and going to the public school there. She made arrangements, with Miguel's approval, to send them to catholic schools in Camagüey the next school year. Dalia (Angel Nuñez' daughter) and Maricusa will go to the Salecianas. Miguelito will go to a boy's boarding school, Artes y Officios, run by the Hermanos Salecianos. He is not planning to follow on his father's footsteps: Miguelito may have figured out that when he grows up there will be more machines around than horses; he wants to be a mechanic. Dalia's brother declined the offer—or his parent's declined for him—working alongside his father will provide all the education they think he needs.

Leisure life in Camagüey revolves around the clubs. While some schools have sports, most of the sports activity centers on clubs which makes it possible to play for a lifetime, or as long as the legs hold up. The closest to us was El Atletico. No fancy parties here or strict membership requirements. This is a place for people that like to play. We had played basketball here after school in El Porvenir but later the craze was volleyball. We took it very seriously even if I was not one of the stars (Lucy was) and even had some out-of-town games. I remember a bus ride to go play Club Vista Alegre in Ciego de Avila feeling very major league-like. For some reason that I have forgotten, we transferred our alliance to the Camagüey Tennis Club, another club right next door to El Atletico, just on the other side of the arroyo and with emphasis on socializing, as well as sports. The Tennis is a woman's club, with an all women directive, but men are welcomed as guests at all times. This is the scene of formal parties competing with El Liceo, the patriarch of all clubs, as well as carnival-like parties during the San Juan season. El Tennis is also the place for debutant parties which for some reason, my sister and I (as well as our close group of friends) never took part in; I guess we never made an official debut. Somehow that was not our thing.

The relative strength of the different clubs' sport teams varies from year to year since many of the same players switch sides at whim. Lucy and I and a few loyal friends played tennis and volleyball at the Tennis Club for a while before switching to the Country Club, known as El Country, which doesn't have a volleyball team, but it has an Olympic size swimming pool. It also has polo. Women never played polo, at least here, but it is a great spectator sport.

Papi had been providing polo horses (they are called ponies, but are horses) to a friend who is one of the star players of the Country Club and the only one who has no horses of his own. When Oli watched a couple of games he said, "I can do that." And found the time for yet another pastime.

It was fair to assume that someday all three of us would marry within our circle of friends, Oli had dated some of our friends and Lucy and I had dated his. The circle was wide enough and flexible enough that there was plenty to choose from. Oli was the first one to choose a partner, or be chosen by one, and it was cause for concern to family and friends. When abuela Consuelo met her future granddaughter in law, she took notice of her flawless complexion and slim figure. But then she gushed, a little sarcastically since I know her well, "She looks like a delicate porcelain doll." The word "delicate" came popping up to describe her; not exactly the most sought after characteristic for the wife of a hard-working, hard- playing rancher, who moved around in a Jeep wagon with either a saddle or a scuba tank in the back.

Marta, my future sister in law, was more than delicate. Like any community of friends, neighbors and second cousins we all know each other's medical history and Marta's was unusual enough to have been widely discussed. I remember her as a little girl in Las Teresianas, several grades behind me, with a bandage on her neck. The word was that she had some kind of growth, inoperable and life threatening. I am sure Oli knew about it but apparently it didn't bother him. It may have added to the romance, sort of a Camille without the coughing. And, after all, choosing a soul mate is not the same as buying livestock, we told ourselves. I was invited to go along when Marta and her mother went to Miami to buy her trousseau. She fainted at Burdine's when trying out wedding gowns; but that is not considered unusual. Getting to know her I could understand why Oli fell in love. She is cheerful and easy to like. They were married in the church of La Caridad in Oct 1954.

For a few years, Lucy and I had been part of a group of friends — all girls, and close in age since I was the oldest and Lucy the youngest, one year range— that we called the sextet. No, we didn't play music; we just spent hours at one of our homes acting silly, gossiping, or doing something useful, like cooking. For a while we even took ballroom dancing lessons. We hired an instructor that came to the house in Cornelio Porro and took turns dancing with each one of us. And we went places together, like Sundays to the movies— always to the Teatro Principal that in my mother's days had been the site for real stage shows, and to the clubs. That way we could go as we pleased without chaperons. The chaperoning rules in Camagüey could be confusing. I think Mami made them up for her convenience. If we were going somewhere where she wanted to go, we needed a chaperon, if not, we didn't. I am being unfair. Actually, our friends liked having her along. I don't remember any of their mothers coming with us. In general, no chaperoning was needed in the daytime or in the evening if in a group large enough. The rules seemed to change depending on how much Mami liked or disliked our date. The worst part was the sister/chaperon. I hated that. It works well with a cute little sister or brother, but not with a sister of about the same age, like Lucy and I. You feel stupid. I wonder how the young men feel. Maybe they like being seen with two dates instead of one. If my explanation of the dating game in our times is not clear, it is because the whole set of rules never made sense to me. I believe it was worse than senseless. It was uncomfortable for all three people involved. I much preferred the afternoon movies when we went on our own, no dates. We talked to boys before and after the movies but didn't even sit together. That was childish fun. We are grown now and finding a husband is serious business.

June 1955 instead of staying in Camagüey for another San Juan season, I accepted an invitation from the parents of my Moravian friend, Shirley, to visit them at their new home in Sarasota. Shirley's father had retired from the army and moved to Florida. Shirley was going to spend her vacation with them and we all thought it was a good time and place to be together again. We had not seen each other since Shirley graduated a year before I did, but letters kept us close.

I flew to Miami and since I had a couple of hours wait for the plane to Sarasota, I called my cousin Aurelia, also known as Bebita, who lives near the airport, or so she said, and she insisted that I have dinner with them. She picked me up alright and I had the new experience of seeing how young families lived in the U.S. She was probably not the typical American housewife, but she tried, and cheerfully managed running a household very different from the one in which she grew up in Havana. She had first gone to Ohio with her Airman —who is probably less dashing as a civilian—but eventually they found their way south, obviously a compromise. Those who know my cousin were not surprised to hear that she didn't get me back to the airport on time. I spent the night sharing a room with several of her six children all jumping up and down on the beds (at least I had a bed to myself). Next morning she took me back to the airport on time for the short flight.

Sarasota is a perfect retirement place: empty beaches and if that is not enough, they have a good museum and the circus's winter home. (This was summer, though). Shirley's parents made sure we had a good time. No parties, just boating and swimming.

To be honest, the reason I left Camagüey during the time of the year when we look forward to parties and a good time, was that I got cold feet. I had never had a steady boyfriend; many blind dates and one time dance dates, but no one for any length of time. Now I had been dating a special friend and was expected to be his partner during the San Juan round of parties. If I stayed I would become his novia or break up with him. I didn't want to do either so I took the cowardly way out. Most of my friends had already had several boyfriends and knew how to handle such situations. I didn't.

Friends were getting engaged; we had despedida de soltera parties all the time. Those parties are not like the "showers" the Americans have. The emphasis is not on gifts — although there is always one from the group — but on having fun acting out a sort of "this is your life." Two members of our sextet were already married (reducing it to a quartet.)

At some point we had switched our alliance from the Tennis Club to the Country Club, probably because they have a swimming pool, although most people here are married. The men and just a few women play golf but the majority of the women stay in the clubhouse playing canasta. There is not much dating going on here.

My first judgment on Chip Tischler was that he is a good sport, or at least, he doesn't mind being made a fool of. He had been a regular at the golf course and had made many friends by the time I came back and joined the afternoon group in and about the swimming pool. The club swimming star is a slim teenager named Pepe Iglesias. Somehow Chip's buddies talked him into challenging Pepe to a race. It was no contest but Chip was anything but embarrassed. If opposites attract, I should have known then. Whether it is caused by personality or looks, people don't tend to notice me. I might as well be invisible and that is the way I like it. With Chip it is the opposite. He enjoys being the center of attention.

Somehow he noticed me. That I was the only unattached woman around helped. We went back to the club that evening with Sam and Betty Grossman as chaperones. They were the most perfectly qualified chaperons. Sam was part of both the old Camagüey and the American expatriate communities. His father had come to Cuba with Teddy Roosevelt and stayed. Sam has a travel agency and is a close friend of my father. There were quite a few English speaking groups in Camagüey at the time. Some mixed with the locals, some didn't. There is a group I met through Chip that had been here for months under a government program called Section Four, here known as Punto Cuatro. The program is supposed to help improve agriculture methods in developing countries. This small delegation of experts has an office, a secretary (a tall blond that Chip had dated) and a tiny plot of land where they are growing pagoda, a new variety of pasture grass. They have kept to themselves and have not bothered to contact the Cattlemen's Association, the local government, or any ranchers. I had the pleasure of telling them that one of our friends already has acres of the same grass and has been experimenting with it for years. Reporting on the progress of those four square meters of wilted grass have provided a good life for this group for years, and will do so for more years to come.

We went out that evening, and the next, and from then on there was no question that this was it. It is hard to reconstruct feelings after so many years, but I must have been really smitten. I have a letter from a Pembroke friend saying "I hope he is as wonderful as you say he is." Lucy and Oli were too busy on their own to voice an opinion. Mami was delighted that at last I had a boy friend, and Papi was worried (of all things!) because Chip didn't blink. I, even then, suspected that Chip fell in love more with the life style than with me, but that was alright. That he was Jewish and I Catholic was no problem either. Nothing was.

I had been taking my ideas about life from the romantic movies we watched. Movies like Carousel where the worst of scoundrels becomes O.K. just because he proposes marriage. In fiction, the wider the differences between the two involved, the more romantic the relationship. A relationship that is supposed to last a lifetime was based on a romantic moment. That was all we were waiting for and all we needed to know: Love at first meeting; no common interests needed. I didn't particularly want to be married but I felt it was inevitable, the thing to do. Oli was married, Lucy had a boyfriend. I would never have admitted it, but since 1950 when I returned from Pembroke my primary job was to find a husband — while pretending not to care. It wasn't easy. For most I was too tall, an insurmountable barrier here. Another phenomenon of our local mores is that women have to stay within our social class. Men don't. Many of the eligible local bachelors already had mistresses. They had a good time with a servant girl and then brought a family-approved date to the Tennis Club party. I don't have figures to back this up, but there were fewer men in my age group than women, and many, like my brother, had married much younger women.

That I could take my life in my hands never occurred to me. If what I wanted was to live in Los Desengaños, why didn't I? With or without a husband.

Chip was part of a team of geologists and geophysicists working for the U.S. Geological Survey. The first Sanchez he met was my uncle Julian, in whose finca was the site of an old chrome mine that was part of their mapping project. From the beginning I must have known that he was not going to stay in Camagüey, or even in Cuba, but, like the war brides of a decade before, I chose not to think about it. Or if I did, not as a permanent good-bye to everything that had been my life until then. I was not consciously running away from anything. I just was not thinking too far ahead. He had applied for a Fulbright Scholarship to the University of Helsinki, Finland (which he didn't get) and even that prospect didn't faze me. When he first went to Los Desengaños, he loved it but I could tell that he didn't belong there. The first time he went riding with Papi and me he had trouble with the horse. The horses he had ridden in the park in Washington responded to shouted commands (he said). To this horse a loud "Whoa" meant "run." When we came back, I could tell that Miguel had been laughing and was trying not to show it. I don't know what Miguel had done, but he was a prankster and the horse running wild was his doing. That little story is just an aside. It had nothing to do with Chip not belonging in Los Desengaños. He was never going to give up permanently the amenities of a city or the career he had worked so hard to excel at. But, I am just trying to explain the unexplainable, why we decided to get married.

In Camagüey, Chip made some good close friends and not necessarily in the English speaking community. One was Gonzalo de Varona, an
ex politician turned builder, who had a contract to build Shell (that he called
"Chell") stations all over the island. Together they travelled to Oriente
province where he introduced Chip to more friends in Santiago de Cuba.
Another of Chip's Cuban friends was Jorge Horstman, a medical doctor just
getting started in private practice, who was one of Oli's scuba diving
partners. Meeting at a place like the Country Club and going out with
married couples met the requirement of chaperoning without ever saying
the word. Anyway, Chip was very accepting of the local ways. He could
have ridiculed that I had to be protected when women my age in his country
are usually living on their own. My friends from Moravian were living in
their own apartments when I not only lived at my parents' but my mother
waited up for me.

In September Marta had a tiny baby girl. Oli had been referring to
the baby as "Pedro" all along and now the whole family was involved in
finding a girl's name. Marta is so good natured that she never said, "She is
our baby, we should name her." Instead, we sat around the living room and
wrote girl's names on slips of paper. All the family names, on both families,
that were not currently used were entered. We threw the slips of paper on
the floor and Bingo, Lucy's boxer grabbed one. When the soggy slip of
paper was retrieved from Bingo's mouth it read "Adriana", the name of
Marta's paternal grandmother.

One of Chip's fellow geologist lived next door to Oli and Marta's
rented house in a suburb of Camagüey. The first time their little boy saw
Oli, he run ran in the house shouting: "I saw a real cowboy."

Marta is, to a casual observer, doing well, but her condition must
have worsened and she is having black-outs. She loves being a mother but
she needed help. They have moved to another rented house just around the
corner from my parents and the baby spends as much time in my mother's
care as at their home, even with the help of an experienced nanny.

It was a bit of a shock when I found out that the geologists' explora-
tion project is coming to an end sooner than expected and they would be
leaving early in 1956. We had been talking about getting married and living
in Washington D.C., but one thing is to talk about the distant future and
another about a few months from now. We had only known each other for
four or five months — and that under strict chaperoning—when we announced that we planned to marry by the end of the year. For years many
families in our circle of friends have gathered at Manuel Barreiro's quinta on

the Carretera Central to celebrate New Year's Day and the host's Saint's Day. Barreiro, a Notario, which in Cuba means a lawyer qualified to perform marriages and other legal functions, was getting tired of hosting those annual parties (or maybe his wife was) and at a party at El Liceo suggested, or maybe somebody else did, that if he married us New Year's Day the party would be at my parents home.

I wondered what Chip's family thought of my family and friends. His parents, his aunt Ann and his teenage younger brother Howard arrived for the wedding. I think Howard was the only one of them who had a good time. You have to be flexible to appreciate a different culture, and mid-westerners usually aren't, except the young. None of them spoke a word of Spanish or had even visited in Latin America but they tried hard to be congenial, and so did my parents. There was Sara, my future mother in law sitting with my mother, trying to make conversation through an interpreter. In that particular case, the interpreter was Marta's kid sister, Maria de Los Angeles, using her school-girl English in her lively style. Sara was enlightening my mother on her newly discovered way of roasting beef, probably not realizing that my mother went in the kitchen as little as possible and couldn't care less about what temperature made the best roast. We never roasted beef anyway. Our daily form of beef was in the form of steaks, fried. At least my father and Chip's father could communicate in the same language, if not on common subjects. There is a snapshot of Ben, Chip's father, at the ranch, standing next to Papi. Ben was in poor health, had already had a heart attack, had also worked hard, but indoors. He looked frail; Papi looked strong, and in charge.

The civil ceremony took place in my parents' living room with Manuel Barreiro sitting on one side of the old mahogany table and Chip and I on the other. Through the whole reading, I could hear Sara behind me crying. I don't blame her. My mother was at her best. She may not be the best of cooks, but she knows how to organize. The whole backyard was set up with tables for a catered reception, and I hear everybody had a great time after we left. In the photos, Chip and I look young and happy as expected, but also a bit apprehensive as we should have been. More than scared, I probably was determined to go through with it, "Now or never." Getting married was something I was expected to do, but it would have been a lot easier had I married someone I could understand and who could understand me. And I don't mean the language.

The choices made by both my brother and I, or that circumstances made for us, were almost a guarantee for difficult times ahead. Neither one of us took the well travelled path. In a group wedding picture, Abuela Consuelo is surrounded by all her eleven grandchildren, some with their spouses. Lucy looks great as always. As far as I knew, she was not with anyone special at this party. Wonder what was in store for her. Oli and Marta have big happy smiles. Marta looks alright, although we knew she wasn't.

. The description of our wedding was not in the society page of El Camagüeyano. It was in the editorial page as a column written by Dario Castillo titled, Impresiones. There is no picture of the bride or anyone else but it is much more descriptive than most newspaper wedding chronicles. His words are florid, in the Cuban writing style, as he touches on the usual: the bride (he calls me princesita adorable), the food, even the tablecloths . . . but what makes the writing special are the personal references to close friends. He describes the looks of at least three of the women present that were regarded as beautiful. I don't know if having designated beauties was a trait of the times, or just of Camagüey. He mentions that someone had been ill and looks well again and that a couple known for having many children are now having grandchildren instead. He refers to Chip by his real name, Martin S. Tischler, carefully copied from the wedding invitation, but doesn't mention the members of his family who were present. The article is not so much about this particular wedding as about marriages in our society. Looking at the names, I notice that a gathering in Camagüey three hundred years before, (then Puerto Principe) would have shown much the same names as this one, except for Chip's. Here we tend to stay where we are born, and where our great-grandparents were born, and our friends are the great-grandchildren of our great-grandparents' friends. But I will be one exception.

For a while we had considered going to Montego Bay, or some other tourist place on our honeymoon, but, since we will soon be traveling at no expense to us, it made more sense to drive to some place nearby and cheap. Our own Playa Santa Lucia is not yet a world class resort, but it has a simple motel and a restaurant. Slowly it has been stealing the name from the much older settlement of Santa Lucia, which has no reason to make itself known to the outside world, so when people not from the area say Santa Lucia, they mean the Beach, not the farms, carefully tended by mostly European immigrants, that produce the biggest plantains in Cuba. It is something like the United States trying (internally successfully) to highjack the name America from the rest of the continent. Another case of "Might makes Right". Oddly we are happy to call U.S. citizens Americans (what else can they be called) but I will never call their country America.

To me a deserted beach with a North wind blowing is as romantic as it gets. Missouri born and raised Chip can not stand the cold. After a couple of days, we packed up and left. I had never crossed the invisible border into Oriente Province so now it was Chip's turn to introduce me to a great part of Cuba I had never seen. He had been to Santiago with his friend Gonzalo, so that's where we headed. We visited some tourist places like San Juan Hill, which is not much of a hill, and the Morro Castle where I never expected to see such a gorgeous view of the bay, and where we shared the castle narrow stairs with giant iguanas. On the way back we visited the church of La Virgen del Cobre, patron saint of Cuba, but mostly, we sat on bar stools with Americans expatriates.

Chip had been living in a rented room in a mansion named Villa Clarita on the Carretera Central. Shortly before the wedding, he moved to a house he borrowed from Gonzalo in a new development by the DobleVia, the road to the airport. We also borrowed furniture from friends in that business so when we returned from our wedding trip we were set for the few months we had left in town. I even borrowed the family's all-purpose back-up helper, Maria Montero. I could have mopped the floors of that little house in five minutes and it was time I learned to cook, but maybe I just wanted company. The first morning Chip took off for work, it dawned on me that I had never been alone in a house before. I took his car and drove to what I still considered my home in Garrido.

When we go to Los Desengaños it is now for me, with a touch of sadness, but just a touch. Unreasonably I will not admit to myself that there is no way that this place will be home again. I just lived in the present. We took another drive into Oriente Province. This time to the North Coast mining town of Nicaro on an invitation from Tony Arruza, family friend and Personnel Manager of Nickel Processing Corporation, the company that ran the operation. The mine had been closed when the demand for nickel diminished after WWII and had reopened a few years ago. A few friends from Camagüey found good jobs there but unfortunately, there is work for just one geologist and they already have one. Chip enjoyed touring the plant and the mine and I enjoyed visiting friends. I also enjoyed the road trip to and from Nicaro. I can't get over how different this area is from the flat country where I grew up just a few kilometers to the West. It is not just the mountainous scenery, but the people in Oriente have their own looks and accents.

Later we drove to Havana, made the required rounds of the homes of my three aunts, and then set out to see the city. I learned that there is more to the U.S. Embassy than what we saw when we went for visas. As a federal employee, Chip had access to the basement commissary: mostly a liquor store where Americans connected with the federal government can buy their whiskey at great discount.

Back in Camaguey, we set out to see nearby landmarks that I could have visited anytime and never considered. We went to see the caves in Cubitas and a sink hole nearby called El hoyo de Bonnet. The caves were important to the Cuban patriots during the war of independence. I hear they used the bat droppings to make gun powder and this was also a good place to hide from Spanish troops. The sink hole gave me the feeling that we were in prehistoric times and could at any time see a dinosaur emerge from behind the tree ferns. I wish I was a better climber. Chip went up and down the steep inclines with no apparent effort, but I have not had much experience at this type of adventure and I am overly cautious by nature.

Very impressive is a place called Los Paredones. Too bad other visitors felt that they had to carve their initials on the walls of clay. Sometimes Lucy went with us, as when we made a second trip to Havana. There, with a cousin of our Havana cousin as Lucy's date, we acted like tourists and set out to see the town. We were not impressed with the newest French restaurant, Le Vendome, highly recommended by our relatives. The food was attractively arranged but the portions were tiny by Cuban standards. At times we joined another couple of newlyweds, our cousin Guille and Irma and drove all over town looking for places that we never found because Guille thought that if we asked for directions it would spoil the challenge of finding things on our own.

We didn't stay in a hotel but had a modern beach house to ourselves at a place called Santa Maria del Mar, on the north coast just east of Havana. It was lent to us by our aunt Zoila, who, with her family was now back in Camagüey in a ranch they had recently purchased and having little time or need for this house. Her husband's fortunes had changed during the Grau administration. He went from being a country doctor, and by virtue of his friendship with the newly elected president, acquired the impressive title of Director General del Concejo Nacional de Tuberculosis. The family moved to Havana and spent the Grau years travelling all over the world. The idea was to see firsthand how other governments handled the problems of public health and the fight against tuberculosis in particular. A worthy endeavor since tuberculosis is a problem here in Cuba and apparently everywhere else.

I have no idea what was accomplished, but at home we said, perhaps unfairly, that he had a botella. The word means bottle, but that is not how it is used in this case. It is the name we give to jobs that elected officials parcel out to their friends. The job may involve a title, an office, even assistants, but no work is required. I doubt that this is a strictly Cuban tradition.

Back in Camagüey, the family was concerned with Marta's health. To Papi, his children's problems are his own. He and Oli talked endlessly about the options. Marta's father, a physician, had died years before and Julia, her mother knew more about the situation than anyone. She must have been of the opinion that something had to be done since Marta was fainting on a regular basis. After some correspondence, Oli and Marta took off merrily for a visit with doctors at Johns Hopkins Hospital in Baltimore. When it was decided that surgery would be attempted, Julia went to be with them, and when the surgery turned out riskier than expected and Marta survival was in question, Papi flew to Baltimore to be with Oli for support. When it was apparent that she was out of danger Papi returned but the news he brought were anything but comforting. Marta had a stroke, or a brain hemorrhage, during surgery and her left side was paralyzed. Eventually Julia returned and Oli and Marta stayed longer so she could be prepared for rehabilitation.

Next time I saw them was when our paths crossed in Miami: Chip and I on our way to Washington D.C. for Chip's next assignment, and Oli and Marta on their way back to Cuba to face a different kind of life. She was almost unrecognizable, her face was twisted which she was assured would be only temporary, but the big change was in her ways. The cheerfulness that makes her what she is was gone for now. It was a difficult reunion in that hotel room. We tried to act natural, as if we were not seeing what was before us, while they explained how she had been trained to dress herself, change a baby's diaper, and even sew, with just her right hand. She could walk with a brace on her left leg, but now she had to learn to laugh again. Over time, that would be mostly up to her. Oli seemed unchanged, or at least tried to be.

In Washington I went through the ordeal of meeting Chip's friends from his bachelor days. Is it always an ordeal to every new wife? What did they think of me, were they comparing me to a previous lover? I tried very hard to be congenial, but there was an added problem: I was afraid to say anything or even think about it, but why was I feeling nauseous?

Next stop was Saint Louis, Missouri. It was much easier there since I already knew and liked some of my in laws. The first meeting had been on my own turf so if somebody was intimidated then it would have been they, not I. At ease in their own home with their own friends, the Tischlers were much more fun and the family interaction made me feel comfortable. Strangely, I realized that Chip's background is similar to mine. Where my family circle is almost totally the old families either in cattle ranching or in businesses related to it, and the rest of society didn't matter, here in the large city of St Louis only Jewish families count and those are all in similar lines of business. The rest of the city, or the country, doesn't exist as far as they are concerned. Aside from Willie, the "color girl" that does the cleaning and laundry, I never saw a gentile in the house. Just as we are non-religious Catholics, this group is non-religious Jews. Aside from some Jewish jokes and Yiddish words thrown around, there is no obvious sign of their faith. They certainly never tried to force it on me.

Chip's aunt, Ann, threw a large garden party in our honor. Again, I suspect everyone there was Jewish. I had a conversation with a group that had escaped from Europe by way of Havana. I had heard about that exodus and that Cuba had welcomed refugees from the Nazis before the United States did, but talking to somebody who was there made it real.

Letters from home began to arrive weekly starting in May 1956, much like they did when I was away in school. But this time, I kept them. I have hundreds of them; so from here on I don't have to rely only on my memory. Like any farmer, to Papi, water is always first, and not only rainwater. He reported that another attempt at having a reliable source of water in Los Angeles failed when a well came up dry. Several years ago, I had watched as a well was dug by hand and, to the workers surprise, they found several meters down, not water but a layer of seashells. Papi tried to explain that we were standing on what was at one time sea bottom. Now, in this letter he writes that he will have to conform himself with collecting rain water in that area. "We will have to dig bigger ponds." He is also buying more land adjacent to Los Angeles. Every track of land is run as a separate finca with its own name, workers and batey. This one will be called "El Muñeco", like our branding iron. If the soil there is as rich as he thinks it is, he may be able to finish beef cattle there for market, instead of taking them South to El Destino.

After water comes the local news and the family concerns. He reported that Marta is improving physically but has a long way to go emotionally. She is able to care for her daughter, but she cries when Oli leaves. Oli has a job of his own which takes him away from home even more than before. He is buying cattle for a Havana slaughter house that specializes in select beef for the tourist trade. Some ranchers are marketing steers again and selling them at a higher price than the government regulated beef. Papi doesn't say so, but he had counted on Oli's help. We all idolize our father, but it looks like Oli is determined not to be just an extension of Papi, at least in the business. He has his own herd of pure blood Cebu cattle in El Destino, and even has his own cattle branding iron. His iron looks a little like El Muñeco, with a hat and without the arms, but it is meant to look like a milk can.

It is reasonable to think that Chip's mother would have preferred a daughter in law who came from one of the families she knows, like the wife of her second son, Gene, but she seems more than happy to have her eldest son safely married off. She can not object to a foreign born bride, since she is foreign born herself. Her family had migrated from Poland when she was five years old. If she had any lingering doubts they dissipated when a visit to the doctor confirmed that I was indeed expecting a child. She was delighted. I wasn't. The birth control method prescribed by our scuba diving/doctor friend had failed. Once I recovered from the initial shock, I started to see the future from a different perspective. I had expected to be living out of a suitcase and calling a motel home. I had anticipated it as our great adventure, but not with a baby. A baby should be part of a comfortable, settled life. Or should it? I suppose babies don't really care. They can be born anywhere. I just needed time to readjust to the new situation. In the meantime, I managed to smile through the many gatherings used to introduce me to family and friends, all the time feeling lousy. On doctor's orders I spent a great deal of the time on a daybed downstairs.

I did feel well enough to shop at the family's own clothing store—they call it a department store, but it is mostly women's clothes. Everyone in the family, except Chip, is involved in the business. They have recently acquired a furniture store next to the department store with the idea of closing it and use the space for expansion. We are the beneficiaries of the plan: we were given furniture and appliances that will be shipped to our next destination.

We drove back to Washington for Chip to get ready for his next assignment. He will be part of a team that will be doing geologic mapping of the whole island of Puerto Rico. We are moving to San Juan and somehow managed to go through Camagüey on the way. During the few days' visit at the house on Cornelio Porro, every friend that have ever been to Puerto Rico had to drop by and give us their opinion of it, which varied considerably from one to another. Alfredo and Dora, both of them relatives, live down the street and visit with my parents most evenings, On one of those visits they sat at opposite ends of the couch in my parents' living room talking simultaneously about their recent vacation in San Juan, one telling how wonderful Puerto Rico is and the other one, how poor and backwards.

Since the plane stops in Haiti on the way, where cases of small pox have been reported, Chip had to be vaccinated. I am excepted because I am pregnant but I was instructed to report to the health department in San Juan after certain period of time to prove I was not infected. We were all vaccinated as children. I have the scar on my leg to prove it, and it is supposed to protect me for a lifetime, but I guess they don't want to take chances.

Puerto Rico

The flight took us island-hoping to Jamaica, Haiti, Santo Domingo and finally the Isla Verde Airport near San Juan, Puerto Rico. It was July 1956. Our first home was a room in a luxury waterfront hotel. That's where I saw, with the last light of the day, a live octopus moving around the tidal pools just under the balcony. I had never seen one in the wild beaches of Santa Lucia and here was this one next to an urban area. This beautiful setting was quickly exchanged for a cheap one: a bleak apartment with high ceilings and few windows, obviously carved out of a large house, that would serve as home during our long search for a more permanent one. Papi's first letter to Puerto Rico arrived at Chip's work post office box. (A relative in St Louis had asked if we liked our apartado thinking that it meant apartment) Papi tries to write weekly but sometimes skips a week if he doesn't get to town or has somebody to take the letter for him. Mail service to Los Desengaños is something we still don't even dream about, although there was a not so distant time when we couldn't imagine driving a car to the batey and parking under the flamboyan (royal poinciana tree) next to the old wagon wheels. Papi's advice is not to rent a large house — too much work for me without help — visitors can stay in hotels. "That's what they are for", he always says.

Our good fortune in finding the house at 790 Calle Diana was the result of someone else's misfortune. The owner of the house was found culpable in an accident. I heard that he hit a pedestrian with his car. The result was a broken leg and a great deal of money to be paid in compensation. The poor driver had to move his family out of their almost new home and go somewhere, probably to live with relatives. As expected, he was not in a happy mood. He had several shouting matches with Chip — but we rented the house. It took a while, but we were not in a hurry; we had to wait for our belongings to arrive. We had furniture shipped from the States: the new furniture and appliances from the Tischler's store in St Louis, and everything from Chip's apartment in Washington D.C. Plus the wedding presents that came from Camagüey. Of those, the most unique was a knock-down bookcase put together with pegs, just the thing for people that plan to move often and take their books with them. It was a gift from Mami and the creation of Alejandro, a most meticulous carpenter: The pegs were numbered and each one was meant to fit in one particular hole on the bookcase frame. He had also built the staircase at my parents' house. There, the steps, risers and rails were numbered; unfortunately, the numbers were not fully erased before varnish was applied so the numbers will be visible in perpetuity

Reparto Dos Pinos, in Rio Piedras, is modern and of no particular interest, but it is close to the University which is always a plus even if neither one of us plans to be connected with it. It is also close to shopping, including El Pueblo Supermarket and a mall indistinguishable from those on the mainland. But the best part is the neighbors, a mixture of natives and mainlanders which even here are called americanos. Strange, since all puertoricans are U.S. citizens. A saying from tío Eliezer (actually my mothers's uncle, not mine) was "tu hermano es tu vecino mas cercano", Your brother is your closest neighbor, and that applied here. Pepe and Chere, next door and so close her kitchen is about an arm's length from mine, have adopted me and showed me who is who and what is what in Santurce, the area inland from San Juan. They befriended Chip also but he doesn't need them as much as I do. He has his job and his co-workers, and he makes friends easier than I do, anyway.

I soon discovered a characteristic that sets Puerto Ricans apart and is the reason they overflowed their island and spilled into New York City: they like to have babies, on purpose. When we arrived I was almost twenty-five and Chip three years older, the question we heard regularly and without preambles was: How many children do you have? Once informed that I was pregnant, that made us acceptable. A pharmaceutical company is conducting trials on the new birth control pill and it is one of the favorite topics of conversation. We may soon know if all those babies were really by choice or chance and parents were just pretending that the unavoidable was wanted.

Births are also regular news from Camagüey. Every letter reported that some friend had a boy or a girl. One of Papi's letters started with "this week nobody died and nobody was born." He worries about Lucy, at times because she doesn't have enough to do and at times because her life is a whirlwind of activity. He worries about Oli, and Oli's wife Marta and he worries because Oli doesn't seem worried enough. But all that is secondary to the animals and the drought. "I had all kinds of animals die of all kinds of causes."

Mami's handwritten letter, in the same envelope, also laments the lack of rain, so it must be serious this year but she is more positive about Lucy's activities. Lucy has always loved kitchens and kitchen gadgets and even cooking some masterpiece now and then. Now according to Mami's letter she has installed a gas stove in Los Desengaños. The old charcoal stove: A table with three burners built in and an ash tray hanging underneath is gone and now they are depending on Butane tanks brought by land from Camagüey. We already had a Butane refrigerator that before sat out on the porch but now it found a spot in the new kitchen. Lucy has painted the new kitchen yellow and Mami reported that she has been baking pies and breads. But they (my mother and sister, not my father) must be always on the move: they were heading back to Camagüey because Lucy is competing at a swimming meet at the Tennis Club. When the family (now just Mami and Lucy) are not with him, Papi usually stays at his little house in La Gertrudis, a place that has not been affected by the new invasion from the outside world. Mami reports several trips to "la playa" which now has taken the meaning of Santa Lucia Beach, not the old boat landing and store at the estuary. According to her there are many new beach houses, but there is still no electricity. Mami seems to use her beach cabin as social currency. She lends it to friends for inexpensive beach experiences. Wonder how long it will take for that wild stretch of sand to become a Varadero or even a Miami Beach.

A simple report of a visit signified to me how much our private world has been changed by an unpaved road. Mami mentioned that tía Amelia has visited at Los Desengaños bringing with her four grand children— who probably had a great time playing in "our" ruins. She doesn't mention how they came but I assumed my cousin Tallo, tía Amelia's son, drove— no big accomplishment, especially in the dry season. What makes this news memorable is that I have never seen my aunt anywhere other than in her century old house in Nuevitas. I thought she belonged there, was part of it.

The letter from Papi, dated 2 August 1956, started wishing me Feliz Dia de Los Angeles, my Saint's Day, and went on to report about the drought that he says is hurting us, but not as much as some other cattle people. He even notes that there are predictions of a depleted aquifer. He completes the bad news with Oli's report that his favorite mare, Socorrito, dropped dead under him on a very hot day. Papi's opinion, "She was too fat", was surprising since he likes his horses with a flat rump, "like a table-top." Socorrito was one offspring of Socorro, Papi's beautiful white Arabian — which I knew only from a photograph and anecdotes. His next letter, on the 13th is handwritten from the ranch. I know it took effort to write such long letter with his bad right hand. He writes, "there is a hurricane around; hope it brings water."

It didn't bring water to Camagüey. It left it all in Puerto Rico. Hurricanes are not that fearsome — some people even throw hurricane parties when they are sure they are in a safe place and have no property to lose. Here we hunkered down in our rented house and waited for the wind to die down. Next day the reports of the disaster started reaching us. A local woman that has been helping me with housework is leaving with a group from her church—I think they are Seventh Day Adventists. She came by to tell me that she is joining a group of volunteers who are going to help repair houses in the countryside. My life is limited to our neighborhood where there is no more damage than a few downed trees, but Chip saw the destruction first hand since his work takes him out on the field and to the mountains that, I hear, are now a tangle of vegetation and roofless houses. People are going around retrieving the metal sheets that had blown off the roofs and there are reports of conflicts as of the ownership of the "tin" roofs strewed on the hills.

By this time, I am on my way to becoming a dedicated "perfect wife." I can exchange recipes and cleaning tips with those who have learned their domesticity from their mothers, not from a book. I take our dirty laundry to the public washers located at a Caserio, a government housing project. Ironing I have not attempted yet. That's where the household helper comes in, but I am learning to cook. At first I had learned how to put together some simple meals. Chip introduced me to the two menus he discovered in his bachelor days: tuna salad (a can of tuna mixed with sandwich spread), and Boyardee spaghetti that comes complete in a box including the sauce and the parmesan cheese. And we eat out probably more often than we can afford. We discovered some great places to eat; Chip's favorite is the Swiss Chalet where I was introduced to fondue, not what tourists expect in the Caribbean, but popular.

The food in Puerto Rico is not that different than in Cuba except that they call things by different names. Their rice dishes are soupier than ours so, appropriately, they are called asopaos. The fruits have different names, which is to be expected because even within Cuba the names change from province to province. The first time I heard a street vendor calling out "Chinas" I had to go take a look; they were oranges. In Cuba they would have been naranjas. Americans can be overly cautious of new foods after been warned of the danger of tropical parasites and such. In Puerto Rico there is a real danger in the fresh water streams but aside from that I see no more need of precautions here than in St. Louis. And when it comes to insects, they are truly paranoid. Chip threw away my first cake just because a few ants found it first. At home we would have just scraped away a bit of icing. He is a little squeamish about our ways but I remind him that Cubans live longer and are healthier than his friends up north.

When you are away from everything and everybody that is familiar, meeting again with somebody from the past is a treat, even somebody who I had not seen in years and was never a close friend. Irma had spent a summer with us at Los Desengaños and then I never saw her again. She called first and then came over. My mother had run into Juana, Irma's mother and they discovered that both their daughters were living in Puerto Rico. Irma has been here for years; she has a husband and a couple of children all of whom came to visit all the way from Ponce on the South part of the island. I would never have known her if we passed on the street: her frizzy, bleached hair, which is what I remembered most, had been changed to sleek dark hair. She probably would have not recognized me either, but we enjoyed the visit. We both remembered the people and the things we had done that summer, and she had not forgotten how she washed her hair in well water on her first day. She was likable as a teenager and still is. If she lived closer we could have stayed in touch, but as it was, we didn't.

Chip likes to say that I am tight with money. —The joke "She squeezes a nickel until the eagle screams" is no longer funny —. He also would say "I don't like money; I like what money can buy." I am the other way around. What I like is the security of knowing that I have the money if needed. Even as children, my brother, sister and I had our own accounts and we often borrowed from one another. My mother had her household account and must have borrowed from me at one time because in one of her letters she included a statement of money she was returning to me together with my dividends from my share in Ganadera El Muñeco. To save the cost of a money order (depression day's frugality is not given up easily) Lucy is bringing it to me when she comes to spend our birthdays together. Our mother's frugality may have rubbed off on me, but not on Lucy. In a letter she mentions that she is not sure she has the money for the trip.

She did. She first managed a few days in Miami where she was watched over (or so our parents liked to think) by Alfredo and Dora who were vacationing there. A letter from Papi, in English, with the latest update on Lucy's trip had a heading in all capitals "AT LAST IT RAINED". It must have been a deluge and lasted several days, because in a seca like the one they have described an afternoon shower doesn't merit declaring that it has rained. Mami reported the event and added that the jubilation was only marred by two unspecified animals (reses) killed by lightening. We have seen worse. Several seasons back, several steers, ready for market were huddled together under a tree in El Destino and were killed by a single bolt Subsequent letters reported mud and flooding instead of dust, but also, what to us was the most beautiful sight, green grass.

Even if the dry season is over, Papi is looking into a puzzle that only surfaces when the grass is scarce and animals forage for anything to eat: cattle that seem healthy, if somewhat thinner, drop dead when excited. The common wisdom is that the culprit is the vejuco. Not any vine, but a beautiful one that stays green when everything else is dry. It grows on fence posts shaded by piñones; its glossy leaves and bell shaped yellow flowers demanding attention. I have never actually seen an animal eating it, but it is easy to see that they would be tempted. Papi had enlisted Chip's help in finding out if the U.S. had information on the vejuco marruguero, as we knew it. He wrote that he had asked Brooks — who we knew as the head of "Section 4" in Camagüey— and he had never heard of it. As it turned out, Papi already had all the information he needed but he was just reaching out to his son in law on a topic that interested them both. He came up with two different botanical names; it was either Urechites luteas or Echites suberecta; known in English as Wild Alamanda. In either case, knowing what killed the cattle satisfied Papi's curiosity, but there was not much he could do about it, other than what he was already doing, not moving cattle in the dry season.

Lucy arrived in San Juan on the 11th of September. The airport is really in Santurce since only the old city on a peninsula is considered San Juan. The choicest real estate, the tip of the land, is off limits, taken by an U.S. military base. We were disappointed several times when in our wanderings we came to a barrier with a warning like STOP or we will shoot you (just kidding). Chip was born to be a tourist guide and welcomed the opportunity to have someone else to show around. Unlike my family where we only go places where we have a reason to go, he feels that if it is there we have to see it. I'm not complaining; thanks to him, I can say that I have seen more of Cuba than the flat cattle country. Even in the city of Camagüey there are some historic places, for example, the churches underground cemeteries, that I only discovered when a friend took me along as a translator when she was showing the city to a British visitor,

Had I hugged Lucy and told her how much I missed her and how happy I was to see her she would have been very surprised. We just don't do that. Although my father and even my mother used the word "love" (querida, te quiere) in every letter, I don't remember them ever saying it in person, or I to them; we don't feel a need for it, it is assumed that we love each other. My sister's visit came at a perfect time for me and maybe for her also. I suspected she was using this temporary absence from Camagüey the same way I used my trip to Sarasota just fifteen months ago— to use time and distance to gently break with a boy friend, or at least, think things over—. So much had changed for me in such short time, but our complex relationship had not. We still were sisters, rivals and partners; we tried to keep secrets from each other, so even if we were not confidants, we knew each other as well as anyone ever will.

In Papi's latest letter he wrote that he was not going to update me on Camagüey news on Lucy's request, so she will convey them in person. I was also advised, as he and Mami had in every letter that I should not be running around all over the island in my present condition. This we disregarded. I was feeling good and at that time was wearing maternity jackets although I was still not large and clumsy. With Chip driving, we went on the mountain roads, which in itself was a treat to us flat-landers. It amazes me that there are no more accidents, drivers just blow the horn as they reach a blind curve as if saying "get out of my way." We visited most of the best Puerto Rico has to offer, like El Yunque rain forest, with Lucy always with camera on hand. We took a trip around the island and spent a few days at Central Aguirre, a sugar mill, while the geologists were working nearby. Lucy didn't feel like a third wheel because Chip's assistant, Pedro, was often with us. He was the junior member of the team and was sociable and a humorist. He was also locally well connected. Thanks to him we were invited to a party at a private local club and met insiders that we may never have met on our own. Lucy's visit lasted a very short month.

I have noticed by reading between the lines in the letters coming from home, and with a mixture of relief and jealousy, that Lucy's position in the family/organization has changed. She has not taken my place as bookkeeper; sitting patiently and quietly would have been out of character. She has not taken my place, but she has carved out a place of her own. Not only I am gone, but apparently Oliverio has not taken the place that was assigned to him from birth. Papi, at sixty five, if things had gone as planned, would be by now delegating some responsibility to his son, but apparently he can not. When he writes "Oli spent the day here" I read it as deploring that, with all the work that needs to be done, he comes only as a visitor. Oli is probably working harder than ever but on his own: he travels as a cattle buyer and he concentrates his efforts on El Destino, which not only has always been his favorite, but is more accessible to town and his family. There he has his herd of pure blood Cebu cattle and his latest passion, beautiful lean hogs; nothing like the almost hairless, pot-belly ones you see around every rancho. (In Camagüey, a rancho is not a ranch but a country hut.) Not that we don't have good looking animals at La Costa, (the collective name for Los Desengaños and the other land near the north coast) but they are mixed breeds. In a letter Papi mentions that he went to San Cayetano and bought two bulls from Federico—a much admired breeder — and jokes that he will be mixing breeds until he gets "green and blue animals." At first I assumed the bulls were Cebu but it turned out that they are Santa Gertrudis. It seems that our King Ranch neighbors have been successful in introducing their breed in the cattle province of Camagüey. Cebu or Santa Gertrudis, either breed, it means that Papi is giving up with his Brown Swiss, Cebu and criollo mix that was going to give him a double purpose beef and dairy herd in Los Desengaños but instead it gave us the ugliest calves I have ever seen. It will take years to undo the damage. In the same letter he mentions, as in passing, that Tony Arruza, the Personnel Manager at Nicaro, had told him that they may need to hire a geologist soon. He will let us know.

Oli's venturing out on his own is probably, at least in part, out of economic necessity: he needs a steady income, not the feast and famine of the cattle business. Papi had mentioned—using slang new to me "comiendose un cable" — that the newly acquired land, El Muñeco, is so far a drain in our resources. Oli has no intention of abandoning his father; he obviously thought that he could handle his new job and still go on as before as Papi's right hand man. But they are all finding out that such schedule is too much even for him since his best clients are in distant ranches in Oriente Province. Most days he hits the road before daylight. With his son not so much his shadow, Papi spends his time with his very able long time encargados: especially taciturn Ernesto — who knows more about animals than most veterinarians and about weather than meteorologists — and cheerful Miguel. Joseito doesn't have the authority of those others who can hire, fire, and award contracts, but he is always in the discussions. Joseito, like Oli, now has a family.

If Lucy can't take my place, she cannot take Oli's either. As far as I can tell, she drives Papi to and from the finca, and at times stays with him in Los Desengaños and probably does the cooking. But I don't believe she rides silently behind him for hours, like I used to, the horses following the single trail carved in the soft ground, Papi planning moves inside his head.

Papi could never put it in writing, but he must have known that someday Lucy would walk out on him the same way I did. The probability of her marrying a guajiro is nil (although it has been done). When we were little he jokingly would tell us that we had to stay and push his wheelchair out in the sun in his old age.

Letters received in October and early November brought me, along with Papi's travel schedule, disturbing news about political violence in Cuba. I like to think that the local press makes the conflict look worse than it is because of the underlying envy of Cuba, the larger and more prosperous neighboring island, you sense in Puerto Rico. Also, the U.S. press tends to ignore Latin America except to report revolutions. My parents' accounts always emphasized that the violence is all in Havana, but one of the worse crimes took place in Santíago, at the other end of the island. Mami, who would never allow the weekly magazine Bohemia into the house because it specialized in "crimes of passion" and anything that was ugly, and chose to live life in the sunny side in the belief that what she ignored was not there, was now forced to report that bad things were happening. There has been "criminal assaults on authorities for which they blame several different revolutionary groups", she wrote, and added "As you know I don't know anything about politics." She was being self-effacing here. Not liking it was not the same as not knowing. Papi was more assertive. He put ex-president Prio at the bottom of all the violence.

Papi visited us for exactly five days; He combined the visit with his annual (in good years) trip to Bethlehem (pronounced Bethlem) Pennsylvania for the Lehigh-Lafayette game. He flew in from New York City, which Puerto Ricans consider next door and we met him at the crowded airport on Isla Verde. Chip would have been hurt if he didn't stay in our guest room, so he did, but I knew he would have preferred the hotel. We made a trip into San Juan and bought a baby crib as his gift to the grandchild. And that was it. He had no interest in seeing the sights and had to get back to work. He just wanted to be sure I was alright.

Papi has been a little concerned because I am not putting on much weight— contrasting me to his pregnant cows — but actually I am doing very well and taking my pregnancy very seriously. Being competitive by either nature or by having grown up in a competitive family, I am preparing for the upcoming event as if my world title depended on it. My coach in spirit was a Dr. Reed and my manual was a book he had written, "Childbirth without Fear." I have a family reputation to uphold: my mother supposedly had smiled through the deliveries. Now she is enjoying her role as future grandmother. In her letters she lists the items she has assembled for the canastilla: matching embroidered jackets and covers, in three sizes that some nuns are making for her at a convent; a friend is knitting a sweater and more. She informs me of what a well outfitted newborn is wearing these days and asks me if I want this and that. As if I knew or cared. All I need is a healthy baby and some diapers.

From Papi, "Chip, write to Arruza (our Nicaro connection) immediately; he said it was urgent."

The big upcoming event in Camagüey is the Feria Ganadera the second week in December. I have been to Country Fairs in the United States and liked them, but they are not equivalent to ours. Ours are serious business. The animals are not individually raised by school boys and girls, they are the best growers can bring and the owners do it for prestige, money or both. The fair used to take place in the small town of Guaimaro, on the Carretera Central just east of the city of Camagüey, but while I wasn't looking, it was moved to the provincial capital and near the international airport. Proximity to an international airport is obviously important because the other large fair in Cuba is at Rancho Boyeros, the Havana international airport. While that location may be good for the general public, it is a long way from cattle country.

But violence in Cuba upstaged the anticipation for the fair. Apparently I had underestimated the militant opposition to the Batista government as isolated and consisting of varied small groups of university students, gangsters, followers of out of office politicians and wild-eyed idealists. The attacks on military and police buildings in the city of Santiago were, by all account, carried out by well armed and uniformed rebels wearing the red and black arm bands of Fidel Castro's 26th of July movement. The attackers were defeated after many casualties on both sides and much panic, rumors and the expected distress radiating from Santíago. Letters from my parents assured me that Camagüey was perfectly calm, and I believed it; we didn't consider this our conflict. But just about a week later it was front page news everywhere that on December 2nd Fidel Castro had returned to Cuba from Mexico. On letters of Dec. 6th Mami insisted that the disturbances were limited to the southern part of Oriente province, around Manzanillo, Niquero (not to be confused with Nicaro which is on the north coast) and the city of Santiago. Papi reported, "The government has Santiago under control, but now there is a group of alzados in the Sierra Maestra being chased by the Army."

All this news and reassurances came intermingled with reports that their granddaughter is too thin; brother in law, Rincon, is recovering from a stroke, and Oli will take pigs, not cattle, to the fair. And, yes, more girlfriends are having babies.

The next few letters were all about the fair which went on as scheduled. Lucy was greatly admired riding British style and dressed as Princess Margaret in a presentation they called "estampas", with riders impersonating figures like Buffalo Bill and other celebrated horsemen and women. Oli showed six pigs, all females, identical except in age, and came away with some cash prizes and seven trophies including one for Grand Champion. Papi joked that that sow will now have Adriana's bedroom and Adriana will sleep in the barn. In a letter written a week later he seemed to be tiring of all the activity and ready to get back to the ranch. That day they had judged the Santa Gertrudis cattle and there was going to be a party for the Texans at El Liceo. Mami declares that the fair surpassed that at Rancho Boyeros in the quality and quantity of animals, but attendance was down because of the tense political situation and fear of violence. Also marring the occasion was a train wreck where several acquaintances were killed. Nobody called it sabotage, so apparently it was an accident.

We had our share of parties in the Dos Pinos neighborhood and also within the USGS group. I have to admit the Christmas holidays are celebrated in Puerto Rico with more spirit than in Cuba. Carolers came around every evening and homes on our street, including ours, took turn in inviting for food and drink even those neighbors we had not met yet. The caroling and the neighborliness I greatly enjoyed, but the more formal parties at the homes of my husband's colleagues I did not. By this time I was big and clumsy with baby due in January and would much prefer sitting quietly at home. I am not good about being a company wife and I have never been a party person. Sitting for hours holding a drink and looking like I am enjoying it was never my idea of a good time. Also, and this may be just my imagination and sensitivity brought on by my condition, Chip seemed uncomfortable being seen next to me and once I was settled down in a corner next to some deaf old woman, he did his best to avoid me. He also had other things in mind and a big decision to make: he had received an invitation to visit Nicaro.

As soon as the fair was over, Papi and Lucy went to Los Desengaños while Mami stayed in town to prepare for Christmas. She sent me the recipe for her unique fruitcake — which doesn't include nuts — with the warning that it was too difficult for me to attempt by myself — at home she usually had three or four of us chopping fruit. She regrets that we will not be with them this Christmas, wishes us happiness and promises to bring our presents when she comes in January. Papi wrote "The political situation is about the same; here you don't even notice. It seems that some crazies have gone into the Sierras and the government doesn't want to bomb them because there are families living there. I suppose they will give themselves up because of hunger; the few who have, as of now, had their lives spared." And on the personal level he was, as always, planning ahead "Arruza tells me that Chip has been invited to visit Nicaro and talk to him . . . if the trip is by boat. You could come also. I talked to the ships' owner and he says they are good enough and it is just a short trip,"

In the same letter dated 21 December 1956 Papi gives this assessment of the situation in Cuba "The worst thing that can happen is that someday Batista tires of all this . . . and leaves us al garete (a nautical expression meaning 'adrift'). We don't know in whose hands we would fall"

*

We waited for the year 1957 at a party in somebody's apartment in the Condado district. That would be the last party for a while and, if we remember the New Year's resolution we made that night, in the future we would not be driving anywhere on New Year's evening. On the way to the party, another car ran over a drunken pedestrian. We saw it happen right in front of us. It was enough to ruin anyone's evening.

Mami arrived in Puerto Rico in mid-January loaded with Christmas presents, baby clothes and full of advice on childbirth. She and her son in law have always liked and admired each other as far as I can tell, and I only have their word for it. Chip has said many times that he looked over his future mother in law, before he proposed to me, to get an idea of what to expect. Not all daughters will look like their mothers after a few years, but in my case, I wouldn't mind.

We talked for hours, mostly about people we knew, Lucy's dates, Oli, his wife and daughter; the last, Adriana, will soon lose her privileged place as only grandchild. She described the new ranch, El Muñeco, which is stretching thin the finances of the family business. All this I knew from letters but it is so much better in person when one can ask questions and make comments. We talked about anything except violence or disturbances in Cuba. And I didn't want to know. The world is different when you are about to become a mother. The focus is inward.

Chip used any time off to give Mami the Grand Tour. I stayed home. Had the baby arrived early, I would have had to take a taxi to the Doctors' Hospital. As it turned out, I had the first signs that something was happening early on Saturday morning 26 of January. This is going to be a considerate person. The traffic going into the hospital in the Condado District of Santurce is horrendous during the week. A week end morning is perfect; Chip will not even have to take time off from work. After a few minutes to be sure this was not just some bodily function, I woke up the others. I took one final look at the empty crib; next time I see it I will be putting a baby in it. For months I had been wondering what that baby will look like. I had imagined a blue eyed girl, something like Chip's aunt Anne. We had a name for her, Diana, named after our street. Papi had been referring to it as Chipito, or Martinsito, Lehigh class of '79.

Dr. Dick Reed and his book didn't let me down. I may not have smiled during the birth as my mother supposedly had, but I didn't feel pain or required sedative either. One piece of advice we didn't follow was having the father in the delivery room. This particular father is much too excitable for that. He waited outside biting his fingernails and, perhaps coincidentally, developed such a backache that visitors found him on the hospital bed and me sitting on a chair by his side.

What was a surprise to me and nobody had mentioned before, either because it is not common or because other new mothers are ashamed to admit it, is the primitive feeling that came to the forefront with the sight of my baby. My instinct was to attack anyone who went near him. Fortunately hundreds of years of civilized behavior won out.

We had a name ready in case it was a boy: Jeffrey. I suppose it was Chip's choice but I had no objection. The German spelling, Geoffrey would have gone better with the German surname, but he will be named after Tomas Jefferson, not any relative. In the Jewish tradition children are not named after living persons, In the Cuban way, the first born is, almost invariably named after the father, (some families skip a generation and name him after the grandfather.) We were trying to keep everybody happy and give our son a usable name. The name Jeffrey also passed another test: It had to be easy to pronounce by both English and Spanish speakers. Chip took the birth certificate to the Cuban consulate and registered him as a Cuban citizen. He can have double citizenship until age eighteen, and then he will have to choose.

In describing new born babies people fall into two categories: the ones that say they are beautiful, precious, or something like that, and the ones that say "a baby like any other; they are all alike." Jeffrey cannot be described either way. He is not a Gerber baby with round face and rosy cheeks; he has lots of soft black hair, even growing on his ear lobes; and he has a disturbing way of looking straight at you. Nobody dared say it, but he looks like a Rhesus monkey.

Mami returned to Camagüey near the end of February. Papi has been writing all along how he has nobody to argue with; Lucy is not argumentative. Although they live in separate houses more than half the time: he at the ranch and she in Camagüey, this was the first time she went this far by herself. I think they both enjoyed it. Next thing they all went to the Fair at Rancho Boyeros and to visit the Havana relatives. Papi is probably wishing for a son in law that could help him. He has been working very hard building another batey from scratch at El Muñeco. Around that time he wrote that he was trying to talk Oli into giving up his job as a cattle buyer and come to work with him fulltime for a salary.

A place always seems best when you are about to leave it. The neighbors are especially friendly now that we have a baby. I am almost sorry to have to tell them, especially to Pepe and Chere next door, that we are planning a drastic move: we are going back to Cuba as soon as the baby is a little older, and arrangements are made to ship our household goods. For me, there are no doubts, no contest; I could shout from the roof, I am going home. For Chip, it is the biggest decision of his career. He is leaving the security of the U.S. Geological Survey where, unless he does something terribly wrong, he would move up, a step at a time, and after several relocations, probably settle down in Washington, D.C. If he is doing it for higher pay or doing it for me, that is a question I do not dare ask He had enjoyed life in Camagüey, but Nicaro is new for both of us.

Nicaro. Almost home

La Nicaro takes good care of its employees. From the moment Chip signed the contract in Puerto Rico, Nickel Processing Corporation assumed responsibility, not only for him, but for me, our child and our household goods. A car and driver will be sent to Camagüey to meet us at my parents' home and drive us to Nicaro. The plant, offices and the company town are on a peninsula named Lengua de Pajaro. The mine where the nickel oxide comes from and where Chip will be working is on the mountains just inland. Overseeing the operation is the General Services Administration, but Chip's paychecks will be coming from Nickel Processing Corporation, known to us as Nicaro, a newly formed corporation owned 60% by National Lead Company and the other 40% by a Cuban group.

Our furniture and household goods will be coming by boat from San Juan to Nicaro at company's expense. They would have taken care of shipping our black Ford also, but we were ready for a new car and had no trouble selling the old one where we were. Lucy has been doing advance work pricing new cars before we even left Puerto Rico. She listed them in a letter to Chip quoting the DeSoto model he wanted at $4,200 and adding that he probably could have it for less since the agent, Raul Lamar, is a friend who, like so many friends from Camagüey, is also a relative and a neighbor.

We visited at the house on Cornelio Porro only overnight. As Papi wrote later, not enough time for him and his grandson to get to know each other (since when does he get close to babies?), but it didn't matter; there will be many other visits. I could hardly believe what was happening. When we left less than a year ago I didn't think there was any possible way we could be back to stay. But Chip will not be the first Americano to become acclimatized (we call it aplatanado), make this his home and be more Cuban than the Cubans. We have an example across the street: Bill, who had gone from aviator to rice plantation owner.

It may have been the baby that made the difference, but I no longer had any need to see the world. I could not even remember what I was feeling less than two years ago when it was fine with me if we went to Finland or wherever. Chip may have experienced the same change. It may be more than money that made him accept the offer at Nicaro, although in his letter of resignation to the U.S. Geological Survey he wrote, with some arrogance, "If I'm ever financially independent, I will be happy to come back."

The Company driver arrived as promised. His name is Victor. He apparently makes this trip regularly to take company managers and visitors to and from the Camagüey International Airport. He explained that Nicaro doesn't have its own airport, but there is a field nearby at Preston, a United Fruit town, that has scheduled Cubana Airlines flights and where private planes can land. He told us not to hurry; he knows the road well and doesn't mind driving after dark, but we wanted to get going. Journeys seem longer with a child. There was no drama to this good bye, Plans were already being made for future visits on both directions, Mami was already in contact with the families of three local couples that had preceded us to Nicaro. There will be much in the way of sharing rides and hand delivering of parcels in the future. And we will be coming this way often and maybe staying longer next time. Even when we moved to Puerto Rico I had not relinquished claim to my bedroom, leaving some of my belongings in the closet and drawers. In a letter Mami had mentioned that my white hat was still hanging on the rack at Los Desengaños. I guess grown children always do that, leave some reminders of them behind. It is a way of saying "I'm still part of this family."

We took off: Chip on the front seat with Victor, the baby in his car bed went on the back seat next to me. At six weeks Jeff had already travelled farther than most adults do in a lifetime. As we went out the gate, I waved to the little group standing under the archway of the porch. Strangely, Mami had a big smile as did everyone else except Papi. He was somber, and why was he worried? But this was just a good bye for now, nothing to get that familiar feeling of loss. I had been writing to this address, Cornelio Porro 54, for years, and will continue to write.

Victor was enjoying himself. At the moment he is the supreme authority on Nicaro's who is who and what we should expect. Chip was his only audience. At this moment I was more interested in what we were leaving behind than in what was ahead, there will be plenty of time to discover that for myself. I know every inch of the road we took as we left the house. After just two blocks, there are no more houses, just the playing fields of the Club Maceo to our right and the much larger Atletico to our left; over a small bridge and under the great trees of the Casino Campestre and then we were on the Carretera Central which can be considered the Main Street of the whole island; we will be on it most of the trip.

I could have named the residents of every house we passed — people in Camagüey tend to stay in the same house for life and then leave it to their children. This is the part of town I am familiar with. In another neighborhood, say, La Vigia, North of the Railroad Station, I would be hard pressed to name two families. That is just the way it is: not better or worse, just ours and theirs. Each family seems to end up in a group in the same neighborhood. Soon tío Ernesto's place was to our left. He had started out with a charming quinta, the kind you expect to find in the tropics with wooden steps leading up to the wide wrap around porches, Then he built modern additions and didn't seem to know where to stop. He made changes until one could hardly see the old house. Finally, he subdivided his property and built houses for his six children, and a modern one for him and his second wife.

At intervals, on the side of the road were tombstone-like markers with Km and a number. A convenient way to give directions to a place on the Carretera Central is to just use that number on the marker as an address. A few Kilometers later it is open country. One of the reasons I am very familiar with the area is because the private school buses came this far for a few students and we all came along for the ride, twice a day. The parents were paying for the service; public schools have no buses. We passed the gate of the Country Club where Chip and I met, and the finca of Jorge, who introduced us. Farther still, we could not see, but we could smell the tannery and, incredibly, right across the highway from it is San Blas, a finca which always seemed to me an ideal place to live. While Los Desengaños is a world of its own, San Blas is a home with animals, you can live here year round and go to school in town. Those living here don't have the problems that come from living in two homes.

San Blas is the home of my godparents. When the wind is blowing from the north, the smell from the tannery may have bothered his family, but not my godfather Carlos Santayana. He had broken his skull a few years back when— in an accident that involved a horse and bottles of beer — he fell and hit the pavement during one of the periodic cattlemen's ride through town to protest government control of beef prices. When he recovered from his injuries he discovered that he could not smell a thing. This had been the only place I stayed overnight as a child, away from my mother and siblings I could not miss my father since he was always coming and going and I was never sure where he was. I must have been four or five years old because the two Santayana girls had not been born yet. That's when I had my first and last experience with what is known as home sickness, I think the trick I learned then had served me well.

My godmother, Olimpia, my mother's stepsister, kept me busy and happy all day. She is a more loving person than my own mother, but come nighttime I felt that terrible lonely feeling getting hold of me. I didn't have to explain anything. She knew what was happening. She said, "Let's write your mother a letter." I talked and she wrote. I was going to see my mother the next day. That was not the point. I was, and still am, the kind of person that has to share every experience, every thought. At that time I was used to following my mother around talking constantly; whether she listened or not didn't matter. I just had to get it out in words. As wonderful as my god-mother was, just talking to her didn't help. I had to tell somebody back home what a great time I was having, and it could not wait until tomorrow.

Victor kept his stories going about life in Nicaro as we drove through cattle country past Sibanicu , Guaimaro, and Tunas —the whole name is Victoria de las Tunas— and then into Oriente Province. At one point Victor and Chip left for a while and went into a store so I could nurse the baby in privacy. At the city of Holguin the Carretera Central turns sharply South on the way to Santiago, but we are not going there. At that point we left the main highway and took a secondary, but also paved and well travelled, road toward the North Coast. My mother has a cousin who lives in Holguin and I plan to visit her soon, but not today.

The only other town we passed before the approach to Nicaro was Mayari. All I noticed there was a row of houses hanging precipitously on the river bank. I'm sure there is much more to the town, but we didn't stop there either.

The most visible signs of poverty I have seen in Cuba (and Puerto Rico) have always been just outside the gates to a prosperous enclave and so it was here as we approached Nicaro. I'm sure there is an explanation, but so far it had eluded me. I don't have to describe poverty; we know what it looks like. If I say "barefoot children and thatch roofed huts", I could be describing a summer resort. This was definitely a poor area on the road to Nicaro. I was told the name was Levisa.

We were travelling through flat low land but could see mountains in the distance to our right. We skirted what looked like a neat hill. It is man-made: a pile of what is called tailings, a byproduct of the operation. I was told that this pile may be processed again since it still contains Nickel, the wonder metal that all this is about. Nothing imposing about the entrance to Nicaro. Sitting by a small bridge in this low area were two uniformed Cuban soldiers, the first we had seen on this trip. They, of course, knew Victor well, exchanged a few words, and we drove on. I'm sure there are more where these two came from, but I was still surprised at their casual attitude. According to the U.S. press, the rebels are still in the mountains to the south of us. I expected Nicaro to be well guarded, maybe by U.S. soldiers, even if this is Cuban territory. The operation is under the control of the U.S. government and it would be a good target had the rebels wanted to make a statement.

It was still daylight but the tanks, chimneys and industrial buildings all shone with a grayish pink cast. Wisely, the residential areas are placed upwind from the plant, and, as our guide explained, only on rare occasions are the families in Nicaro bothered by the colorful smoke going up from the chimneys.

As in any company town, every building belongs to the company, and is assigned by the person in charge of housing. The residence goes with the job: you are promoted and you move to another house. The company would provide the furniture if needed. I think they preferred to since it was probably cheaper than paying for shipping. In our case, the house that went with the job of Geologist, of which there was only one, was not ready. Since we are bringing our furniture, almost everything in the house is going to the warehouse and the house cleaned and painted for us. I would have been happy staying in the house where Victor brought us that first day but to Chip it was important to move to the higher level area as soon as possible. While in Camagüey your social standing depends on the family you were born into (with money a contributing factor) in a company town it is all about the job description, and the house assigned to you is the most visible sign of it.

With no car and a small baby, I would have been isolated for a while were it not for the friends Disnalda and Elia Maria from Camagüey, who had preceded me to Nicaro. (The latter had to use a double name in Camagüey to distinguish herself from her mother, Elia, but here she was free to drop the "Maria" and call herself Elia.) Those two were married to plant engineers, therefore, at my same level. And Silvia, who was a tennis partner in our single days, and related by virtue of her sister being married to my cousin, was in the top company echelon because her husband was top management. As a non-working wife, my position was that of my husband. That I knew. I probably had much more to learn. I had heard much about company towns from classmates and relatives who had grown up in cen-trales, or sugar mill towns. I knew that a company town was a world of its own with its own hierarchy (should we say royalty?); a country within a country and Nicaro was more so since it was operated and partially owned by the U.S. government. When you lived here you did not live in Cuba, you lived in Nicaro.

The house assigned to us is a modern one, obviously built when the plant re-opened and not one of the original and more charming ones closer to the water. There are eight of them, identical, built along a high road that runs like a spine along the center almost to the end of the otherwise flat peninsula. Our house is going to be the fourth after the climb. Serge, the mine superintendent, a bachelor, has the first one, the only one on the left of the road, and Silvia and Tony Arruza, the next one, first on the right side. All the new houses have perfect view of the docks and the bay, over the rooftops of the older houses. It is such a choice location that I wondered why nothing was built there before, until I heard that few automobiles could be brought to the original Nicaro in the 1940's and our hill was not a good place to live if you had to walk to it. After a few days, we moved, or rather were moved, into our house before our furniture arrived.

Since we would not have enough furniture of our own to fill the three bedroom house, some company owned furniture was left in place, and the rest was taken to the warehouse. We had beds, but no baby crib until ours arrives from Puerto Rico. Jeff slept in a dresser drawer for a while.

Elia's house is directly below ours and I wore a trail through the tall grass to the street below. We had many "remember when" conversations before we started on the issues of the time. There is a difference in relationships with people we get to know, like my neighbors in Puerto Rico and school mates at Moravian and people you have always known, like Elia, whose parents are friends of my parents since childhood and we have visited many times at each other's home in Camagüey. I had also been a visitor at her parents' finca although she had not been to Los Desengaños. Not many people have. The first time I went to her Nicaro house she had just returned from Camagüey and had a letter for me from Lucy in which she claimed that now she (Lucy) was as cheap as I, using a friend to save the cost of postage. Using friends as couriers is more an old custom than anything else since, as far as I know there is no problem with the regular mail, although it is addressed to the office, not delivered to the houses.

Elia had already been in Nicaro for over two years. She knew everybody and everything that was going on without stepping outside her house. Her main concern was babies; she was on the third one in so many years and was a faithful follower of the instructions on her Dr. Spock book. With all that, she still had the time and interest to know of the most resent act of terrorism and government reprisal. They had a television set, but that was not her source of information; it was always on when I was there but the flickering images were only of comedians or children's cartoons.

Our belongings arrived by ship from Puerto Rico in early April and soon after that Chip went to Camagüey and came back with our new car. Since he has a company Jeep, the DeSoto will make a bigger impact on my life than his, even if he had chosen it with such great care and to me a car is a car. This model is made solely for export. Those who know of such things commented that it was more a Plymouth than a DeSoto. It is sky blue; made to resemble a convertible (which it isn't) and the first car I have had with carpeting, which I think is a bad idea.

Now that we had our furniture, books and dishes I was once again ready to be a house wife but I discovered that doing one's own housework was something unheard of in our part of town known as the Numero Uno — other areas had more colorful names, like La Pasa, but ours is simply number one. The newly arrived American housewives had probably never had to supervise household help before, with the possible exception of those coming from some areas in the South or from very wealthy families, but without exception they adopted the system and they all have live-in help. It is so convenient; the houses are built to accommodate at least one person from outside the family with a bedroom and bath by the back entrance. In Nicaro, unlike St Louis, or even Camaguey, most domestic workers live in because the town is closed to the outside. Workers and visitors have to come past the guards at the gate. I suppose it can be arranged, but a live-in baby sitter is great. How else could we go to the movies every evening? Also, to the housewives who speak nothing but English, bilingual Jamaican cooks can open the doors to the Spanish speaking side of Nicaro.

It is easy to make friends or at least get acquainted very quickly; we have so many common interests. The husbands all had the same employer — almost, but not quite. Aside from the U.S. Government and Nickel Processing Corporation, there were several companies represented there: Nicaro Nickel Company, Freeport Sulphur, National Lead. . . , I hear the names mentioned but have no idea who works for which. We all shopped at the Commissary, were vaccinated at the Company Hospital and those who had school age children sent them to the Colegio Americano or to the public school. With a small baby at home I probably didn't get to know the town as well as the ones with school age children, but what I saw made me think of a summer camp for adults. There are several social clubs; I don't know if you joined the closest one or, like the houses, they went with the job. Ours was Las Palmas; we actually can see the palms from our terrace. It has a large swimming pool, a lending library and, of course, a bar. I didn't see the women playing cards there by the hours as they do at the Country Club in Camagüey. Here they played in private homes. I declined to join them, but I did make an effort to learn to play Bridge with Chip and his friends as resigned instructors. We in Camagüey preferred dominoes, a fast and noisy game more in harmony with our character.

Those who are working, mostly men and a few single young women certainly don't see Nicaro as a summer camp. My friends Elia and Silvia are each familiar with a different area of the operation because of their respective husbands' position. Elia's husband, Manolo had come to Nicaro during the plant expansion. He is in charge of one of the several plant operations and Elia knows all the engineers, their families, and what is going on at the plant. The talk now is about the new rail line where Manolo will be in charge of construction.

Silvia's husband, Tony, who is one of my father's buddies regardless of the some thirty year age difference, is top management. Silvia is by nature good at her job of hostess to company visitors. I never have liked the term "entertain" as used for enjoying the company of guests. It makes me think of singing and dancing for them, but whatever you call it, Silvia knows how to do it. She can spend hours preparing some tidbits. Like the miniature pizzas she prepared one morning, and later served on the terrace, with the aid of a maid, to a few of us and the out of town guest she was "entertaining", a woman she had never met before, probably the wife of a company executive or a politician on a fact-finding mission. I remember that particular gathering not only because it was the first for me but because of a telling comment made by one of the local wives. Our visitor, sitting there with the bay of Levisa as a backdrop, admitted that this was a lovely place to visit but was curious about our lives here without the amenities and distractions of the urban areas. To which one of the Nicaro wives replied, "Just because one lives in London doesn't mean one is having tea with the Queen."

I had heard, if second hand, about the plant and the administration office from my friends, but what interested me most was the mine, that was the reason for all this, and where Chip went every day. Unlike the plant, tanks, warehouses, residential areas and offices that were located in a compound on the Lengua de Pajaro peninsula all within the gates, to go to the mines one had to venture into the hills on the mainland. I was impressed the first time I rode in the Jeep with Chip and it never ceased to impress me on later visits. Mountains, of themselves, are the stuff of fairy tales to me but here they had great expanses of moon-like pinkish naked earth where green mountains once were. To keep things in proportion we could look at the match box size dump trucks carrying ore to the platforms from where it was pushed by bulldozers directly into the train cars that will carry it to the plant. Chip's job was basically to keep the ore coming by drilling sample holes ahead as markers. That showed the operators of the huge machines how much soil they had to remove to get to the ore. I was told they will return the landscape to its original condition. I tried to believe that.

As to be expected, the most regular visitors to our house are from the mine. I never learned for sure what was Serge Marinkovic's country of origin. He was equally comfortable in English and Spanish and probably a few more. Here he was chief Mine Engineer and people in that profession tend to be international in outlook; home is where the mine is. Chip had known him at the Rolla School of Mines of the University of Missouri but had not kept in touch or even mentioned him until they met again, which is not remarkable since, to my husband it is "out of sight, out of mind." Serge had worked in South America for several years before ending in Nicaro when the mine reopened. While in college, he had lost his left arm at the shoulder when the car he was riding in rolled over. He said he went back to classes while still bleeding which is believable since to him a lack of one arm doesn't seem to be a handicap. One day I was sitting holding the baby when he came in and handed me a folded piece of paper, a note from Chip. When I fumbled trying to unfold the paper with my one free hand, he took it back, gave it one quick shake to unfold it, and handed it back to me. He gained my admiration and I learned a new trick as useful to mothers as to one-armed engineers.

Serge's second in command, Red Wells, had also worked at several mines in South America before coming to Nicaro, but in his case that was a return trip. He and his wife Elizabeth had lived here, although not married to each other, when the mine first opened during the 1940s. From them we heard of how it was before Nicaro was connected by road to the rest of the Island — a condition I could compare to that at Los Desengaños. When everything came by boat there was no point having a car that could not go very far, so everybody had horses. Elizabeth still keeps a horse which she rides occasionally around town amongst the cars —So far I have not seen a good looking horse in Oriente province, but these scrawny horses seem to be sure-footed. Maybe the beautiful horses from Camagüey would break their necks on these hills. Elizabeth is the kind that doesn't mind being different or talked about. On the first tour here she was married to the company doctor but somehow ended up married to Red. That probably gave the community something to talk about at the time. Now we don't even bother with such petty gossip; between the reports in the U.S. press and the local bolas there is enough violence and intrigue to keep conversations flowing. Red and Elizabeth had been in Colombia in 1947 at the time of an attempted communist takeover known as "El Bogotazo" in which a very young Fidel Castro had participated. Of all the Americans with whom we have contact, the Wells are the only ones who have not the slightest sympathy for the band of rebels on the Sierra. They tell anyone who would listen that Fidel is a communist. It is an endless argument. To me personally, communist or social reformer makes no difference, The rebels taunting the army or the students throwing Molotov cocktails at the police, are all ruining my beautiful, if imperfect, country.

All the time I was in Puerto Rico my father down played the disturbances in Cuba as a counter balance to the inflammatory reports I was reading elsewhere. I thought he didn't want me to worry about the family and friends back home. But it is more than that. He and most ranchers and business people want normality so badly that they try to make trouble go away by ignoring it. In letters dated 26 April both my parents promise a visit for next month and plan to bring Elia's sister with them. Mami writes about a new diet and exercise plan at the Country Club and wants to know what I want her to bring. She is still not sure what to call the baby. Sometimes it is Yefito, Jefesito or Jefito and sometimes she says "el nene" with the accent on the first syllable, as they say in Puerto Rico. Papi stopped saying Chipito and now writes "Jeffito." He sounds like he has more work than he can handle; or that he should be handling at age sixty-five. Because of the distances involved, he is always on the move trying to be in several places at once and he is still trying to convince Oli to give up his second job as a cattle buyer and work for him full time. He doesn't resent the time my brother gives to playing polo or scuba diving. Polo can almost be considered part of business since he shows off our horses. Then, after writing that nothing important is happening in Camagüey, he writes "a small bomb went off night before last but no damage was done. Yesterday they arrested some boys that, it was said, were planning to attack the Cuartel Agramonte with sticks and stones."

The promised visit was postponed three times until they finally came at the end of May. One delay was because of illness, Papi had a kind of flu we call the gripe. Then he was busy with his latest endeavor; the local cattlemen have formed a cooperative and now are planning to build a slaughter house of their own. For that they are issuing bonds. The third delay was because of something that was not supposed to happen anymore: The road to Los Desengaños was impassable. The rains came early, and they had so much that the river had again washed away most of the bridge. Papito, our driver (not to be confused with Papi) had to turn back but Oli could always get through in his red Jeep wagon, el Tomate. He has a system for sliding it across what is left of the bridge, the lengthwise supports, on improvised runners, while pulling it with the Jeep's own winch. According to Mami, they were busy moving cattle to higher ground. She didn't mention any dead animals so I hope there were none. Papi knew the land he bought last year is low but figured he could work with it. So far lack of water, not excess, has been the problem; all attempts to dig wells have failed.

What bonds Chip and Papi, other than their relationship to me and the baby, are their cigars. Papi is never without one and Chip actually smokes them. Papi has a source of cheap cigars, without brand or rings, which is what makes them cheap, and he now buys them for Chip also. In a letter announcing the visit, he tells Chip that he doesn't want to be shown rocks or mountains; he just wants to sit around and get acquainted with Jefito. That was not to be. Chip's specialty is to show visitors the sights which most everybody enjoys even if they claim otherwise. There was also time to observe the grandson, from a safe distance; the verdict was that he looks Cuban. The visit was very short; just a weekend. Lucy played with the baby, Mami gave advice, and they were gone.

On the return trip they were going to visit Mami's cousin Mary Alvarez in Holguin. Mary had lived there for years and, as everyone in that family, is gregarious and likable. Her husband has a tractor dealership and between the two of them they know people of all social levels. Mami is going to ask her cousin to send me a good sirvienta. I have had two disappointing experiences in the two months I have been there. The first one was Cuca, unassuming black woman, older than me, and nothing outstanding about her. At age twenty-five, I was still more used to taking orders than giving them, and the relationship would have worked out weren't for an "only in Nicaro" kind of problem. I had half noticed several times when I expected to have left-over food and we didn't. How much could that small woman eat? One day when I knew she was gone, I heard noise coming from her room. I said, "Cuca, are you there?" No answer. I went and found the extra key and opened the door. There was nobody in the room. Then I opened the closet door, and there, almost filling up the tiny closet, was a man. I should not have been surprised, but I was startled. As for him, he was scared. He said, "Please don't turn me in." I should have, but I didn't. The precautions against sabotage have reasons to be taken seriously in Nicaro. Cuca tried to explain, but I played the unforgiving boss and dismissed her. She didn't go far; soon afterward I saw her working at a neighbor's house. Again, I said nothing.

The second try was a beautiful young Haitían girl with "good" hair, long and shinny and skin like melted chocolate. She was too good looking for her own good. After a couple of weeks she told me that she was taking a bus to Havana. A friend had convinced her that she was wasting her talents here; she could earn much more money in the capital. I didn't ask, "Doing what?"

Mami's cousin came through: she sent us Maria. Maria has a family in Manzanillo but since traveling to that area is becoming hazardous she moved in with us and became part of the family. The baby is old enough now to recognize people and he immediately accepted Maria, maybe because she looked more like me than the others. Our lives changed for the better because of her.

Once again I received letters promising visits and then explaining why they didn't happen. Lucy wrote that Disnalda had offered her a ride to Nicaro but she had already made plans to spend most of the summer tutoring "her children" in Los Desengaños. Miguelito has some catching up to do. His teacher at the Salecianos School has given her all the books and materials needed so she can prepare him to enter sixth grade in September. She plans to also work with Maricusa. No mention of Dalia, so she must be dropping out. Dalia has mother and father so she is not Lucy's charge as much as Miguel's children. Miguel is hand feeding an orphan calf in the house and has named her Adriana. It must get confusing when Adriana (my niece) is visiting. With so many names to choose from why repeat them in a household. But then, there were cows named after both Lucy and me.

Marta had a four and a half pound baby boy June 6th who was named Adolfo Rene. Mami wrote reminding me that I had the opportunity of naming Jeff, the first grandson, "Adolfo Rene" as she wanted, and added "you don't like to carry on family names, but I do." Actually, I do, but my father's given name goes better with Sanchez than with Tischler. We had a joyful letter from Marta in the old tradition of offering the new baby to friends and relatives. Everybody has commented on Marta's amazing comeback. She takes care of her home (with servants, of course) and her child, and now will be caring for the baby as well. I wasn't around enough to know how the change came about but my guess is that the solution came from within, not from psychiatrists. Her innate cheerful character came through and won over her disabilities. Her letter was signed Oli and Marta, but Oli has not written to me once since I married and moved away. I have not seen a letter from him since I was away in school. We have talked on the phone several times and he has promised to come to Nicaro with his Scuba diving buddies, Jorge and Jaime. He has an invitation from another diver, Phillip White, son of our General Manager to go diving on the ocean side of Isla Saetía.

I was receiving more letters from Mami and Lucy than from Papi because they are at Los Desengaños most of the time and his trusty old typewriter is in town. It never occurred to him to buy another one. I guess that one was too much part of him. In one letter he writes that he came to town just to take care of some paperwork and left his glasses in Los Desengaños, "something that Consuelo (my grandmother) would do." He had borrowed from Alfredo some old reading glasses with a missing leg that kept falling off. In the way of news he writes about his business as if it has a mind of its own, "This year the Ganadera El Muñeco has gone crazy and is in debt up to the eyes because it has bought a tremendous number of cattle and now Felipe Labrada wants to sell us Las Cabreras, the finquita behind Las Gertrudis and it is almost certain that we will buy it." I remember it as the place where I was bit by a dog and then cried (not unusual for me) when the owner tried to punish her. It had been my fault since I stepped on her while playing blindfolded a game we called gallinita ciega. I still have the scar on my leg. Papi's letter ends, "I have tried to talk Lucy into going to Varadero, Miami or Nicaro, but she is determined to stay and tutor the children… you know how she is when she is into something. They are leaving now but I have to stay and meet a shipment (of cattle)…"

Wonder if Papi read the last issue of the magazine Bohemia before he went on his buying spree. We didn't buy Bohemia, but as usual, had no trouble getting the information second hand. What everybody kept calling El Manifesto was the first declaration of purpose from Fidel since he set himself on the Sierra. Bohemia had printed the whole text of the document sent to them by courier from the Sierra. Ours is a very peculiar dictatorship that allows the press liberties to the point of irresponsibility. The document was titled "Pact of the Sierra" and was signed by Fidel Castro, Raul Chivas (brother of Eddy and now head of the political party started by his late brother) and by Felipe Pazos, an economist from Santiago. Most of the text was pretty mild, even altruistic: end of regime of force; individual rights; free elections within a year of taking office. Nobody can argue with those promises, the economic part of the proposals was the disturbing part. The terms "Agrarian reform" and "redistribution of land" could not go over very well in Camagüey. Elia and I found those words disturbing..

The new U.S. Ambassador Earl Smith came to Nicaro late in the summer and we all met him at a banquet in his honor at the Club Las Palmas. He has been much in the news since his appointment in June. He had come to Oriente Province to see for himself what was going on since several journalists from U.S. newspapers had made the journey to the Sierra Maestra and written extensively about the rebels. Fidel Castro had been interviewed and quoted in the New York Times and other U.S. newspapers usually showing him and his cause in a positive light. Readers up north are treated to a more romanticized version of Fidel and his band of rebels than we are, At the same time, Batista, who is now an elected president, even if he was not always so in the past, is always referred to as the Dictator and the (very real) excesses of his government and army reported with relish. In Santiago, Ambassador Smith was witness to an incident probably orchestrated to test him. When the new ambassador arrived in an eight car motorcade, a group of women demonstrators dressed in black were waiting for him. The occasion was the funeral of Frank Pais, a rebel leader that had just been hunted down and killed by the police. The ambassador witnessed how the police used a water hose; women were rough handled and some were arrested. In the press conference that followed, Smith, not a career diplomat but a business man, spoke out in the heat of the moment criticizing the government and the heavy handed tactics of the police. His remarks did not make it to the Cuban papers or radio, but since he was followed by U.S. journalists, the whole world, including us in Nicaro, heard about it. Officially the U.S. Government, which owns Nicaro, is supposed to be supporting the Batista Government but that support is fading.

At the banquet we were seated according to rank as expected. I was still not familiar with the ranking of the different positions within the company, or within the several companies that were involved. It seemed that the rankings were of more interest to the wives, who didn't have much say on the matter, than to those who were ranked. We were placed at the table with Elia and Manolo, and several other engineers and their wives.

Silvia and Tony, who apparently ranked higher, were at the head table with the Ambassador, the owners and the top managers. I am new to the company town culture but I am quickly learning and noticing the difference between this and "normal" communities. For one thing, this is nobody's hometown. Some had lived here for years and their children were born here; some, like the Wells had lived through a plant closing and came back when it reopened; but nobody can count on this being their permanent home and that of their descendants. The world demand for nickel dictates our future as a town. We have a reminder just across the bay of the fragile nature of a company town based on a mineral: Felton. The Fe in its name is the symbol for Iron (just like Ni in Nicaro is the symbol for Nickel). I had not been to Felton yet but I was told that there is not much left of the town. Probably mostly fishermen had found it possible to make a living there now that the iron and cobalt mine is closed, and the Bethlehem Steel Company that processed and exported the ore at Felton has pulled out.

Silvia and Tony are leaving Nicaro next year. They will be missed here but for me it won't be a definite goodbye since there are several points of contact in our lives that will keep us in touch. The same with Elia. We will always be friends regardless of differences. Around here nobody seems to have heard of the rule about not mentioning religion or politics in social gatherings. I don't know if anything along those lines was discussed with the Ambassador at the head table, but at our table the inevitable topic was the conflict. Is there a possible solution? Not only politics, but religion came into the discussion. Several individuals and groups have surfaced lately with conciliatory ideas for bringing peace to the country. Those include a committee headed by Cardinal Arteaga — the first Cardinal in the Americas and a distant relative on my mother's side, but probably senile by this time — and Perez Serantes, Archbishop of Santiago and Fidel Castro's godfather, who supposedly started the process. They call their group The Committee for Harmony. In a Catholic country like this, one would think that their words would carry weight, but they don't. Not if our table, mostly Cuban and mostly catholic, was representational of the country as a whole. Even to some of the very religious friends sitting at this table, the rebels were on the side of the church, if there was such side. After all, Fidel has a crucifix hanging on his chest, and, if reports are correct, they even have a chaplain on the Sierra. The Harmony idea didn't get far: The insurgents thought the committee was on the government's side, and the government thought it favored the opposition. The last was probably closer to the truth: some priests had been criticizing the government from the pulpits, and one in

Havana, in a much repeated statement, blamed the problems on the loose morals in the higher levels of society.

The letter from Papi dated August 7th looked peculiar: no capitals. He explained that he had broken his left arm which in his case is the good one. Dr. Saez, who had set my broken elbow almost twenty years before, had set his. Now instead of typing with his two index fingers (which he did quite fast) he is typing with just the one of his crippled right hand. The broken arm was still swollen and hurting but he wanted to tell me right away "before someone else did and made it sound worse than it was." Actually, Mami's letter dated the next day told first how she and her granddaughter cavorted in the surf at Playa Santa Lucia. Then she went on to say how Bingo, Lucy's adored boxer, became very ill, they rushed to town, and Jaime (veterinarian and husband of her niece) diagnosed it as distemper. Only after explaining the prescribed treatment she went on to inform me that my father had broken his arm.

In her next few letters Mami reports that my father is restless; complaints that he has nothing to do. His only expressed regret was that he can no longer go out alone because he needs somebody to hold his horse to mount and dismount. "Now I can't ride alone and meditate while wandering around Los Guanales." He wrote. The Guano, or palmetto, is useful for roofs, but an indication of poor soil while royal palms supposedly grow in rich soil. Los Guanales has more than palms. It is a thickly wooded area that was never cleared for pasture land. Some breeding stock is kept there so obviously they find something to eat, and single trees are cut and hauled out by oxen power when timber is needed, but the area still looks wild enough. It is my favorite place and maybe my father's also because he often followed the narrow cattle trails through those woods when there was no apparent need to do so. Maybe this was as good a place as any to make plans and he was thinking business all the time.

While Papi's planning revolves around moving cattle, Mami's has to do with people. In August she reported helping Lucy in outfitting the children for school, which should not be hard to do since they all wear uniforms. Maricusa will be in third grade, Dalia in fourth and Miguelito in sixth. I was surprised that Dalia was returning. Lucy reported that she was the only one homesick last year, but then she is the only one to have a real home to miss. Then Mami's attention turned to our visit in September. She is planning a birthday party for all the September birthdays, Oli the 12th, Lucy and I the 15th and Adriana the 21st.Mami had everything arranged as in a military campaign: Luz Maria has measured her little room to accommodate a bed for Maria who, Mami insists, should go with us. She has borrowed a contraption called a Kiddie Koop for Jeffy. It is an enclosed crib, top and all; sort of a chicken coop for babies. These last letters came by Elia Maria's parents who were in Nicaro for the baptism of her third child. On our way to Camagüey we stopped in Holguin for a few minutes break at Mary's always welcoming open porch. Here as well as later in Camagüey we heard about all the opposition factions competing for attention in Havana; there is even supposed to be a second front in the Escambria Mountains in Santa Clara Province. Of all the groups and individuals trying to replace, undermine, or whatever their undisclosed intentions, the Batista government, Fidel Castro was the only one that had captured the popular imagination. People are talking about him, but from him and the rebels in the Sierras there is silence now.

Everybody looked good to me in Camagüey: Papi is regaining use of his arm; Mami loves being a grandmother; and they both seem to have developed a good relationship with Lucy. While having two single daughters at home seemed to me that at times was a little irritating to my parents and to my mother in particular, having just one is very different. Lucy is respected as an adult and a partner in this household — although she is still chaperoned by Mami. Oli and Marta walked over from their home just around the corner. She is no longer wearing a leg brace but has developed her own way of moving dragging her weak left leg and, this day, leaning heavily on Oli. They both wear big matching smiles. Anybody who feels sorry for Oli would be mistaken. They are both happy now. At the moment Marta is taking great joy in caring for the baby; she had missed much of Adriana's babyhood. Adriana and Bingo competed for the center of the stage but this day it belongs to Jeffy. A maid brought over baby Adolfo Rene (who said all babies attract the eyes) and nobody paid much attention to him. But Camagüey is more than one household and one family: we are part of a tribe and they all paraded through my parents' living room. I find myself starting to call this house my parents' home, not just "Home", but that company house in Nicaro cannot be home either. Where is home? We could have gone to Los Desengaños for a quick visit, but we didn't. Miguel had sent word that he wanted to see the baby; maybe next time.

Lucy went back to Nicaro with us. On my last day in Camagüey, a close friend had taken me aside to confide a secret. She said in a whisper even if we were alone in the room "People are saying that Lucy and (a familiar but unexpected name) are getting married." I laughed and said something to the effect that there was nothing to the rumor. When I told

Lucy about it, she also laughed and said that people like to talk about others, which didn't confirm the rumor but didn't deny it either. She was right about people in Camagüey talking about the private life of others, but I will not call it vicious gossip as it is often characterized. I think it usually just proves that we care about others. I would not like to live in a place where nobody notices and talks about their friends and neighbors. There are others that would prefer the anonymity that is, perhaps erroneously, associated with living in the big cities.

In Nicaro, Lucy and I spent time with the friends from Camagüey doing pretty much what we did a few years back, except now with babies in the background. I tried to play matchmaker with Lucy and Serge. Single or married, everybody is attracted to Lucy but I'm beginning to think that being gorgeous is not as desirable as it is thought to be.

When she hitched a ride back to Camagüey, Lucy took letters, parcels, and requests from our little community of Camagüeyanos. I don't know if this pony express went on before or was started by my mother but now most of my mail comes by courier-neighbor. Not only we all make occasional trips back home but every time any of us has a visitor they bring at least a letter to each of us so hardly a week goes by when something is not hand delivered to my door. Why do we do this when there is mail service? All I can say is that it has always been done. We call them encargos, small favors asked of anybody going to the local store or across the world. My father has three sisters living in Havana and nobody in our circle of relatives ever goes to the capital without taking letters with the line "favor de Xxxx Xxxxx" this being the name of the traveler handwritten below the recipient's name. I suppose some have been annoyed by such imposition and may have even refused to be carriers, but it is one more way of tightening our bonds. At least that's what it did in Nicaro. When I first moved here, we knew Disnalda only because she lived next to a friend. Now my mother mentions her in almost every letter. She has been taken into the circle. It is the same with the way we deal with merchants. When Lucy went back to Camagüey she was entrusted to buy a washing machine for us. The furniture and appliances provided by the company doesn't include washers. We only had a small portable one we had bought in Puerto Rico for diaper duty and are in need of one. No doubt washers were available somewhere closer, like in Holguin, but we bought appliances at Casa Mendia in Camagüey for the simple reason that there is where we have always bought them. Lucy soon reported that the price was $300, but the guarantee did not extend to Nicaro. We bought it anyway.

The promised October visits were cancelled at the last moment: one of my mother's step sisters was having surgery; Oli's diving buddy, Jorge, was bit by a rabid dog and was undergoing what seems to be very uncomfortable treatment, and, everybody has Asian flu.

Serge has a girlfriend. In a break from the hierarchy rules in effect in Nicaro, he is dating the daughter of a laborer. He always seemed perfectly comfortable alone at company functions while everybody else was paired off. I never saw him with any of the several single secretaries — who seemed to enjoy making us, housewives jealous. I never had seen Elsa until he brought her along on a sailing excursion and it was obvious that she was his one and only. The first time he visited at her parents' home he commented on how tiny it was and crowded with a large family. As befitted his position in the company he has one of the largest houses which has been a source of whispered protests from some of the wives who thought it unfair that a single man should have more house than many families. Soon that won't be a problem.

In Nicaro we look toward the sea rather the mainland for weekend outings. The company has several boats at the disposal of employees (I'm not sure if they were available to any group of employees or only to executives). There is a smaller launch that women often use for day shopping trips to Preston, but the larger one, a two decker called "Molly and me" was the one a large group, mostly Americans, borrowed for an all day trip to Antilla. During the week, my associates are my friends from Camagüey, but when Chip and I go out as a couple for evenings and weekends, we are part of the American community. With them, the conversations are different; their president is Eisenhower rather than Batista, and they can be detached in their assessment of the rebels. Though their livelihood is in Cuba, and some genuinely love the country, they can always go home. Since last February when the New York Times published a series of articles by journalist Herbert Mathews portraying Castro as an idealistic patriot, the U.S. press, and therefore any American that reads it, views Castro favorably. Why Mathews and several other reporters who followed him can find the way to Castro's hide-out and the Cuban army cannot is a mystery. Batista's army and police do nothing to even compete in the war for people's minds. The people on our boat have never met other soldiers than the couple who stand bored at the entrance to the plant, and probably never a policeman, but they have definite ideas of what they are like: cruel torturers of innocents.

The water in Levisa Bay is calm since the mouth to the open sea is so narrow the bay is almost enclosed, more a salt water lake than a bay. But once we go through the narrow entrance and out on open waters the voyage to Antilla changes. And it is rough; the kind of sea where the boat seems small deep in the trough and the waves high above it, giving the illusion that the water would go over us at any moment. I had been in seas like this before, but some of our companions, newly arrived from the mid West, had not. To me Antilla is special from the moment we dock; there is a tonina (dolphin) playing by the pier and it is obviously such a common occurrence that nobody pays attention, except us. The town gives the impression that it has been closed to the outside world since colonial times. When the sea was the main connector of all the population centers around the island and the gates to the outside world, this must have been an important town. It looks a little like a flat Nuevitas. The Carretera Central has shifted the center of commerce to the center of the island, but personally, I am partial to the seaports. I imagine myself living in one of the houses behind the high open porches and wonder what they are like inside.

I didn't find Preston particularly interesting. We didn't go by boat. Although we could have; we went by car with our next door neighbors. It was tiempo muerto when the grinding is over and many of the larger homes were shuttered. This is a United Fruit town and, unlike Nicaro, managers are all foreigners and locals are employed only as laborers— at least that's what my neighbor tells me. The other town on that side of the bay is Felton, now just a quiet fishing village. It is hard to believe that this was once a busy port shipping out iron ore. That is one of the vagaries of the mining industry.

Halloween in Nicaro was not only for children; there was a costume party for adults at the Club Las Palmas. With my innate urge to excel I worked for days making costumes for Chip and me: we turned out as very believable rag dolls. As Raggedy Anne and Andy we did win a first prize, but I had forgotten that the purpose of a party was to have fun, not to be admired. The costumes were impossible to wear: the padded heads where I had carefully embroidered faces were hot and difficult to keep up. We soon discarded them and were just a couple in funny clothes.

News from Los Desengaños included that the bull known as Arroyo Prieto (after the place where he was bred) had to be sent to the slaughter house because of some undisclosed injury; somebody ate some pretty valuable chunk of beef, probably in the form of sausage. Mami had found a cook willing to go to el monte which seemed to include both the ranch and the beach house. Lucy thought it was a waste to keep Luz Maria,

166

who would not go out of the city, when the family spent more time away than in town. This newly found young woman was a niece of Marina, a neighbor on the street behind the Camagüey home and the first black person to work at Los Desengaños. Mami was delighted with her. And finally, Papi reported that Oli had left his job as a cattle buyer and will be working only with him. At the moment, though, he was fishing in Santa Cruz. Papi would never say anything critical of any of his children, especially Oli, but, since to him his work is also his source of enjoyment, he has trouble accepting Oli's need to spend so much time underwater. An accident on one of the recent dives when one of his companions was pierced by a spear (released by the boy's own father) did not cool Oli's enthusiasm for the sport. On the contrary; he was proud that they had removed the spear themselves.

Papi does break away for a few days each November "to keep curujeyes (air plants related to orchids) from growing on me." He pulls out his one suit and tie for his yearly treat, a trip to Bethlehem, Pennsylvania This year Mami and Lucy are going with him as far as Miami where they plan to shop for themselves and, of course, fill out some encargos for others. Nobody can go to Miami without a long shopping list. Mami wrote from Biscayne Terrace, their home away from home. "The stores are beautiful, already decorated for Christmas, and the food is wonderful." Several friends are there on the same mission, including Silvia who will be following Tony to his new job at Central Violeta after the holidays and must be shopping for her new home. Papi stopped in Atlanta on the way to Miami to visit his sister Catalina who has moved back where she once lived. (I believe one of her six sons and some grandchildren live there. I have more cousins than I can track) Then to Miami from where he, Mami and Lucy flew to Camagüey together.

His trips are usually fast, of that I was not surprised, but lately he has been especially nervous about been away too long. That is the only indication I had that the countryside in Camagüey was not as secure as he would like me to think. Everybody's letters, including mine, give no hint of anything happening out of the ordinary. It is our conspiracy to sound relaxed, normal. No mentions of bombs, arrests or threats. Nothing but family news and platitudes. We try to ignore the gorilla sitting on the living room couch. Following those self imposed rules, the report on the 1957 Feria Ganadera was only that the fair went on, but only for the participating farmers and cattlemen. In that respect it was successful, but there was nothing for the general public. Oli's pigs had ribbons again and his right hand man, Titino, had an award for the best kept stalls. What I read in that message was that there have been bombs, or what can be just as disruptive, threat of bombs, and it would have been dangerous to assemble a crowd.

Now it was my turn to make excuses for not going to Camagüey for Christmas. They tempted me with memories of Christmas past. Even tía Pepilla got into the act, "we missed you last year…" For a non-religious family like ours, Christmas has a secular meaning, and as that it was our only formal holiday. This was turkey time (we have no thanksgiving in Cuba) not lechon asado time. Mami tempted us with a roast pig at El Destino on the 28th. She also wanted to personally give us all the presents she has bought in Miami instead of having to wait for the next "courier" or bring them herself. But we stood firm with our "no." Did we want to assert our independence as a separate family, or was it too dangerous to travel?

Second year in Nicaro

We started the year by celebrating our second wedding anniversary with a large party at our home. When we married, we had promised our friends in Camagüey that the New Year's Day gathering would be on us. We ambitiously were hoping to replicate the parties that for years had taken place at the Barreiro home on New Year's Day but so far we have not been in Camagüey for out anniversary. Last year in Puerto Rico we had to keep the celebration subdued because I was not in shape (physically) but this year there is no such excuse and we went all out. I worked more than needed by making tablecloths, centerpieces, and preparing some of the food even if we could have had everything catered from the club. The bartender of Club Las Palmas was in charge of drinks since he knew most everybody's preferences. Even with all my work and outside help there is no way that a party in a company town can emulate the fun of one in a community of friends and relatives. Maybe next time I will try making it a family affair with children included. Time to start thinking of our son's social life.

My parents and sister came for a short visit. They, as well as I, were disappointed that we didn't go to Camagüey for Christmas now that we were within driving distance. It seems that we are forever giving each other excuses. Oli hasn't been here yet, but I can understand that, because although Marta is managing well at home she understandably likes to stay in familiar territory. He is still promising to come with Jorge and maybe other divers. The local divers are looking forward to taking them to what is supposed to be a great diving area near Playa Cristo on the ocean side of Cayo Saetía. Oli and his friends have been pioneers in the use of the Aqua Lung in eastern Cuban waters and local divers are interested in diving with them and sharing experiences. For one thing, they first located an unidentified early warship near Santa Lucia that started a controversy amongst divers. Oli and his group had been careful to make drawings of the wreck, showing the measurements and location of the cannons, but not touching anything. When another group of divers found out about it they went to the site and removed an anchor which they have been exhibiting. All I know is that that's an ongoing saga.

Mami wrote as soon as she was back, congratulating me on the success of the party (she seemed surprised) and reporting on the progress of my encargos which included fabric for drapes. What she found she thought was too expensive. Because of the configuration of our house, we are going to need lots of fabric. This house is H shaped with the cross bar of the H, the living and dining rooms separated only by a built-in planter, almost entirely walled in glass. I like it just the way it is, with a view of the bay on one side and the garden on the other. The previous occupants obviously had no problem with the glass walls either, but Chip would like to be able to close the rooms to the outside. This is one of many of our genetic differences and points of friction. All my life I had been able to look out open windows. But drapes were always closed at my in laws' home in St. Louis. There is where I first learned I was claustrophobic, or at least I like to say I am.

The drapes gave me a good reason to spend a day shopping in Holguin. A good friend from Camagüey had just moved there and was just as happy as I was doing what so many take for granted: chatting and walking around town with a friend. Marta (not to be confused with Oli's wife) had been Lucy's best friend since they shared a double desk in second grade, and by extension, was my friend also. On top of that, she married a relative of ours on Mami's side, and her father, a widower is very close to my parents. That is the way things are in Camagüey. Holguin boasted a branch of the El Encanto, a chain of department stores that included the words "Havana-Paris" as part of its logo. That's where we headed and where I ordered the fabric and the hardware needed for my project. Marta had already made friends with my mother's cousin Mary; both their husbands are in the tractor business. There must be much demand for farm equipment in the area, not affected by the looming disturbances coming from the hills. Now I have two friends from Camagüey in Holguin. It is a comforting thought.

My in-laws are finally coming for Jeffy's first birthday. They had a trip to Puerto Rico planned to greet their first grandson when we left rather suddenly and the trip was cancelled. Just as well; Jeffy is much more enjoyable now than he was as a newborn. I have been sending them photos about once a month so they can see him grow. Ben and Sara Tischler already have two granddaughters living near them, who I'm sure they enjoy, but in Jewish tradition, grandsons are especially important, and still more especial, the first born son of a first born son etc., which Jeffy is. Don't know why. It isn't as if he was going to rule a kingdom. First born or not, Jeffy is a wonderful baby, healthy and loving. He picks up new words every day and I'm not a bit resentful that his first word was not Mami, but Aeea (for Maria). He is still not walking unaided. He probably could if he tried but he still has not made up his mind about it. For now he prefers to hold on to something.

But he is a champion crawler, fast as a dog. He has the run of the house and even the yard as long as somebody is watching because he would eat anything. Like one day on the terrace I thought I saw him pick up something; when I reached out my hand and said "give it" he pursed his lips tight and I had to fight him for it, it was a roach. I told the story to my parents but not to my in laws who would have been shocked. Papi just said, "Good source of protein."

The Tischlers flew to Camagüey, spent a day with my parents, and then were driven to Holguin where we picked them up. Howard is interested in everything; Grandma just came to see us. Grandpa had been reading horror stories in the papers (usually true) and was worried. Thanks to having a child, now I know what to call Chip's parents. In some circles it is considered rude to call in laws by their first name; Mister and Mrs. is too formal, and I was never comfortable with Mom and Dad which is what their other daughter in law calls them. Now I can safely say Grandma and Grandpa even if Jeffy doesn't say it yet

For Howard, going swimming in January is treat enough. He and Chip are very fond of each other even if — or maybe because — they are eleven years apart. Poor Grandma became sick almost immediately with the tourist ailment known in Mexico as Montezuma's revenge. Here we don't have a good name for it but it can equally ruin a traveler's plans. She stayed home under Maria's care while Chip gave the rest of us the grand tour of the mine. Grandpa Tischler had a pre conceived idea of a mine, maybe from watching the movie Snow White. He kept asking, "Where is the mine? Where are the miners? There was no way to convince him that this is it; that he is in the middle of the mine. He looked in vain for men coming out of a hole with picks on their shoulders. The moonscape with heavy equipment pushing rocks unto railroad cars is not his idea of a mine.

We celebrated Jeffy's first birthday with a few neighborhood children posing around my masterpiece of a cake. Grandma insisted that we had to have three candles one for good luck and one to grow on. I never had heard that and thought it was a silly idea but went along. Next day we drove them all the way back to Camagüey for their return trip. I hope they left with less concern about our safety than before. It was fortunate that they didn't travel through Havana where the chances of running into, or hearing about, acts of terrorism are greater than in Camagüey. If Chip's parents blame me for being responsible for their son having a life, that to mid Western city dwellers must seem exotic and risky, they have never hinted of it. If our roles were reversed I probably would.

It is polo season in Camagüey, The new popularity of the sport has surprised me. There used to be only one team, at the Country Club, and they played exhibition games with teams from Havana. Now every social club has a team. Oli is playing for El Liceo, a club in the center of town with no playing fields of any kind. I think they all play at El Country where they can keep horses nearby and where lights have been installed so they can have night games. Papi likes any competitive sport; in his youth as a player, now as a spectator. Lucy is involved in a Squash tournament, according to my mother, "With her usual fervor."

To make the war of nerves even more bizarre, in February the rebels started broadcasting on what they call Radio Rebelde. Every evening they start with the words: "Aqui Radio Rebelde transmitiendo desde la Sierra Maestra, Territorio Libre de Cuba." Translating to "Here, Rebel Radio, transmitting from the Sierra Maestra, free territory of Cuba." I purposely try not to listen too much for fear of falling under Fidel's spell like so many others, apparently thinking people, have. The speeches are, like the Siren songs of Greek mythology, impossible to ignore. The rhetoric is vague, probably on purpose, so everyone hears what they want to hear. He promises things like peace, and justice, and jobs. Who can argue against that? I cringe at the words "agrarian reform" but can see they are useful in appealing to a crowd, after all, who doesn't want free land, whether they can farm or not.

The government is still trying for general elections in June. Batista cannot run for office again, his term ends on February 1959. In a sane society the solution to our problems would be simple: a meaningful opposition that would promote the elections and come up with serious candidates. But since here everything is accomplished through rumors, the anti-government factions are trying to convince the general population that we don't want elections. I personally don't understand why Batista's 40,000 man army doesn't bring down the few hundred barbudos from the Sierra. I think they are afraid of Castro's popularity. But, here where I am, the government has already lost the popularity war. They cannot be more disliked than they already are. So why not go for the jugular. There is a cruel but effective way to stop an insurrection in the countryside and in Cuba there is already a precedent: it was called La Concentracion de Weyler. Whether the country people living in the Sierras sympathize with the rebels or not they are preventing the army from all-out warfare. What the Spanish Governor Weyler did in 1896 was to order the country people to the cities (where many starved to death) and destroyed their crops. That won the war for Spain —temporarily. Ramon, my grandmother Consuelo's hijo de crianza, sort of a foster son, came to her after that war—along with a girl who didn't stay — when they were left on the streets of Havana with hundreds of other children. Guided by what little memories he had, he searched for his real family all of his life but he never found any. Now on the twentieth century we could come up with a more humane tactic that would serve the same purpose: remove the civilians so the government can attack the rebels. That would take care of the insurrection at this end of the island. I have no suggestion for dealing with the violence in Havana, but those hyperactive students, gangsters, and out of favor politicians don't hold the public popularity that Fidel has.

The inhabitants of the Sierra, the people who I was planning to move around like pawns, are a mystery to me. I imagine they look like those we called orientales who did seasonal work in Los Desengaños. According to our history books, there are no indigenous people left in Cuba; the European newcomers exterminated them and, together with the African slaves, replaced them. But by their looks and even by their tone of voice, the orientales can be mistaken for Mexican or Central American natives. They speak Spanish like the rest of us, but in a softer more musical tone. We like to say hablan cantando: they sing as they talk. My uneducated guess is that the natives that survived in the mountains had just enough contact with Europeans to learn their language and costumes, but didn't become as racially mixed as my ancestors did on the plains. Now, through no actions of their own, they are having close contact with people that to them must seem as strange as if coming from another planet. I hear that the rebels (or Mao Maos as we have been calling them equating our revolutionaries to those in Africa) have been holding classroom lectures to indoctrinate the peasants. Out of one of those unexplainable personal idiosyncrasies, I hate the word "peasant" and its Spanish equivalent, "campesino." Where I grew up, it is guajiros, not campesinos. The difference? Guajiro is what we are: rich or poor, farmers or artists. It is the country that defines us, not the occupation. The word campesino is often used by people who are trying to change them.

There are many stories circulating in Nicaro about the interactions between rebels and the people they are trying to indoctrinate. One so funny that I hope is true: a group of mountain people listened to Fidel through one of his endless diatribes about "setting them free from the tyrant." When he paused, his listeners cheered "Down with Spain!" They had not heard the news: they thought they were still under Spanish rule. We fancy revolutions being fought by the common people rebelling against the elite, but this is an upside down revolution. Castro's followers are mostly professionals and university students. Lawyers predominate. They are also very young. The common men are on the other side: poor uneducated soldiers quickly recruited and trained when the need for a large army arose. I fancy them to be scared and take their courage from the rifle they carry. It is said that there is nothing more dangerous than a coward with a rifle.

The insurgents are now in an area closer to us, a mountainous area named Sierra Cristal. Radio Rebelde calls it the Second Front. They said they have fifty armed men lead by Fidel's little brother Raul Castro. To those of us within Nicaro, they are still phantom figures, but rebels have already made contact with the miners at Mina Ocujal and those working higher on the mountain, on the rail line being built to Ramona, a newly developed pit mine. Chip, as the mine geologist, moves ahead of the others and not only have seen rebels, but had them pose for a photo which was the first view that those of us that stayed close to home had of those mysterious creatures. What kind of a war is this? The pace of the conflict has accelerated. We hear that an armed group from Miami landed at Playa Santa Rita, near Nuevitas. Hope they are not planning to start trouble in Camagüey but plan to move on to join the others in Escambrai. There is enough trouble elsewhere that in mid March the government suspended civic liberties and established censorship. After trying in vain to convince outside organizations like the U.N. or the OAS to supervise the elections, they were postponed from June until November, I don't know why they think that the country will be safer in November. Batista still promises to hand over power to his successor on 24 February 1959.

My father still reads the New York Times and has asked us several times what is known here about an inquiry going on in Washington on Nicaro. I suppose the General Services Administration's local representative has been reporting that their investment is in ever increasing jeopardy. Cuba is also in the news up north in connection with arms sales to the Batista government (the only government we have) which is becoming unpopular with the U.S voters since the rebels in the mountains are depicted as "freedom fighters." There is talk of an arms embargo to the military but nobody can stop the illegal shipment of arms to the insurgents. Cuba's geography has always made it possible to bring in clandestine shipments from the United States or from other Caribbean countries to our thousands of coastal landing sites. Now we can add to them many small plane landing fields.

Encouraged by the latest bombs and mayhem, Castro started talking about a final push: A general strike in April that would paralyze the whole country and would be followed by a general uprising. He greatly overestimated the organizational ability of his followers. There were plenty disruptions to be sure, but not nearly enough to bring the country to a standstill as he had predicted. This is what went on in the city of Camagüey, as for Mami's account: "As you must know, the revolutionaries ordered a strike but nobody here paid attention. The only businesses that closed were Valdesuso (furniture store) and Anderson (farm equipment) administered by Felix Miret who later gave all sorts of excuses. Many mothers ran to take the children home from school; in the morning they had assaulted some milkmen (on their way to town) and spilled their milk but they didn't get Mola (where they get their milk delivered daily). I hear the telephone employees didn't show up, but the service was not interrupted and neither was the electric service." Papi's letter dated the 19 of April said that he was at the ranch and missed what disruption there was. When he came to town it was all over. "They didn't manage to have a strike and people didn't pour out on the streets as expected. Now people are coming out of mourning", he assured me. "The movie houses are packed. The Tennis and the Country Club are going to start having dances again." And he adds "The problem will be when Batista leaves."

There is something going on that to my family is as serious as any revolution. Mami had been hinting in a couple of letters that she could not think clearly, there was something occupying her mind. I had assumed that it had to do with the present situation: a friend imprisoned or something of that sort. She finally managed to put it into words. "Lucy is again en relaciones with THAT man and we have given permission for her to receive him at home. Your father thought it would be worse if she was to see him elsewhere. I have been trying to take this the best possible way but I still can't accept the idea that she will end up marrying him." Had Mami been able to use profanity she would have used it here as she described her prospective son in law. An outsider reading that letter may have assumed that Lucy was seeing a convicted ax murderer. Parental opposition, with or without justification, has a long tradition in Camagüey. I could name a few more or less happily married couples who at one time faced the wrath of their parents and now all those involved wish the whole episode forgotten.

Papi is mostly hurt that his younger daughter has not been truthful with him. Their pain is my pain. I can see why they are unhappy but at this moment Lucy is the one that needs support. Gonzalo is a member of one of the "good" families of Camagüey, but he is divorced and double Lucy's age. (At least he was when Lucy was twenty two and first drew his attention). She has had three years to think about it and has apparently made her decision. She is the one that will be affected by it. According to Papi's letter, she looks happy; why shouldn't she? But in his hurting mood, he attributed her good mood to "setting herself free of us." I can only imagine what Lucy and Gonzalo are facing. People like both my parents, whose normal expression is a big smile, when they attempt to look solemn can look fearsome. Lucy wrote that she counted on my support, but advised me not to get involved. "It will only hurt them more."

Maybe my parents have put too much of themselves into their three children; maybe all parents do. The choices we make for ourselves, we make for the whole family and the same goes for even the smallest of victories: my mother was ecstatic every time one of Oli's pigs received a blue ribbon; when I gave birth to a perfect baby or when Lucy was admired when modeling at a charity fashion show. If they think about the spousal choices that Oli and I made, they could see that they are potentially more damaging to the family than Lucy's. Oli's wife will always be a worry to everyone around her and certainly not any help to him. My choice was even worse. As hard as my parents have tried to see the best in Chip once I made up my mind to marry, they have seen examples of his out of control temper. Also, because of his profession, our possibilities of ever living near and helping my parents are close to nothing. Nicaro is the best we will ever do. I think part of the reason for the opposition to Lucy's choice is what we call in Camagüey "el que diran" or the, what will they say. In that, they are mistaken. There have been much larger social scandals in Camagüey and they are soon forgotten. Gonzalo is well liked, successful, and well connected in the capital. That may have impressed Lucy, but as we all know, you don't have to have a reason to fall in love.

Papi also wrote that they were worried about the health of Abuela Consuelo, my mother's mother. Seems that she is seeing blood where it should not be. My father is very fond of and an admirer of his mother in law but I understand that Abuela at first opposed his relationship with her daughter, for what reason, I can't begin to imagine, maybe this is a local tradition. I trust that someday Gonzalo will be accepted, and, who knows, maybe even liked.

Chip had a birthday party with games and music and attended by hundreds. His birthday, 20th of May, is Cuban Independence Day and Nicaro went all out with the celebration. If there were festivities like these last year, I missed them, but probably the organizers this year tried to compensate for the incertitude in which we are living. The Field Day started with the school children, preceded by the school band, parading into the baseball stadium where the track and field competitions were to take place. This is one of the few places in Cuba today where a crowd can gather without fear of disruptions and violence. But the violence is moving ever closer to us. Two guards at the mine have been killed and the mine office broken into and ransacked. Precautions had been taken for our Independence Day party. There are a few uniformed guards in evidence but our safety comes from being closed to the outside world, everyone in the stadium either works for the Company or depends on one who does. To damage Nicaro would be to damage our livelihood. Come to think of it, that thought has never stopped a dedicated revolutionary.

First we had the required speeches. Bob White, the General Manager read perfectly a speech in Spanish, written by someone else and probably not understanding much of what he said. The beauty of the Spanish language is that it is so easy to pronounce, once you learn a few simple rules, that nobody can tell that you have no idea what you are saying. Chip was one of the judges, or officials, of the competition. He had a good time and he needed it. Driving out to the mountains everyday not knowing what to expect is taking a toll. There have been several kidnappings of Americans by Raul Castro's group. So far nobody has been harmed. The hostages are kept for a few days, lectured to, and released to carry back the rebel's message

Chip was not kidnapped; the rebels were after bigger fish. Three of our top managers, including White, were grabbed when they ventured outside the plant. The families were distraught even knowing that the other victims had not been harmed. In this situation nothing is certain, but the pattern seemed to be to show us and the world that they could do harm if they wished but didn't because they were the "good guys." Chip's knowledge of the terrain became an asset. He contacted the kidnappers, or they contacted him, and served as a go between. Several anxious wives came to our house for reassurance and to send clean underwear and shaving things to the prisoners. This is a strange war. The Company managers were finally released unharmed but looking bedraggled in spite of Chip's efforts. Whether they learned anything from the rebels or the rebels from them, I have no way of knowing. The outside press made the most of the kidnappings as expected.

Lucy's marriage took place in my parent's living room May 31st at 1:30 in the afternoon. Mami informed my father at one o'clock, as he was getting ready to take his afternoon siesta that the ceremony was going to be at home. He quickly showered and dressed to stand stone faced next to my mother who was wearing dark glasses to make sure everyone noticed she had been crying. The ceremony surely will not be reported in El Camagüeyano. No photos were taken; no food or drinks were offered. Present, besides the marrying couple and my parents, were Gonzalo's son (close to Lucy in age), the Notary and his secretary, two witnesses, and Marta. Oli didn't go. We were not invited or notified of the date, since apparently it was not set until the last moment, but Lucy had written that she was going to move the date forward to put an end to a difficult situation. Mami wrote that she wished Chip and I had been there "to smooth things over." Papi wrote dramatically "they drove away and we may never see her again." Of course they will.

Marta suggested that I could spend some time with my parents to try to console them; fill the void and sadness for the way their youngest had left them but in the next mail I had letters from both my parents. They had been at Los Desengaños since the day after the less-than-joyous occasion and were spending Sundays at the beach cabin in Santa Lucia. Mami has always loved the ocean but as far back as I can remember Papi has never gone in it— that from somebody who spent a summer as a lifeguard in Atlantic City and has the photos to prove it. He was always busy elsewhere or used his own excuse: his acquired pot-belly kept turning him belly side up in the water. No more excuses, "She even forced me to go swimming", he writes. They seem to be having a great time together even if each one claims to be doing it for the other. Sounded like a honeymoon to me. Papi has more than enough to do and think about, but to Mami, this is the start of a new phase in her life. She spent years chaperoning, bossing and worrying about her daughters. She has been the mother too long; now she can go back to being herself again. She became active in an organization called Damas Catolicas and quickly became the president. She took over the responsibilities of looking after the children from the ranch that Lucy had in boarding schools. One thing she never even considered was learning to drive, even if her sisters Olimpia and Zoila drive in and out of town all the time. Mami prefers to be chauffeured or take the buses that have replaced our beloved trolleys.

As soon as my parents stopped worrying about Lucy, they started worrying about Oli. He is limping and hurting badly. He thinks that he was hurt pulling a boat out of the water. Papi's diagnosis is that there is a pinched nerve, probably at the head of the femur. Not bad from a chemist—

turned rancher. Tío Julian, a gynecologist-rancher thinks it is a nutritional problem and prescribed a special diet. Oli is hoping that it will go away on its own, but for now he is driving and riding as little as possible. A new television set is now the focus of attention at my parents' living room in town and Papi reports that now they don't go to bed with the chickens; they stay up late. When there is no baseball, there is boxing; my mother still gets her novelas on the radio. Oli and Marta walk over every evening to visit and Oli throws himself on the couch. Sitting has become painful.

The word now is that there are insurgents operating in the Santa Lucia area. Mami invariably refers to them as the Mau Mau. Apparently they don't need mountains for hiding. I wonder who is giving them cover. According to Papi there are rumors that the insurgents have had encounters with soldiers from the army post in the town of Santa Lucia. "Everybody is claiming that they are all over the place, but I go there at least once a week and have never seen one." Papi is still trying to convince me, or convince himself, that the national reign of violence doesn't extend to Camagüey. And apparently he is not the only one trying. It would take more than bomb threats to keep baseball fans away from an exhibition game. On the next letter he wrote, "Yesterday I went to Moron to see the Cubans play Buffalo. There was a tremendous crowd."

Not everyone is that calm. Mami is looking for a new cook because the one she has been raving about will not go to la costa because she is afraid of the rebels. People seem to believe that there is more danger in the country than in the cities even if most of the attacks and killings of civilians have been in Havana. Until Mami finds a more permanent helper, she is going to rely once again on Maria Montero, who will go anywhere and do any kind of work, as long as it is not permanent. That Maria (not to be confused with our Maria in Nicaro) is the common law wife of Titino, Oli's cook and friend at El Destino. Maria and Titino could have been the model for the Cuban stock comedy act of the gallego and the mulata. Theirs is a loose relationship; Titino lives full time in El Destino, he doesn't trust himself to go into town and not drink. Maria's son Periquin also lives in El Destino. Maria, with her daughter, has stayed with us for months in Los Desengaños several times; Titino has never been there. Still they consider themselves a couple even if I don't recall ever seeing them together. These two have a long history together, including having owned a restaurant at one time; my parents will be eating well for a while.

When I say that Titino is Oli's friend I mean really friend, not just an associate. Oli and Papi have different management style, probably because of the difference in age and upbringing. My father is always friendly, but dignified. At La Gertrudis where he spends the day, even when the family is at Los Desengaños, he doesn't eat with the men; he has his little table to one side. He is called "Don Adolfo." It would be ridiculous, by men who had seen him grow up, to call my brother "Don Oliverio" and, of course, he eats at the large table with everybody else. Every ranch owner or manager has a different style. We have heard that fellow rancher Manuel Parrado sits at the head of the table like in a boarding school. He serves every plate and makes sure every worker eats. His argument, according to the story, is that if someone is not eating enough, it's because he is not working enough.

Marta is going to spend the summer in Havana having some kind of physical therapy. Surely not very intensive because she is pregnant again! She, her younger sister Maria de los Angeles and the children have a couple of rooms in a residential hotel in Miramar called the Rosita de Hornedo. Oli left them installed and turned around the same day because there were cattle to be shipped at dawn. After a few days, Marta wrote, "So far the children have broken a lamp and three glasses . . . they are cheap, I will replace them before we go. Aside from that, they have not been any trouble . . . there are two sea water swimming pools with water flowing in and out . . . today I started going to the Ornsi (?) because the doctor I had planned to see is in the army and has gone to the Sierra . . . we went to visit Tía Gloria. She is worried about you because you are so close to the fighting." Tía Gloria is Papi's sister and dedicated Fidelista. Her home in El Vedado is easy to find, so all the relatives from "the Interior" make the pilgrimage to her house when they go to the capital for any reason. Marta doesn't mention Oli's problem with his leg. Maybe she is so busy with the children that she hasn't noticed, but both my parents discuss it in every letter. Several treatments have been tried but he is not improving.

The army is trying again to round up the rebels in the Sierra and if we can believe the word of mouth reports, the only reports there are, there have been some real fighting and many casualties, mostly on the army's side. The rebels have no prisons; it is believed that when they take prisoners they indoctrinate them and then release to "go and spread the Gospel," (my words.) In Nicaro we expected something to happen on the 26th of July (a date that should be taken out of the calendar). Those who have appointed themselves local representatives of the Movimiento sent the word that we should all turn the lights off that evening as a sign of support. What if we didn't? The implication was that the house would be targeted or something evil would happen to its occupants. Our house on the hilltop shone as usual and nothing happened.

My parents came to visit again in July. According to plan we met them in Holguin at Mary's home. Visiting her was an extra incentive for the trip. Then their driver returned home, probably eager to get away from Oriente province. Papi joked that they had never even been stopped at road blocks, "they must have considered us too insignificant," Chip is getting stressed out; he didn't bargain for this: doing geology work in a war zone. His latest work is in an area called "Pinares de Mayari." The area was abandoned by Bethlehem Steel when the iron ore ran out. When I went along I found it one of those places, like the town of Antilla, where you feel that you have stepped back in time. Of particular significance to us, because Papi's connection to Bethlehem and Lehigh, is a monument to the Lehigh Civil Engineers who worked in the construction of the rail line. Wonder if the Lehigh men are also responsible for the ingenious water system: the flow of the water itself pumps some of the water back up and into a tank. The pump is working constantly as it had for years with no outside source of energy. The constant pumping sound is eerie in the abandoned site.

I need a new driver's license. The rules at government offices in Camagüey can sometimes be flexible and sometimes very strict, depending on who you know and also on your approach: if you have the right touch, you can say "mi amigo", slap the clerk on the shoulder, and service improves. If you offer cash, it may work or it may backfire. The concept of a driving test hasn't taken hold here. We decided that I would send the required photos to Oli and he will get mine when he renews his. People just naturally like him and I'm not sure about me. Chip has a long way to go: he goes from one extreme to the other, either tremendously helpful, or he gets angry and becomes insulting. He just had an unpleasant disagreement with Papi. They were having a friendly interchange about what is right and what is wrong with Cuba and Chip came out with the assertion that Cuba is hopeless because the quality of its people, quoting the old saying that people end up with the government they deserve. Considering what has been going on around him, he has every right to think that, but saying it to his father in law was not the right thing to do. Papi is not overly nationalistic and often compares unfavorably the way things are done here to the way they were in his second Mother Land, the U.S. But today he must have been feeling particularly patriotic. Even if he is the first one to criticize the Cubans who have succumbed to this group madness, he didn't like hearing Chip make a blanket statement that all Cubans are no good. Mami and I had the good sense to stay out of it, and soon they were sitting on the terrace smoking their cigars and talking baseball.

By mid-August the fighting in the Sierra had stopped. We heard it from Fidel himself who talked for hours on Radio Rebelde. He invited the ordinary soldiers to leave the army and join the insurgents. He can make a very compelling case for his side of the conflict. The government doesn't even try to compete in the battle for the good will of the public.

Mami writes that Marta and the children are back, "Marta is heavier (which is supposed to be good) and Adriana is thinner, if that is possible . . . the houses in Santa Lucia are filling up for the summer. People are losing their fear of the Mau Mau which hasn't been seen for some time. Some say they have moved on to Cubitas. . . still hasn't rained. As you know, the seca drives your father loco . . . Oli's leg is still hurting him...." These last two items are part of every letter. Whether it is raining enough, too much, or not at all, has always been a controlling fact of our lives. Oliverio's pain that refuses to go away is now central in Mami's mind. Also in almost every letter she informs me about the latest traveler to Nicaro she has been able to commandeer to take a supply of cigars to Chip or (in this last one) little bathing trunks for Jeffy.

This year there will not be a joint September birthday party in the Sanchez household. Oli will be starting his twenty-ninth year in Baltimore where he is going hoping for a diagnosis on his leg problem at the Johns Hopkins Hospital. We always say "leg" because that seems more delicate, but the injury, or whatever it is, radiates from the buttocks and down the leg. X-rays have not shown bone fracture and several treatments prescribed locally have not helped. Johns Hopkins came to mind because just two years ago Marta had surgery and was hospitalized at that hospital. Oli spent so much time "hanging around" the ward that, as it often happens, became much at home with the place and made friends with the staff. Our family connection with that hospital goes farther back: Papi had surgery there on his broken hand after his encounter with a wild bull. Unfortunately, neither medical intervention was a complete success: Papi's right hand is frozen stiff, and Marta lost use of her right side. Some problems are beyond the ability of the best surgeons. We are hoping for a better outcome with Oli's problem. I'm not sure where Lucy will be for her birthday. She wrote from her new home in Camagüey, but mentioned that in the last couple of months they have made three trips to Havana and three to Santiago. She has been shopping for the house in Camagüey which she says is almost empty, but the apartment in Havana (at the famed FOCSA building) is fully furnished and equipped. We will probably just go to the movies on my birthday, as we do almost every evening, and I'm sure they will have something at home for Adriana's third birthday.

I did have one large present. We have a tile floor terrace on the East side of the house where we like to sit, often with our next door neighbors. It has a panoramic view of Levisa Bay and it is a perfect outdoor sitting room, but only when the sun goes down. It has no shade whatsoever and I have often said so. Probably too many times, because on the day of my birthday Chip showed up in a pickup truck with a couple of helpers. In the truck, standing as if it had been growing there, was a flamboyan or Royal Poinsettia tree, with its orange/red flowers in full bloom. Bringing it, digging the hole, planting it and staking it down against the wind was a huge job. Keeping it alive will now be my job.

Early in October we left Jeffy in Maria's care for a quick trip to Camagüey and were reprimanded for not bringing him. It was partly a business trip; I had to sign some papers for La Ganadera in which I am a minor partner. We had been cautioned about traveling but there were even fewer soldiers visible than on the previous trip. Still, these are times when we should stay together; hang tight to our children. Our Maria is a very calm person; that is one reason I trust her with my child, but she is getting worried about her own children in Manzanillo. There is no communication with the rest of Oriente Province south and east of Holguin and she hasn't heard from them in weeks. We have more options than she has: if the road out of Nicaro is closed, we can always take the Company boat to Preston and fly out of there, either by commercial or private plane.

Oli returned from Baltimore, still limping. The test results and final evaluation will be mailed to him and he may be going back for treatment if appropriate. He didn't think he should stay away any longer under the present circumstances. For one thing, their third child is expected next month, or anytime now, if we remember that the other two were born prematurely. Marta has carried this one longer and looks healthier than she ever did

October 13 is my parents' thirtieth wedding anniversary. I don't remember it being a big occasion at home but, of course, if it was celebrated it would have been just between the two of them, maybe a trip to the movies. This time I sent them a card and to keep it light I sent it in Jeffy's name to his abuelos. Papi replied, "Thank you Jeffy for having remembered that today your grandparents celebrate thirty years of marriage. You have better memory than I because I only found out when we had a breakfast of hot cakes at Oli's house and Adolfito brought us some magnificent presents"; (looks like I'm not the only one who uses a toddler as a surrogate) "a ring for Mami and a beautiful suitcase for me. I will have to start traveling now." Papi had used the same pig-skin valise for his trips north and to Havana as long as I can remember and I dare guess that he will keep on using it.

The letter continues with the usual, "Elia Maria brought us your letter, Ange, and today we received another (in the mail). I am very glad that Jeffy is well and eating much. Today we saw Julian (my uncle and doctor) and he told us that it (reason Jeffy had not been eating) was from teething, but don't mention that in front of other doctors....Oli has us worried because it seems that he is getting worse with his leg, or at least he is not improving. Today he is going to El Destino and tomorrow we are going to the Coast...At last it is raining, plenty...at la Costa there was a tremendous flood. At Las Becerras (neighbor to the East) a bull valued at $20,000 drowned along with many other animals. It is a good thing that Ernesto is not one of those fancy encargados; the day before, he moved the cattle out of the potrero that was in danger of flooding.

I won't write more because Papito is waiting to take me shopping. We have to buy some things to take to the finca tomorrow.

"Thank you again for the presents and I wish that you two reach thirty years the same as we have because in all this time we only have had one great sorrow, that, even if you blame us, you are mistaken.

"This afternoon Oli and Marta are coming here for steaks and I'm sorry that you two cannot be here with us. As for our trip there, I will let you know with time. If everything is going well, it will be the 16th of November. Los Quiere, Adolfo"

What my father refers to as their "great sorrow", is Lucy's marriage. Did they over react? Protective they were, but domineering? I don't think so. We were trusted and treated as responsible adults and allowed to make choices much earlier than other children and now when it came time to make the most important choice of our lives we were expected to make wise ones. What happened? The choices made by the three of us were almost guaranteed for difficult times ahead. None of us took the well traveled path. In my case, suitors were not exactly lining up at my door, but with a little effort on my part I could have found a local young man willing to put up with me. Instead I married a foreigner and went into a marriage that will always demand more compromises than if I had married a family friend. Yet my parents never said a cautionary word to me. I believe that Oli was warned that he was marrying a woman with a serious health problem, but that was as far as it went. He went ahead and married her and has had nothing but support.

The strong opposition to Lucy's marriage is painful to watch and difficult to explain. It has a different basis on each parent. My father has an incredibly strong set of ethics and morals. He also is a firm believer in discussing things openly; that there should not be secrets between members of a family. He could have accepted whatever decision his daughter made, if only she had been truthful with him from the beginning. At least that is what he implied. Lucy caught him by surprise announcing her plans without even pretending to seek his advice.

While the root of Papi's disappointment was the break in the code of conduct he had set up for his family, Mami was disappointed in her daughter's choice. In Camagüey it is not only the animals at the fair that are judged on their physical attributes: everybody is, but mostly young women. Some of us found it annoying; most ignored it, and some let it go to their heads; or in this case, the mother's head. Lucy had style, we were told, or, as they said, had "It." We had heard so much about her good looks that we thought she could have married anyone she chose or her parents chose for her. My mother was the one waiting for a prince for her beautiful daughter but her daughter knew what she wanted and he was not her mother's idea of a prince. Not long after he made those bitter statements, my father acknowledged that Lucy had restored his faith in true love. Mami never did.

We are the News. It can't happen to us

Except for the wild rumors circulating, life went on pretty normally for those of us inside Nicaro nearly until the end. Not so for those like Chip who climbed in his Jeep every morning and drove outside the protected area of the plant. By October, the climate of fear at the mine was such that operations ceased. In my idyllic isolation all I knew was what I heard from a highly excitable husband and from the mostly Fidelista friends. The information that Chip shared as he ran in and out of the house now that his job had disappeared, was that the company officers in Nicaro had been having discussions with their counterparts at the General Services Administration in Washington. Those working at the mine thought that it was too dangerous to continue operations and managers at Nickel Processing Corporation that operated the mine under contract had backed them up. GSA, wanting to preserve their $100M investment, downplayed the danger and wanted operations resumed.

The excitement around my Cuban friends came from a different point of view. It focused on the advance of the revolution rather than the economic survival of the mine and the processing plant. Elia's husband, Manolo, had been promoted to an office job once his work as head engineer of the rail line to La Ramona was finished. He, like Chip, brought home news and rumors as they reached his office. Raul Castro had already shown that using Americans as hostages was part of his strategy. It follows that a large American owned plant will make an even better hostage. The rumor is that he and about forty men are lurking just outside the entrance to the compound.

After days and even months of expectation, when things happened, they happened quickly and without warning. On October 20th, the nearest army garrison withdrew, leaving Nicaro to the rebels. Was it all a plan? All sort of theories reached me before and after the event, all I know is that that same day we saw carloads of barbudos moving around our roads as if they owned the place; which for now they did.

Seeing a barbudo for the first time is like seeing something that had been described to you but you were not sure existed, like the Haitían tonton macute, or the Tooth Fairy. They could never be confused with soldiers, and not only because the soldiers wear kakis while the rebels are in olive green with the 26th of July black arm band. For one thing, there is all that hair that earned them the name of barbudos, the bearded ones. Facial hair and bushy shoulder length hair; I swear, they even have hairy arms. I am told that Raul is easily recognized because he is smooth-faced, unlike his bearded companions, but I never saw him. Another difference between these creatures and real soldiers is that, apparently, they have no restrictions as to what they can use over their uniforms: vests, scarves, and anything that can hang from a chain. And what is probably the most important difference: the casual way they treat their weapons. Do they know that they are real? I am afraid to look at any of them too closely. I am afraid to find some nice young man from Camagüey under all that grime.

The rebels want to be sure that what happens in Nicaro stays in Nicaro. Telephone communications had been cut off before they even came in, and as soon as they took over, they went out (on our boats) and placed explosives at the narrow entrance to Levisa Bay. The war of nerves continues. What do they want? They may look scruffy but they have some organization and some plan. For four days they were in the office negotiating with management. Our General Manager, Bob White (given name is Sherman) is also negotiating, or rather, taking orders, from the U.S. Embassy in Havana by short wave radio.

In those days I kept hearing the word "evacuate", a word, or rather a concept, that Americans seem to love. After years of working, living and playing side by side we had suddenly split into two separate communities with separate interests: U.S. citizens and everybody else, and I was in both and in neither. It came home to me when Chip announced that we had to start getting ready to evacuate. At that time he brought home a small American flag which he attached to the radio antenna of our DeSoto. That magic piece of cloth was going to protect us from all evil.

Americans have an undying faith that their government will get them out of whatever mess they get into. We Cubans don't expect anything from our government and least of all, in our present situation. Right now the question is "When?" When will the Cuban government react? When and how will they try to drive the rebels out of Nicaro? The more anti-government factions are afraid the military will not care much if civilians got in the way. As for the U.S. government, it has made it clear in the last months that they no longer supporte their old friend Batista by placing an embargo on the sale of arms to his government. Public opinion in the U.S. has been turned against Batista by innumerable reports of crimes against civilians while reports about the opposition, and especially those on the

Sierra, are mostly favorable, finding their crimes justifiable. U.S. intervention now seems certain to us. How can the powerful neighbor put up with this affront? But apparently the rebels were better informed than we were or they would never have taken the chance with such confidence. The message from Ambassador Earl Smith was to just get every last US citizen out of here, and apparently, once the Americans are out, their government doesn't care what happens to the rest of the people in Nicaro or the operation itself. For the evacuation of US citizens to take place the rebel leaders have to give their consent since they are in charge now, and apparently they have. What they received in return, we could only speculate. My guess would be that thing that smooths all conflicts, money.

I am not the only Cuban here married to an US citizen. I know of at least one other who, together with his American wife chose to stay in defiance of orders. I was sure that my father was already working out a way of sending for us. Many rancher friends have small planes that they would without hesitation put at his disposal to fly us out of Preston and back to safety in Camagüey. We were in no more danger than the few thousand other Cubans sequestered in Nicaro. But here at home, orders were obeyed. I was told that I could stay if I wished, but my twenty-one month old son was a US citizen— as well as a Cuban citizen — and he had to be evacuated. I wondered if he had noticed anything askew in our routine. The evening of October 24 we had dinner and put him to bed as normally as I could. I then remembered that his little friend, Bruce, was having his two year birthday party the next day. No ice cream and cake for the children tomorrow.

I tried hard to get some sleep that night. I know how lack of sleep affects me; I walk around like a zombie after a bad night. I needed to be at my best in the morning and prepared for a day that now we could only imagine. I wanted to sleep but I also wanted to hear what was coming from our Zenith short wave radio placed on the bookcase headboard of the bed. That radio is one of Chip's favorite toys but tonight it was not used for amusement. The reception was perfectly clear. We recognized the voice of Bob White. He wasn't getting any sleep either — I wondered if his wife Phyllis was next to him, or at home, wondering like me, if we could get some sleep tonight. White was talking to somebody on a ship identified as the U.S. Navy transport Kleinsmith that apparently was waiting just outside the entrance to the harbor. There were other voices, maybe from the ship's home port of Guantanamo. The voice giving the orders came from the embassy in Havana. The Navy is to take all U.S. citizens to Guantanamo from where they (us) will be flown to Miami to wait "until the situation here stabilizes", their words.

As we eavesdropped on the radio conversation my mind was moving in all directions. I wasn't sure whether to treat this as a permanent move or as an unplanned get away. I thought of the most trivial problems: the philodendron climbing out of the living room planter; it should be watered before we go. My new tree will die without rain. The film I had left to be developed; a dress at the dry cleaners . . . Maria will not stay in the house alone and I cannot promise her that we will return. All the food in the refrigerator will spoil . . . I thought of the fragility of home. The only thing that was holding our lives and this house together was Chip's job. Will I ever feel securely at home anywhere but in Los Desengaños?

The light that I saw when I woke up was not daylight yet. Chip was adding papers to the two suitcases we had packed the night before. Somehow that gave me the impression that he was not counting on coming back here. What is the proper attire for evacuees? I left the unmade bed, dressed and went to the kitchen. Maria was frightened and was not afraid to show it. I felt like a heel, abandoning her like this. She doesn't have anybody in Nicaro but us. I told her, "I'm not going to the U.S., just as far as Guantanamo. When I get there I'll get in touch with my father and he will send for me. Maybe you can come work for us in Camagüey." I don't think she felt any better. Nobody is making plans for her immediate future, but both of us took care of the present. I went to get Jeffy while she fixed his breakfast: always the same, oatmeal. Chip shouted toward the kitchen, "There is no time for that." We ignored him and went about the morning routine, only a couple of hours earlier than usual.

Jeffy was awake, standing in his crib and talking to himself. The whole room looked a pale gray in the reflected light. I went about as if this was another day. The hugs and laughter; the trip to the bathroom. He is toilet trained but wears diapers at night, just in case. By now he knew that we were going someplace because I dressed him completely before leaving the room, even to his white boots that are suppose to prevent him from being flat footed. Normally he only wears shoes if we were going out. He ate his cereal sitting in his high chair while his father paced around and reminded me that we will surely have breakfast waiting for us on the ship. Then he went out, loaded the car, and called, "We have to go, Now!" I wiped the oatmeal off of Jeffy's face and Maria carried him to the car. As we took off Jeffy said, "Aeea crying."

The few neighboring families drove down the hill like a diplomatic caravan, our little flags waving: the Daubenspecs, the Morrisetts, the Anastacias... We can see the wharf down our hill and toward the East, but to drive to it we go from the other side. We take a downhill hairpin curve and, once on the flat ground, we drive past the Commissary and turn right with the ammonia tanks to our left; then over the rail lines and toward the docks. Somebody was directing traffic. As the cars arrived they were parked in a neat row and everybody started walking on the lower level where the small boats are docked. Are all those cars going to stay parked there waiting for our return? Surely the Company has it all planned. It always has. I had been told that every single U.S. citizen was supposed to be evacuated, but I could name a few who are not here. On the other hand, the international mining community being what it is, some of those here are from countries other than the U.S.; at least Canada and Sweden are represented. I wished I had been stronger and refused to join this party. This same group has boarded the same boat many times for pleasure trips, but there is nothing festive about this trip: we carry suitcases, dress somberly, and we are watched. A row of barbudos sat on the edge of the higher dock, only inches away from us as we walk by; their weapons dangling casually from their hands, as usual. Nobody talked to them or they to us.

White and Jay (another manager) are farther down the pier directing the operation. With them there is another small group of barbudos in one of our boats. They talked, and then the boat took off, full speed, toward the entrance to the harbor. Our two managers came back and explained to us what is going on. According to them, the rebels on the boat are on their way to remove the explosives they have placed earlier to mine the narrow entrance to the harbor. We were to be ready to depart in our own boat as soon as they give us the "all clear" signal. For some diplomatic reason the U.S. Navy ship was not to come into the harbor; it is waiting for us on the open waters just outside the entrance. Some jumped in the boat and some were helped, but in minutes all of us had taken our places in the benches on both levels of the pleasure craft. It always amazes me how obedient Americans are, and how quiet; I wondered how a similar group of my compatriots would behave in these circumstances.

We waited, and waited. The sun was up, promising a beautiful day for the beach — or whatever. For the first hour or so, there were many questions and comments. Then we settled down, each with our own thoughts. My situation is different from the others'; it is almost the opposite. First, I am not scared of the present danger as some are, and second, I

191

am not relieved by the prospect of being taken away into the unknown. That magic word, evacuation, is not the cure-all for me that seems to be for some of my companions. Looking around at the faces of the other women on the boat I wondered if they were thinking about unfinished household projects, as I was. Then I looked at the rebels sitting, just a few feet away, on the edge of the higher dock. They were sitting as before, but the morose attitude was gone. The weapons were not dangling but held firmly. They were not looking at us, but looking toward the distance beyond the end of the docks, and they were mumbling amongst themselves. With no warning, they stood up, turned, and ran toward land. The ones that had gone out on the boat came roaring back, hit the dock and jumped out without bothering to turn off the engine. They too ran past us, and would have shoved aside anyone who got in their path. If children in our group had been standing by the boat, as they had a few minutes before, they would have been trampled.

The leaders in our group immediately grasped what was happening even if I didn't. Someone shouted, "To the plant!" By that time we were behaving as a troop — an odd troop made up of people of all ages and physical condition, including the old, the obese, and a pregnant young Canadian. We scrambled out of the boat, ran to our cars, and backtracked toward the plant.

We heard explosions but knew not where. From the distance I saw that preparations had been made to protect the civilian population in case of attack. A giant white cross had been painted on the metal roof of the largest building and that's where we headed. In almost two years in Nicaro I had never been past the main gate to the plant. Now the whole town was pouring in. There must have been some advance planning for everybody to know where to go. We abandoned all the cars in an open area and ran indoors. Now, what really was a disturbing sight was to see the armed barbudos running in to hide with the civilians who they had endangered. Even their supporters must have felt like telling them, "cowards, go out and fight" But I doubt anybody did. We ran from here to there trying to stay as a group and trying to stake out a corner of space for ourselves for what looked like a long siege.

Soon the word got around that the explosions we had been hearing came from the cannons on the deck of a Cuban warship that had slipped into the harbor when the rebels removed the mines. Apparently they had waited out of sight for such opportunity. How did they know when the mines were removed? How could they watch the rebels without being seeing? We guessed that they had intersected a radio communication. I wished I could see the warship. I knew Cuba had a navy, many Cubans didn't — in my previous life I had even dated a graduate of the Cuban Naval Academy, who was as out of place at Los Desengaños as Chip was. Why do we need a navy? Maybe the answer is here right now. How about an Air force? We were still milling around when the planes started flying low over us. They are firing at nothing because their targets are here inside with us. Is this what wars are like? Lots of noise and indiscriminate firing just to feel they are doing something.

I saw a movie once titled "Trial by Fire" in which two women reversed their character at a time of danger: the supposedly tough one broke down in panic and the meek one took charge. The reactions I see around me run the gamut from hysteria— in a woman brought in from our hospital— to complete unconcern. There are surprises: an American neighbor who always professed to love Cuba and Cubans was standing right next to me warning her son not to ever leave the United States again "the only civilized place there is" and wishing Nicaro was like Preston where Americans "are kept separated and protected from the Cubans." But most parents around me are not thinking of the future, but are just trying to keep their families together. I came across Elia and Manolo with their three small children, the youngest just days old. That's when I thought that nobody should have more children than they have hands to hang on to them. When it comes time to run for your life, you should be able to grab a child on each hand and run. As children started to feel comfortable, the older ones began to move around the crowd and explore. That's when I saw many parents frantically rounding up their brood.

We claustrophobics fear nothing coming from the outside; at least it is always preferable to the feeling of being trapped inside. So after several hours of sharing the floor space with hundreds of apprehensive people who, like me, are caught in this situation of which we have no control, I decided to take my chances with the strafing airplanes outside. Of course, where I go, Jeffy goes. I made sure Chip was not around or he would have accused me of endangering our son's life, and I slipped outside to a partially uncovered pathway. I was not the only one. Claustrophobic, bored or curious, at least a dozen people were out here, and I joined them to watch the fireworks. Here I learned that in all the confusion, the rebels had left Nicaro and the government forces are now in control. But maybe they didn't know it because they kept on shooting for hours at non-existing targets. A man in the group gave Jeffy a piece of candy, a Life Saver. He had never seen one. He turned it around in his hand for a moment, but it didn't take him long to figure out what to do with it. It has been a long time since that bowl of oat meal.

Quietly the group of prospective evacuees was rounded up. The administration had established contact with those now in charge and obtained permission for us to try to leave again. We headed to where we had parked our cars. All through the day, news and rumors had traveled around the crowd in the most efficient manner and now, before we reached the cars, a mob had gathered around them to keep us from going. Here we saw the little American flags at work. They are a liability since they serve only to identify our cars. I saw our almost new DeSoto's tires being slashed. This mob was not made up of strangers; these are people that I see at the commissary, the movies and the ball games, but fear has taken over. The word is that as soon as U.S. citizens are out of the way, the government forces will bomb Nicaro in retaliation for having harbored the rebels — as if we had a choice.

The places where we had stood or sat on the floor all day may not have been comfortable but at least they were clean. Now our group was imprisoned in an area called "los hornos", the ovens. The windowless tank-like room, where apparently ore was processed, was coated with the fine pink dust that is the trademark of the Nicaro plant. We had no idea what was going on outside or even who was in charge. All we knew was that the bombing had stopped and it was very quiet. We were in for more hours of waiting.

When the door was opened and we were ordered to step outside it was by a kaki uniformed soldier. He didn't care if we were Cubans or Americans, he was looking for rebels. We joined the crowd outside. It was my favorite time of the day, just before the sun goes down. Then I saw why we were moving so slowly toward the plant gates: soldiers at the gate were allowing the women and children to walk out but were waving all the men to one side. Chip had been carrying Jeffy on his shoulder and now turned him over to me and joined the other men. I thought it chauvinistic of the soldiers to think that no harm could come from women, but maybe they were looking for somebody in particular. I held on to Jeffy's hand and we started walking, joining other women and children in a gloomy hike toward our hill and home. We half listened for shots in the distance, but none came.

Maria was at the house. Wisely she had never left but took her chances with the bombs. Our house had taken a couple of hits from the gunboat. There was a hole in the wall of my bedroom and another one in a corner of the kitchen, both facing the water. Maria's rooms are on the other

194

side. I was beginning to think about food and a shower when Chip ran in. "We are going", he said, and we went.

This time we walked on the foot path at the end of our hill to the dock down below, and it was pitch black. This was the darkest and quietest night I had seen in Nicaro. Apparently there was no electricity and people were trying to stay out of trouble. There was a different boat waiting for us this time: a U.S. Navy landing craft and there were uniformed U.S. sailors manning it. A woman in our group gushed that just seeing those uniforms she felt secure. Her faith in her government had not wavered. I just wished I could stay home. Mine is a cat mentality: I will stay in a crumbling house rather than face the unknown.

The waves outside the bay were huge as usual and even more impressive at night. The Navy ship waiting for us was not designed to transfer out of shape civilians of all ages in a high sea. The sailor who took Jeffy from me at the railing said, "What a brave little boy." Many other children were crying, including Jeffy's little playmate, Bruce. It took four sailors pushing and pulling to haul fat Mrs. L aboard. Another decision made on the spot: I will never get fat.

The bunks assigned to the women and small children were inviting, but first, a quick shower. Quick by necessity because we all had the same idea and there were others waiting. I did what I had never done in all my years in boarding school: throw aside my Cuban modesty and take a group shower with women of all ages and several toddlers, including my own. We each grabbed a bunk and settled down for what was left of the night. Jeffy had never shown any emotion through the long ordeal. He seemed to be just observing with interest, but not distressed. But as he drifted off to sleep, I saw him suck his thumb for the first time.

There were no portholes in our bunk room but when the lights went suddenly on we took it as a sign that the night was over. After hours in an ore tank and a night deep inside a ship, I will never say again that I panic if I can't see the sky. Still, it was wonderful to go up on the deck after breakfast — how do they cook such good food in such a tiny kitchen. This was definitely not a cruise ship. It was set up for able-bodied seamen that knew better than to fall overboard; the only thing that separated the deck from a drop to the waves below was a cable strung around the perimeter. Jeffy was as delighted as I was to be out in the fresh air again, but I held him so tight that I left finger marks on his arm.

We had cruised East during the night and rounded the famous "Paso de los Vientos" or Windward Passage that separates Cuba from Haiti.

Now the coast of Cuba was to our North, and, was it beautiful! The ocean is extremely deep along this coast (according to my geography books) and that makes the water a deep indigo blue, very different from the turquoise water outside of Nuevitas and Nicaro. We could see that we were approaching a large naval base because we had already come up to several military vessels.

The Bay of Guantanamo has an interesting history now mostly forgotten. In the 19th Century it was an international vacation spot for the very rich. They were sort of the jet setters of the time, except that they didn't come by jet but in their own luxury yachts. That era came to an end when the new Republic of Cuba let the United States keep Guantanamo for a military base. There is a more modest, small town of Guantanamo outside the base. My uncle Miguel Agramonte met and married his beautiful Corina when he was district judge there. She came to Camagüey and became one of us. I like to think that she is the inspiration for the popular song "Guantanamera."

Getting off the ship was much easier than getting on it: we walked a plank to the dock, but, were all these people here waiting for us? Coming forward from the crowd there were Red Cross workers armed with clipboards ready to question each one of us. And military families from the base, as it turned out, were not here out of curiosity but because they had either volunteered or been commanded to take the evacuees in as their house guests. I should have been grateful like the others, but I wasn't. It was difficult being polite to the Red Cross woman, "I am not a refugee. This is my country, Leave me alone and I will find my way home", I was thinking. My only request was to get in touch with my parents in Camagüey but she could not help with that. Communications within Cuba were disrupted. Now I had the prospect of pretending to be grateful to the young military couple who put us up for the night at their home, even moving their son out of his bedroom, and prepared our breakfast the next morning. Everything these kind people said rubbed me the wrong way. First, they were whole hearted Castro sympathizers so they had a different view of what had happened to us. And second, they kept referring to the rest of the island as Cuba as if Guantanamo was not in it. As, "We don't go to Cuba anymore. . ." To argue my case I said, "If you rent a room in a house you have the use of the room as long as you pay the rent, but the room is still part of the house and belongs to the house's owner." They were not convinced, "This is a United States Navy Base" pronounced slowly and with great pride. I don't know why I start arguments since I never change anybody's view.

Besides I was still tired. I said so and we went to bed. I had slept better in the ship's bunk.

We were rounded up and delivered to the base airfield in the morning. It appeared that the others had established a much better relationship with their hosts than I did. There were many hugs and promises of eternal friendship. The plane waiting for us had United States Navy on its side but inside it was just like any passenger plane. Only, it was not large enough for our whole group so it was decided that the women and children will fly to Miami in this plane and the men will follow in a cargo plane. A few of the older children begged to wait and go with the men, and were granted the privilege of an uncomfortable flight.

We took off toward the ocean — there are high mountains inland — and then skirted the coast for a while before crossing the island and heading North toward Miami. By now, we were all clean, well dressed and outwardly composed but inside all of us were still apprehensive, if by different degrees. We were the dependents of men who may have lost their jobs, but after months of a war of nerves, some were glad that it had come to a head and they were moving on to something else.

We landed on an area of the Miami International Airport reserved for military planes and were escorted to the very familiar terminal. We had been warned that we would be questioned by reporters but I never imagined there would be this many. We walked silently in the sunshine surrounded by reporters with flashing cameras. The fight over Nicaro and, most of all, the ordered evacuation of U.S. citizens had been big news the last two days. We had been instructed to refer all questions to a designated spokesperson, who will be in the next planeload. Arrangements had been made for the whole group to stay at a motel on the North perimeter road of the airport, but first we had to clear customs like anybody else. I found myself in the uncomfortable position of the lady without a passport: Chip had all our papers. While the other women and children moved on to the large waiting room, Jeffy and I waited on the other side of the counter. There I discovered how resilient my child is (and maybe other children as well). Up to this point I had been a by-the-book mother. Bedtime routines, bath, meals, everything planned and on schedule. He was taking the changes in his life in stride; much better than I, maybe because he doesn't think far into his future. He is making friends with a couple of airline attendants and they are all laughing as he gives them a lesson in Spanglish; they had never heard the word shoepato as in "shoepato susio." He was wearing the white boots that have become a status symbol for Cuban pre-school set; only, they require daily whiting and his were dirty with nickel ore.

After a while somebody vouched for me and we joined the others for more waiting. We were all tired and bored at the same time and a couple had the first signs of a cold. The children were feeling better than ever and kept asking the classic "how much longer." As if we knew. Then, after a long silence, my neighbor Ruth Anastacia provided us with much needed laughter by saying, "Do you know that some people pay to do this for fun?" Soon after that, the rest of the group arrived, papers were produced, and we found taxis for the short ride to our next home, an airport motel and restaurant.

We could guess that Chip's parents and mine, as well as friends and relatives of everyone in this group, had to be frantically trying to find out where we were. This was our first access to a pay phone, and for that we had to wait our turn. Chip's parents wanted to know how soon we could be in St. Louis. We assured them we were fine where we were and would go visit soon. Then I called my parents. It was easier than expected; strange that we could talk from Miami but not from Guantanamo. As I had guessed, my father had been busy trying to find out where we were. From the Embassy in Havana he learned that our names were on the list of those ordered to evacuate, but was told that not all of them did in fact go. Our names were not on another list of U.S. citizens and dependents who had chosen to remain in Nicaro. Then he contacted Tony Arruza, now at the Central Violeta in Camagüey Province; Tony called his friend Lito Gonzalez (a Cuban part owner of Nicaro, whose role I never figured out) and finally heard that we were in Guantanamo. That night I wrote a long letter to my parents with my account of the last two days. I wondered how it would compare with the several other versions they had heard.

The next morning The Miami Herald had a photo of the group of us walking away from a Navy plane under the headline "58 Tense Americans Flee Here After Castro Release." Under the photo there is this caption, "Americans Released by Rebels Are Weary Upon Arrival Here- Cuban shell fire and tension left them bitter". That is an attention catching headline, but the reality was quite different and if publicized may have caused problems later within Nicaro. We were not held prisoners by rebels; we were thrown into that ore storage by fellow Nicaro residents to keep us from fleeing. Some facts are best forgotten. The text of the story continues, "Fifty-eight Americans whose U.S. Nickel mine in Cuba was overrun for five days by rebels, flew into Miami Sunday. Shell fire and tension left them weary and

198

tight-lipped. Some were fearful for the safety of the fourteen, including two women and four children, who remained in Nicaro . . ." Now, I don't know who made that last statement, but I found it disturbing. I can understand that the U.S Embassy is only interested in the safety of U.S. citizens, but these people have been working for years with the people of Nicaro, their children go to school and play together, and now, they are only interested in the safety of the precious few who have U.S. citizenship papers?

The first letters from Camagüey addressed to the motel were dated Oct. 26, the day we finally talked. Mami recalled all their efforts trying to get in touch with us, including amateur radio. Papi and Oli were ready to try to drive to Nicaro when they found out that we were gone. She adds, "That night we were asking ourselves, how is poor little Jeffy sleeping and how is he taking this." She goes on to practical minutia: fabric she bought for me that she will be returning; a pattern she had for an unspecified friend of mine . . . and then "I regret in my soul that you had to leave Cuba, but not for that we will stop reuniting once in a while. Even if I don't like to travel I will have to do it to see my grandson. Here in Camagüey the Fidelistas have not been able to dominate, but they have done enough harm. Send me instructions of what you want from Nicaro that as soon as something is clear we will try to resolve anything we can."

Then her religious side came up (or it may have been just a form of speech), "Let's pray to God that he illuminate the minds that are confused in Cuba, and in the whole world, and that he shows us the best road to follow and gives us courage.

"Count always with our invariable love. Mami "

In his familiar one page typewritten letter on his letterhead and in his usual take-charge style, Papi wrote "I thought you would be coming to Camagüey to retrieve your belongings from Nicaro, but since you are going to St. Louis, as soon as it can be done, I will try to bring your things here, or at least, the car.

"There is still no telephone communication with Nicaro. As soon as there is I will call Sergio (Serge Marenkovic) or Manolo to see the condition of your house because as I understand it, after you left, the battle continued until the army dislodged the rebels." (I don't believe so; by the afternoon of the 24th the rebels had disappeared.) "Now everything is quiet in the opinion of Carl Lowell (Company executive) with whom we talked yesterday thanks to Arruza, who has been very helpful.

"Let me know if you want me to wire the money you have here, and if you need more let me know.

"Tomorrow I will be going to La Costa. I have not been there these days because I knew things were going bad where you were and it was not possible to communicate. I don't know why you didn't come when Disnalda's sister came and brought your letter, because she told Angela that things were getting bad over there.

"Around here the rumors continue and the terrorist acts of propaganda, but aside from that we are alright and waiting for elections, hoping that with the election of Marquez Sterling things will calm down some.

"I can only imagine what poor Jeffy has gone through.

"Oli still has trouble with his leg. He is not getting any better and I don't know what else to do. We will probably go see a doctor in la Habana.

Los quiere, Adolfo"

*

I tried soaking the white dress I had worn on the last day in Nicaro in the bathtub of our motel room but I ended up throwing it away. Some of the others are planning to keep their stained clothes as reminders that it was that ore that was supporting us all in Nicaro. Our motel is comfortable; it isn't even noisy since the planes usually take off over the residential areas to the South, but it is not one of the vacation hotels in Miami. After a couple of days, my next door neighbor, Janet, had the idea that we needed to treat ourselves to a day in town. We extracted all the information we needed from a helpful desk clerk and feeling confident and cosmopolitan, boarded a bus to downtown. After a few stops and moments of indecision, we found what we were looking for as the bus deposited us in the center of super modern Miami. In Burdines we started with the beauty shop. Neither one of us is a regular beauty shop customer but we felt that we deserved a treat. Then we shopped for a couple of hours until we figured it was time to find our bus again, we stepped outside, and…it was pouring rain. We arrived back at the motel looking like drowned rats, or, even worse, lost, bewildered and homeless. To cap this misadventure, when I showed Chip my only purchase, a pair of red shoes, he saw red. Apparently red shoes mean something to him that they don't to me. I obediently went back the next day and returned them.

Our last hope for a peaceful solution was the election scheduled for November 3rd. It was a very faint and unfounded hope. Batista's request to the UN and other international organizations to send observers had been denied. It was probably deemed too dangerous to send outsiders, and with reason. Candidates had been assassinated and threats of violence were circulated. The several anti-government groups, both urban terrorists and the rebels in Oriente Province, El Escambray (and increasingly in Camagüey) had made it clear that they would not accept the results. Still we hoped.

The little group of evacuees assembled in the hotel lobby for the televised evening news. Many in the group knew little about the candidates but their futures depended in part on the outcome of this election. They may have known that ex-president Grau San Martin apparently had not had enough and was running again. Batista's chosen successor was Rivero Aguero who, on his own, would have been worthy of admiration: a poor orphan who had risen against all odds. But he was Batista's candidate and as such, he would never be accepted even in the off chance that he won on his own merits. The opposition was ready to declare the elections rigged. The only candidate that could be considered legitimate in normal times was Marquez Sterling, and, even if I knew little about him, all my hopes for Cuba returning to normality rested on him. He had no connection to Batista's or any previous discredited administration. All the rebellious groups that had brought so much grief to the average Cuban in the name of patriotism would have a hard time justifying attacks against him.

It was reported that only 30% of eligible voters were expected to vote, and in Oriente Province, as few as 10%. Voting is mandatory in Cuba but the fear of violence is stronger than that of a fine. The opposition strategy was not to vote any particular way, but to keep people from voting by any means possible including destroying ballot boxes. At the same time they spread the word that the election was rigged and that duplicate ballots had been printed and marked by the soldiers. I could not believe that Batista could be that stupid, but apparently he was.

I may have been the only one surprised when the results came in: Rivero Aguero had a decisive win, with Marquez Sterling second and Grau a distant third. We were not going to hang around to wait for the charges and counter charges or for the 24th of February fake change of power. We went to our room and packed. We were heading for the St. Louis, Missouri home of my in laws with not the vaguest plans of what to do next. The group at the Miami motel began to break up. Some were waiting right there for the opportunity to return to their abandoned homes; some were actively looking for employment; and some, like us, used the forced opportunity for an extended visit with relatives. Jeffy's little playmate, Bruce Fluesmeir, and his parents, also headed for St. Louis. Once there, a reporter from the Saint Louis Post Dispatch interviewed all of us. This time the headline was "Two

St. Louisans Tell of Day of Terror under Fire in Cuba" over posed portrays of the two family groups. The Fluesmeiers look happier than the Tischlers.

Chip did most of the talking during the interview. He told the reporter that Oct 24 was the climax of an ordeal which began last March as he tried to conduct exploratory drilling operations in rebel-infested mountains 30 miles from the protection of federal soldiers at the Nicaro plant on the northeastern Cuban coast. "The real trial, though, began Oct 20 when the federals pulled out of Nicaro for reason known only to themselves and let the rebels move in. We had halted exploratory drilling and pulled out of the mines weeks earlier after getting a warning that the rebels were out to seize us. We had insisted on staying in the plant area although the General Services Administration, which owns the plant, kept sending word from Washington that everything was safe and that we should resume operations. The plant management backed up our position. . . " Arsdel Fluesmeir declared that he had enough and had resigned from his job (as a chemist) and was job hunting. Chip said that he also had enough but was technically on a paid vacation and was hoping for a new position with National Lead, the parent company of Nickel Processing Corporation. Actually, that was just wishful thinking.

The senior Tischlers once again gracefully opened their home to us. They had moved since we first visited as newlyweds. Just like my parents, they had moved from the home where the children grew up into a more modern house. My parents had traded a rented one story — not really our main home, which was Los Desengaños — for a custom built home with upstairs bedrooms as nostalgic reminder of the houses of Papi's youth. The Tischlers had gone the other way. The house where we first visited was the usual two storied house of the cold North. Their new house was one of the now in vogue ranch-style houses, nothing like real ranch houses I know, except that it is all on one level; in this case with a full basement, the domain of Willie, their "colored girl." Unlike the criadas of Camagüey who are part of the families they serve, colored girls go home when their workdays is finished. I see them waiting at all the bus stops. Also, Cuban criadas come in all different colors. If Jeffy lost his loved Aeea he soon became attached to Willie and spent time talking to her in the basement watching her iron. Just like my parents had treated themselves to some new furniture to go with the new house, so had my in-laws and theirs was not child proof. Jeffy (also known as "fingers") had to be constantly watched. He also gained an equally dedicated friend in his Grandpa Tischler — He even discovered a resemblance of his grandfather to the man on the Quaker Oatmeal box. Jeffy would point to the bald old Quaker on the box and say "Grandpa." Chip did as he always does in times of crisis; he put his nose in a book, and kept it there.

The first set of letters from Camagüey was dated Nov. 5th.

Mami starts "Dear Angelita, fortunately I have good news to give you..." and then goes on to report that on November 3rd Marta had given birth to a "precious baby boy, healthy and well developed." The last was worthy of notice since the previous two children had been born prematurely. It sounded like a press release; "Both the mother and child are doing well." They plan to name the baby Pedro.

Oli had talked about "his son Pedro" even before their first child was born. Since that child was a girl there was no arguing about it and we ended up with Adriana, named after a great-grandmother on Marta's side — in our tribe you are always named after somebody, that's why there are dozens of Angelas in my family tree and it is so easy to get lost on its branches amongst identical names. The use of two surnames helps some, but not when cousins marry cousins. Oli and Marta's second child was indeed a boy, but stronger forces prevailed and he was named Adolfo Rene after the grandfather. This baby will be Pedro, but he is not being named after the family patriarch, my great-grandfather Pedro Sanchez Dolz. A branch of the family in Havana, not in the cattle business but owners of the department store Sanchez-Mola have the duty of carrying on Papa Pedro's name. Oli is naming his child, as promised, after Pedrito Carbajal, his friend and mentor who was the encargado of El Destino and had died childless. The baby's second name will be Oliverio.

Mami writes that she and Oli are still trying to convince Papi that he should make his yearly trip north. She argues that he needs to take a break more than ever to "remove himself from the tense situation that we are living in." She would come with him and use the opportunity to go to St. Louis to see me (and her grandson) but they are putting her mother, Abuela Consuelo, in the hospital to prepare her for surgery. She mentions Elia Maria. So my Nicaro friends have made it back to Camagüey. Probably drove down the Carretera Central as before where we took the long tortuous way out. Then Mami asks me to tell Sara Tischler that the dress she left for Adriana fits beautifully and was worn to a neighborhood birthday party.

Papi starts his letter by acknowledging that they finally received the long letter I wrote from the Miami motel. He goes on "We lost the elections. Some say it was fraud, and some say it wasn't. The truth is not known."

"Here in the campo, things are bad. Day before yesterday, Raul Castro's people went to La Gertrudis and took my bulldozer, but yesterday Oli and I went and he followed the tracks for three leagues and found it broken. He was able to repair it and take it back. Today I am going to try to take it to Camagüey. That is, if they haven't gone back and burned it down. They had been using it to tear up roads. They have also been burning the bridges."

"We received a card from Jeanne (my boarding school friend has recently discovered that in France, Jean is a man's name, and became Jeanne) asking for your address. Here is hers. . . Denver 3, Colorado."

"I see that you have decided to stay there for which I am glad, because even though (here) in town there is no physical danger it is bad for the nervous system. You know that for us it is a very great pleasure to have you here any time and for as long as you want.

"Monday, Consuelo enters La Colonia (Colonia Española, a hospital) and I don't know when the surgery will be so I may not be able to go to Bethlehem or if I go, it will be for just a few days and I won't be able to go to St. Louis.

"Oli just came in. He still has the problem with his back (it was his leg before). I believe he will end up having to have surgery. Marta and the niño are doing well. She can hardly believe such a large and strong child.

"Your car has not been brought and I don't believe Manolo has the key because all he said was that it was alright.

"I suppose you know about the crime of the airplane at Preston; maybe now the government in Washington will pay more attention because the authorities in Florida are allowing the conspiracy that is going on in Miami. . . you should see the instructions they left for me at the ranch, they are purely communist.

"We'll see if Jeffy fattens up now (once a cattleman. . .) and also Chip with the tranquility there. I believe he should finish his PhD and stay there as a professor and not roam around mining camps anymore. Of course, that is an opinion and not advice because nobody follows them. Regards to Chip's family. Adolfo"

Chip's family give every indication that they are happy to have us for as long as it takes but it isn't easy. We cannot help being tense about our uncertain future and the present perils of my family and friends. Also, I was beginning to discover a father-son relationship completely different from the one in the home where I grew up. Is this love Jewish style? I broke into tears the first time my father in law said "my no-good son" before I realized that he admires his oldest son's education, although he never let him forget that it had been paid for by the labors of a man with a sixth grade education. If hugs and kisses are signs of love this household is way above ours in Camagüey, where we hardly ever touch one another. The kissing includes the parade of close friends of the family that come calling regularly, more now than ever out of curiosity since we were in the news, but also, I presume, to meet the grandson. Sara humors me by telling her friends "Angela doesn't want anybody to kiss the baby on the lips", and then raise her shoulders as if saying "isn't that odd?"

Papi's letters follow a common pattern addressing subjects in short paragraphs. I have noticed that they are arranged in order of importance. In the first one, he either acknowledges having received my letter, or not, and, if he had, comments on it. On Nov. 13, the second and third paragraphs are about Nicaro; Manolo and Elia Maria are in town and, like us, don't know what to do next. He has received orders from White to return but he is not eager to do it. Nobody knows where our car is. Papi wonders if our insurance would cover it if it is lost.

Next, "I may go to Bethlehem on the 22nd. You may write to me at the Hotel. If I can, I will go see you; that depends on how Consuelo is doing. She seems better now because she had a blood transfusion. They have desisted of operating on her because they don't think she can take it.

"The elections went normally until 6 (P.M) and then they did as they wished. I believe Marquez Sterling could have won with the votes he had because there was lots of enthusiasm for him, at least in Camagüey. Now I think things will be even worse.

"Things are going badly at the finca. The Mau Mau are around but they are not doing much harm; there is a bad seca and the langosta have eaten what grass there was." "Langosta" can be lobster but in this case it is a more formidable creature, locust. Papi and Oli are considering taking what, to us, is an extreme measure; move some cattle out and place it a piso, (boarding) probably south where there is still some grass. And then he explains why he is planning to be away from the ranch under these dire circumstances. "Oli's family is alright, but he is not any better, that's why I am going to Baltimore, to talk to his doctor.

"Armando (my uncle) was sick but he is alright now.

"I am not giving you any news because there are so many lies circulating that nobody can tell what is true. El Burro (undignified nickname of a family friend) says that they have destroyed Levisa (small town just outside Nicaro) but I imagine it is just his tale; you know how he is. Regards to everyone and you know I love you" Adolfo

Mami's letter was dated three days later, "Querida Angelita, I suppose you are a little more at home and Jeffy is adapting to his new life." Then she relates the same visit with Manolo and Elia Maria with the new twist that the two of them may go back to Nicaro and leave the children in the safety of Camagüey with her parents. Knowing Elia Maria I know that she would never agree to that. They must be desperate to even consider it. Then Mami goes on with the report on my grandmother's condition. Her doctor, Miguelino, who happens to be my mother's relative, is not sure of the outcome of the planned surgery and together they have decided not to make Abuela suffer with an operation of doubtful outcome, since right now she is not in much pain.

She seemed more certain of Papi's trip than he was. "Adolfo plans to leave next Wednesday and on the return trip he will go by to see you. Then he will tell you how things are going over here, although I will advice you that in Camagüey we are as always, not counting the displeasure with the general situation.

"Oliverio [going] from bad to worse but he continues to do everything. Some things hurt him and others don't, but nothing makes him better.

"If you want to take advantage of this forced vacation to travel a while, send Jeffy back with Adolfo (Ha!). You can do it with the certainty that it would give me great pleasure . . . Grossman wants to know what to do with Chip's money that he is holding, and I ask the same about what he deposited in my account. It is all in Cuban currency"

"Greetings to Sara and Ben and receive muchos cariños de Mami".

Letters from Camagüey are taking anywhere from three days to a couple of weeks. Amazingly good service considering what is going on at the other end. But when these last letters arrived I had already had a call from Papi. I didn't think of asking him where he was, but assumed that he was in Bethlehem. He was canceling the promised visit to St. Louis and flying directly to Miami and from there to Camagüey. I was not too surprised at that since he is not fond of going to new places. Bethlehem, Philadelphia, Baltimore, New York, that's where his friends are and where he feels at home. If we stay here he will eventually come to visit, but not yet. This time he has a valid reason to cut his plans short. There are rumors of an upcoming airline strike and he doesn't want to find himself stranded. He was already having second thoughts about leaving during these troubled times and anxious to get back.

I believe it was that same day, or maybe the next, when tío Julian called. Tío Julian, of my father's five brothers is the closest to him in age and temperament. He is a medical doctor who should have been used to telling bad news, but this time he couldn't. He probably figured that when he told me that Oli was badly injured I would hear it as "was killed", but I didn't. I didn't want to. Next came several long distance phone calls to find Papi (known as Sanch to his Lehigh classmates and D.U. brothers). Some conversations that took place on that day I remember word by word, but I don't remember how I told my father what little I knew when we finally talked. Anyway, I don't think he read "injured" as "killed" either because he says that in another phone call, to his room at the Miami Colonial Hotel, where he spent the night before the morning flight to Camagüey, it finally hit him. He turned down the invitation to spend the night at the home of Enrique Biosca, a friend living in Miami who didn't want him to be alone, and sat all night in a chair in his hotel room wishing he could be dead instead. Later he told me, "I don t believe people can die of grief or I would have died that night."

When Mami called me later that same day, she assumed that I knew that Oli was dead. In my father's family we don t believe in theatrical displays and my mother tries to follow his example even if it is not her nature. The phrase that stuck with me from that conversation was "se volvieron fieras." And for a while I didn't know who she meant. Who turned into wild beasts? She mentioned the names of three men, two of them, Joseito and Miguel, our long time ranch employees who were as close as family. The third one, Juan Pantoja, was the fairly new cook at Los Desengaños and I didn't know him. Were they the ones that went wild? Finally I learned that they were all dead. What had happened?

1959. Land of Love and Hate

I don't remember sobbing or having any of the usual expressions of grief; before grief, came the feelings of shock. Not even my husband could understand what I could not explain. More than pain, it was disbelief: This could not have happened; not to us, not in Los Desengaños. Bad things didn't happen there. Here I was being observed by kind people with only indirect interest in me but who still wanted to help. They looked at each other, looked at me, and whispered. For a couple of days I did nothing until another call from Mami woke me up. She said, "Just come. You need to be with us."

I left Jeff for the first time in the care of his father and grandparents. From St. Louis I flew to Miami and then to our small international airport in Camagüey where I was met at the plane by friend and airport employee Benny Arteaga and maybe others, (funny how one remembers one face and forgets others.) Thanks to the prerogative given to me by the family tragedy I was spared the formality of going through the perfunctory questioning and baggage check in the international arrivals part of the building. Benny escorted me around the building side to where my father's chauffeur, Papito (Antonio Portal in the paychecks I had written to him in the years I was the book keeper for the family business) was waiting by the car. Lucy was sitting in the back seat.

It was the same airport that I knew so well since the days when I came home from school and yet this time it was completely different. Not only because I didn't go inside the terminal to go through customs or claim luggage which I suppose somebody had done for me; but the air itself seemed different. Joyful anticipation was not there but an unreal feeling had taken its place. The ride home was also the same; Papito drove on the Doblevia, the only four lane road in Camagüey, crossed the railroad tracks by the station and then along narrow streets to the new bridge and to the leafy part of town. This trip, I associated all the landmarks with my brother: the massive building of the Escuelas Pias, also known as Los Escolapios which Oli attended for a few years after Los Maristas which is on the other end of town. Come to think of it, he attended every boy's school in town but not because he was a poor student. He was not top of the class either. There is no reason to push yourself hard when you know well what you will be doing in life. The Carretera Central here curves right as it crosses in front of the Instituto de Segunda Enseñanza (sort of between a high school and a junior college). Years ago Oli had suffered a double fracture of his right forearm when he and friends couldn't resist the temptation to roller skate down the marble (or was it concrete) ramps on the sides of the steps on its Greek Revival facade. We turned left by the Instituto and crossed the Casino Campestre, over a small bridge on the probably polluted stream where Oli, as he admitted later, had swum. A road with (white) Club Atletico to our right and (black) Club Maceo to the left, took us to Cornelio Porro 54, the second house on the second block.

On the way Lucy tried to describe the situation at home, and prepare me for it. Our strong father is broken with pain and beyond consolation, but Mami has not shed a tear. She told me about the funeral, which had taken place two days before. Government troops had been stationed at every intersection along the route in fear that the funeral would be used to start an uprising. Oli, in death, had become a hero to the revolution that he and the rest of the family despised.

The layout of the house has been temporarily changed. When the living room was used for the funeral some of the furniture had been taken out of it. Now, most of the furniture was back in place but slightly skewed. I imagined that everything had been pushed aside to make room for a casket in the center and folding chairs for a velorio, or an all night vigil. I felt ashamed for not having been there.   An upstairs sitting room has been created in what used to be Lucy's bedroom, and that's where I found my parents. I suppose one can never have too many friends, but someone has found it necessary to create a haven where my parents can have time to themselves and leave the duty of talking to visitors downstairs to other relatives. My only thought when I first embraced them was, "how could I ever leave them again?" To my surprise and relief, Lucy is again part of the family. Which is good, they are going to need her. They talked freely about her and even her husband as if there had never been a break.

Next, I alone took the short walk to see Marta and her new baby. Her house is in disarray with untrained and unsupervised servants chatting outside, two children, one of them still in diapers, running around and a baby in the crib. But Marta seems calm and in control. Ironically, her source of strength is the new born. She confided on me that she forces herself to keep calm because she wants to keep nursing this baby. I wondered how long that technique will serve her, and if she will fall apart when she can no longer push aside the reality of her loss. But for now her system is working.

210

The baby is healthy; Adriana and Adolfo Rene are surviving without their Papun. Adriana is old enough to ask, but she is not asking. I believe that she has overheard enough to figure out that something terrible has happened and it is best not to know.

The story came to me in bits and pieces over the next few days: I had known that rebels had been operating in the area of Santa Lucia for some time. Papi referred to them as the Mao Mao after an equivalent group in Africa that had been in the news. He had mentioned Raul Castro in connection with the stolen bulldozer, but without specifying if somebody had actually seen him. We were all aware of the danger of being caught in between the soldiers and the rebels but until now senseless killings was something that happened somewhere else, not in Santa Lucia. The rebels must have been camping in Los Desengaños or somewhere near. What they were doing there, as everywhere, was to cause disruptions to anybody and in any way they could. The people at the ranch were caught in the middle; they had no choice but to cooperate with both sides. Those concerned with work — mending fences, caring for animals— had no choice but to tolerate them. You don't argue with armed people convinced theirs is a just cause, which justifies any means. At the same time, the ranch people had to stay friendly with soldiers from the barracks in Santa Lucia who came every morning to get (free) milk not knowing, or wanting to know, that the rebels they were supposed to be chasing were camping in the same pastures that milk came from. The first shot was fired by the rebels— not caring that they were endangering the lives of the people who apparently were giving them asylum—and killed a soldier. The other soldiers retreated but came back with reinforcements.

It is impossible not to speculate if things could have been different if my father had been in Los Desengaños. He blames himself for having left, but what could he have done? I like to think, perhaps erroneously, that he could have been the voice of reason and save the men's lives. Aside from the soldiers, there was only one witness, another employee named Ramon Diaz. Either he was either out of sight or somehow was not considered involved, but he was spared. As soon as the soldiers left, he rode to San Miguel to tell relatives. What he told was frightening to people who had been hearing for months about acts of extreme cruelty perpetrated by the army. The three men in Los Desengaños had not only been arrested, but he had seen when one of the soldiers hit Miguel with his own milking stool, before leading them away. The transformation into beasts that my mother had mentioned had already started.

Once the news arrived in San Miguel a way was found to notify those in Camagüey. My mother was alone at home when the news came that our three employees had been arrested and taken to the army garrison in Santa Lucia. She can be quite resourceful when need be; she managed to locate Oli, who had been south of town near El Destino. Then she found Papito, the driver. Together those two drove to San Miguel in my father's car. What they found in San Miguel was chaos. The three dead bodies had been found just thrown on the road by the gate to La Amelia just next door to Los Desengaños. Miguel, Joseito and Juan Pantoja together were related to half the residents of the Municipio. The general consternation can only be imagined. If this can happen to such decent people, it can happen to anyone.

Oli sent Papito back to Camagüey by bus and continued alone by car to Los Desengaños. He was not seen alive again. His body was found next day, November 23 thrown at the cemetery in Santa Lucia.

We had an account of how he was killed from a civilian who, strange as it seems, had hitched a ride on a truckload of soldiers. This man was a member of the Masons or some such secret society. He wrote down what had happened and left it at his Lodge for safe keeping. He saw Oli chase the soldiers and cut in front of them. Then he stopped at the gate to Los Desengaños and dismounted. Angry words were exchanged; the soldiers opened fire. He was taken, wounded, together with the car to the army post.

Our neighbor from the King Ranch, Lowell Tash went back a couple of days later peacefully and retrieved the car. The killing frenzy was over. He thoughtfully cleaned the interior of the car before returning it to my father.

Our friends at La Concha restaurant at Santa Lucia Beach witnessed as some soldiers discussed their deeds and divided amongst themselves the contents of Oli's pockets and his silver belt buckle, a gift Mami had ordered from Mexico.

I didn't want to hear any more but could not help wondering if we were victims of a random act of cruelty like the many others we had heard (and sometimes disbelieved) taking place in the capital or we were singled out to create the martyrs needed to fuel a revolution. Now, on top of his grief, Papi was faced with the chore of having to prevent his tragedy from being used in the ongoing war of words. The propaganda value of these killings was immense. Nobody could accuse any of the victims of being anything but hard working private citizens. If any of us still had doubts of the government's army being out of control, now we knew what they were capable of doing, but, we argued that the rebel army was not the friend of the civilians either. When Papi received a letter from his sister Gloria, Havana resident and dedicated Fidelista, asking him for a photo of Oli, suspecting her motives, he complied, but he wrote across Oli's big smile, "Another victim of this maldita revolucion."

Work in a finca cannot be neglected for even a day and Papi for the moment didn't want, or was not capable of making any decisions. I knew that his strong sense of responsibility would soon kick in and he will be back in charge. He is needed now more than ever with so many orphans depending on him. Running the Ganadera El Muñeco is complicated business with five separate bateys supplied and financially controlled from the home office in Camagüey, but run independently by the trusted encargados, or bosses in residence. There will not be disruptions in three of those locations, but El Destino was personally managed by Oli and Los Desengaños, without Miguel or Joseito will have to be redone from scratch. They had been there so long that they knew every animal and the location of every tool.

Most everyone has love for their spouse, children, parents, siblings and maybe a select group of friends and relatives. But Papi's circle of those he cares deeply about has a much larger radius. It includes school friends, second cousins, employees, and people that were part of his life before I came along. And that concern, love if you will, extends to all their children. He manages to keep in touch with them all, cheers their successes and suffers with their pain. He is particularly close to some of his relatives who are in the same business and now he is being helped without him asking or even being aware of the help. For now, my cousin Roberto is the one that seems to be handling concerns as they arise. If he stays as Papi's assistant it would be a case of giving a job to the busiest person. Roberto already has a ranch of his own and manages one for his father, my tío Armando.

I had agreed to limit this visit to a week. The day before I was scheduled to leave I drove my parents to Los Desengaños. Just the three of us. It was probably a mistake, but it had to be done sooner or later. We stopped in San Miguel to see Carolina. Joseito's widow was nothing like the young woman I remembered. She was not expecting us and was caught unprepared. She didn't have much to say and I wished I could guess her thoughts and offer some help. She will be getting Joseito's salary and she has the support of relatives. Is that enough? She has two small children, and one on the way, and no husband. Her blank look may be one of extreme sadness, fear or even resentment. She, like Marta, may be trying not to think at all. She certainly will not be thinking about school for her children, but for some time now Lucy has been making all arrangements for the schooling of Miguel's two and also Dalia, from La Gertrudis and Joseito's children will be included when they are old enough. But Lucy has been in Havana most of the time and now that responsibility falls on Mami.

The only thing I remember about this visit to Los Desengaños was the entrance gate. Somebody had hastily painted it with our all purpose gray paint. You could still see the splintered wood where bullets had hit. When I walked back to the car after swinging open the double gate, Mami was crying in Papi's arms. As I said, this is something that had to be done and it wasn't going to get any easier by waiting.

On the flight from Camagüey to Miami I sat next to a family friend who was known as a Fidelista. It was a particularly bumpy flight. Or, rather, we hit a depression or something that took the plane straight down as if on an elevator. I thought we would not stop until we hit the water. But we did; the stewardess picked herself up, passengers crossed themselves or laughed nervously, and the flight went on as normal. Maybe prompted by this incident, my traveling companion started to talk. He was carrying cash, lots of cash, in U.S. currency. He was confident in the success of the revolution. He was planning to come right back and participate in it. But he was opening a bank account in Miami. Just in case.

It was night when I arrived at the Tischler home in St. Louis. Jeff was awake when I went in to see him. He gave me his biggest smile and soon went to sleep. He seemed healthy and I was told that he had been happy, so I was not as indispensable as I thought. I wrote home and told them that Jeff had gained weight in my absence. It doesn't matter to me, but to them gaining weight is important, be it a child or a steer. Chip has been getting mail from Nickel Processing Corp. They are trying to round up their employees with plans to restart the plant.

The next letter from Papi was dated Saturday December 13. My letter about Jeff getting fat arrived as he was writing his. Angel Nuñez had come all the way to town to report on the situation at la costa, our collective name for all the lands near the north coast. His other reason for making this, now difficult, journey is that his daughter Dalia is in Las Salecianas in boarding school. The ranches to the north are now accessible only on horseback as the last bridge has been burned. I can understand that Angel would be nervous about having his daughter so far from home at times like this.

Papi writes "Here in Camagüey there have been several assaults and reprisals. I don't know how long this can go on. It seems to me that out of humanity somebody should intervene because the two armies don't fight, the only thing they do is chastise unarmed civilians."

"Since yesterday, all communication with Havana by train or highway has been cut off, so I can't ship cattle."

"I understand that Nicaro employees have returned or are returning. I can't imagine how with the situation as it is. Manolo Lopez Blanco went back by small plane."

Then he sends me the mailing addresses of some of his friends in Bethlehem, Friends have been writing to him but he is finding it difficult to reply at this time. At his request, I had been writing letters for him to his friends I knew from my days at Moravian, so I guess I should write to the ones I don't know also.

And finally, "Sergito, Chichi's son (and tía Amelia's grandson) escaped and arrived in Barcelona. So the poor woman is now happy. She was able to save her son (who apparently was involved) while we, without being involved in anything, have lost our poor Oliverio." I suppose I should know what this Sergito was involved in, but I don't. His father was a union organizer and probably a communist so it is not hard to imagine how my relative was caught somehow participating in the revolution.

There was no letter from my mother in that or the next envelope. I imagined her writing something, regretting it, and tearing up the letter. Or, maybe she could not bring herself to write at all.

I notice that Papi now addresses his letters to me "Querida China," China was Oli's nickname for me and nobody else called me that. We tried to keep it secret and he never used it in public. Except one day during a volleyball game at the Tennis Club, we were teammates and he was trying to encourage his distracted sister. He yelled," Dale China", not once, but several times during the game, "Hit it, China." Our secret was out, but, fortunately, except for a few who tried it that day to tease me, nobody else picked up the nickname permanently.

The letter dated December 23 marked one month since Oli was killed. "It still seems untrue to me, I always think that I am about to see him, and that I will hear him talk. He was so attached to me in my work that besides being my son he was like a partner."

"Lucy left yesterday for Havana for a few days. Also out of town are Roberto and Alvarito that were coming to see us every day. The rest of the family is still coming to keep us company."

215

"Nothing from Nicaro except that Manolo sent a radiogram to Elia Maria saying that he was alright and working in the batey."

"We received a (condolence) letter from Marcial from Blair (Academy) and another one from Scrap Johnson, both very nice and remembering Oliverio. If you can, please write to the D.U. (Lehigh fraternity). I haven't done it and I am not in the mood to do it."

."We are thinking that Marta may build in the back of our lot once she gets the insurance money and sells their car and a parcel of land she owns." I wondered if Marta was included in the collective thinking. My impression after talking to her was that at least for now she is not thinking of a future. She has found a hiding place in her religion and her children. But that will not last forever, when she comes out of it she is not going to let anybody do the thinking for her. I hope she understands that Papi's sense of duty makes it imperative for him to try to solve his children's problems and is not offended by it. We are used to it and love him for it. Now his concerns include mine and Chip's future. He continues:

"You haven't said if Chip is negotiating to return or find employment somewhere else. I may not have said it before, but this house is as much yours and Lucy's as it is ours.

"Things here (are) about, the same. They say that the zafra will take place but I don't see how. There is no communication with Havana except by plane, so no cattle is being sold. Can't drive to the finca because all the bridges are down, even the big one in Sta. Isabel.

"Angela and Marta just left for the cemetery but I didn't go because my hermanos y sobrinos (the Spanish nouns cover relatives of both sexes) always come at about this time."

I had not written to them about Chip's plans because I had no idea if he had any others than to wait and watch for developments in Cuba. As the Christmas Season approached we received cards from some of the former Nicaro residents that left with us. A few had returned to their jobs but without their families. I suspected that they may have been promised large bonuses to take such risk. Or they had such faith in the resolution of the Cuban situation that they judged that it was worthy of sacrifice. My concerns were more on the daily human tragedies than on the long term survival of a Nickel plant.

Never in my life had I been so much in need of someone with whom to talk. Someone who knew what was really happening in my country and my family. Instead, they were trying to distract me. Being with people who had no idea what I was feeling was worse than being alone. And then the thought came to me: some of the older family members had firsthand experience with human cruelty and destruction. They were Jewish, European refugees. One particular one, Aunt Lena, was especially kind to me. She hinted that her husband had barely escaped from Europe with his life but they had learned not to dwell on the past.

To me, it was not the past I had to deal with, but the present. Every letter, every news report, brought reminders of the ever escalating violence in Cuba. One day I read a newspaper column in which somebody referred to Eleanor Roosevelt as "Everybody's Fairy Godmother." Had I stopped to think I would have realized what a silly idea it was to write to her, or to anyone else for that matter, but I thought the widow of a president could possibly have the ear of powerful people, even if she had no power herself. I found the perfect seclusion in the guest powder room, a pretty room with bright daylight coming from a round window facing the street— I'm still not used to using artificial light in the daytime — and sat on the only available seat with a paper tablet on my lap. Nobody interrupted me except for a timid tap on the door to ask if I was alright. While I left to the grandparents the joy of protecting their belongings from a busy toddler I tried to explain in written words what was happening to Cuba and Cubans, not to ambassadors, politicians and rebels, but to people like my parents. Was I so naïve that I could think that a letter could make a difference? Probably not, but I felt I had to do something to remind people in the U.S. what a close friend Cuba had been. Why are we abandoned now? I was writing to a woman whose husband's death was mourned in Cuba as much as in the U.S. We helped him fight his wars. She must have known that.

I came out of my hiding place and rejoined the household. Nobody asked me about the letter. Writing it didn't make me feel better or worse but it was just something to do. Sara informed me that a tree had been planted in Israel in Oli's name. I had to thank her. In Cuba it was Masses. My mother finally wrote and included a list of people who had dedicated (paid for) mass in Oli's name. "I had made a firm promise to myself that I would not go another day without writing." She wrote "We feel very alone without you since Lucy is in la Habana. We go to mass every morning (I wondered if that included Papi). The one this morning was given by Ana Maria (de Miranda, friend) who went with us and Marta and Pepilla also Lolita Lavernia, who have been to most of them, and Marta Balais and. . . ." she names more relatives and friends who either join her in mass or keep them company at home including some who I didn't recall ever seen at our house. I hope they think kindly of the two daughters who are away. Then she goes to the usual news: Elia Maria had a baby boy (didn't she just have one?) and so did my cousin Alicia Agramonte. Manolo has reported that things are going well in Nicaro. He left his car at my parents' place with the intention of returning with ours. She ends by asking me to thank Sara for her kind letter. She must have written about the tree.

In a short handwritten letter dated Dec. 25, Papi takes note of our third wedding anniversary just days away and, even if there will not be celebration this year, he wishes us future happiness. We had not thought of anniversary celebration or even about Christmas presents, but the idea of a present for my parents came to Chip while we were at a downtown department store. It was not exactly a shopping spree but Chip is one man who likes to shop and for me, just wandering around the large store was entertaining. Within the store there was a portray artist studio. I stopped to admire the high quality pastel portraits which gave Chip an idea. He talked to the artist who agreed to paint a likeness of my brother using as a source only a couple of snapshots. When we came back a few days later we were impressed with the finished work. He made a few minor corrections— I thought the hair was too long on the sides. He then sprayed it and framed it. A piece of chalk covered paper will be a poor substitute for a person, but that may be the only face his children will see.

Papi wrote one of his usual typewritten letters just two days later on Dec. 27. For the first time he says that he hopes that Chip finds a job in the U.S. Apparently he has lost hope that we may return to our home in Nicaro. He included the address of his friend Enrique Biosca in Miami and asked us to send the framed picture to him, that he would find a way to get it to Camagüey. He adds that El Liceo is giving a mass for Oli at the cathedral the next day and the whole town is expected to be there. Group demonstrations of affection seem to be of some consolation to him at least for now. If the soldiers had set out to find and murder the best loved young man in the province, they could not have done better.

I find it disturbing that there is not a word about the fincas. Is he going to turn his back on his life's work? Who is living and working in Los Desengaños? If I know our guajiros, somebody, probably one of his relatives, has stepped in quietly and taken Miguel's place. I know that because of all the destruction cattle cannot be moved now, but cows still have to be milked, pigs fed, and the water turned on and off, — or maybe not.

The one paragraph about local happenings reads, "In Camagüey things are quiet. They haven't killed anybody in several days, and no arrests either. It looks like things are happening in Santa Clara now. Some believe that this is about to end, but I doubt it."

This time my father was wrong. By the time his letter arrived there was no fighting in Santa Clara or anywhere else. The revels had leapfrogged the province of Camagüey and there has been some serious bombing in the province to our West which the news agencies had been following. When we awoke on the first of the year 1959 expecting to hear more of the same, we were greeted with the news that Batista had given up, resigned and left the country. He had officially resigned at 3:00 A.M. "To avoid further bloodshed" and turned the office over to the oldest member of the Supreme Court, Carlos Manuel Piedra, as provisional president. Of course, nobody counted on a civil transition of power. We, personally, didn't know what to expect, and the U.S. government apparently was caught by surprise as much as anyone else even if they had facilitated the demise of Batista's regime with the arms embargo and other one sided decisions. Public opinion in the U.S. had made a hero out of Fidel Castro ignoring the several other groups involved in the overturn of the Cuban government. It was not a given conclusion that, when things settled, Fidel would come out on top.

Apparently Fidel Castro's personal popularity both in Cuba and abroad was enough to put him over the top. But in my mind I always held him and his adoring followers equally responsible for our tragedy. When a response came to my letter to Eleanor Roosevelt congratulating me for the "happy resolution to the problem in Cuba" I found it so heartless that I crumbled it and threw it away. Had I saved it I would have an important historic document.

The next few days there was an overabundance of news from Cuba but the one that concerned me, that my parents were alright, came by telegram on Jan. 5th. A letter, written that same day came a few days later. Papi reported that the one death in town on Jan. 1st happened to be in our family. Dr. Rogriguez de Leon was married to my cousin Clemencita. This was definitely a case of being in the wrong place at the wrong time. A slightly deranged man (one of the many to surface during this conflict) went on a shooting spree to celebrate the fall of Batista. He wounded one and killed tío Ernesto's son in law who was just walking by. My tía Pepilla, with no children of her own, considers Clemencita more a daughter than a favorite niece, so I wrote her a letter of condolence. She replied with a detailed description of the killing — one bullet to the neck and one to the abdomen —, which one would not expect from a gentle, secluded, old maid. Polite, social conversation in Camagüey now includes bullet wounds.

Again to Papi's letter,"Here everything is quiet and the people are very cheerful, except for those of us who have lost somebody, because the death of poor Oliverio is not compensated by any good that they can do for Cuba."

"We have already been able to arrest everyone who took part in the assassinations at Los Desengaños and I have hopes that they will be executed (by firing squad). Everyone in Camagüey is very interested that it is done."

"Fidel spoke last night at the Plaza de la Caridad for about four hours and has offered many things. We'll see if he can deliver. The best he has done is not give participation to Prio and his old politicians."

"I suppose you will be able to come by soon, for things are fairly normal. Lucy has been in la Habana through all this and we still have not heard from her."

I had assumed that my father would not partake in the wave of revenge that had to follow the fall of an out of control regime but evidently he and a group of friends had been quietly preparing for it. They had been doing more than going to daily mass. They had found witnesses and secretly put together names and evidence sufficient to convict the culprits, and then waited for the right time. The time came with the new year. What had to be done quietly while Batista and his army were in power could now be done openly and even encouraged by the mood of the populace and the revolutionaries moving into positions of power. Everything was done fast before soldiers shed their uniforms and blended into the shifting crowds, and while memories were fresh. It was cowardly of me, but I was glad I was away. Nobody described the trial and the killers remained faceless and nameless to me. Not only I don't know their names and faces, but I don't even know how many participated in the crimes and how many were tried and executed. Papi, The Avenger, is preposterous, but it makes sense only when you think that if allowed to live such heartless criminals would be living with the rest of us. Once they were identified, they had to be killed. But I think of the time when soldiers were in such a high state of alert that anybody they suspected as sympathizing with the rebels they saw as their enemy. They could be seen as cornered vicious dogs more than as criminal minded humans.

There is no doubt that many undeserving went to The Paredon as the places where the condemned stood before firing squads were known (whether there was a solid wall behind them or not). It was a great opportunity to dispose of enemies and rivals. But I was assured that those accused of the killings at Los Desengaños had a trial and evidence that would have stood in any civilized court, even if this one wasn't.

The world cameras descended on Cuba, mostly on Havana. The scenes they filmed for us to see were mostly joyous ones. Fidel took his time traveling from Oriente Province to the capital making speeches along the way, I had already heard about the one in Camagüey. Some of his people, mainly Camilo Cienfuegos and the infamous Argentinean doctor known simply as El Che, went ahead preparing the way for him. Here in the U.S. the revolution had been all about Fidel Castro, but in fact, there were other groups involved, like the Directorio Estudiantil, and the followers of ex president Prio, and it was not a given which group will be assuming power. It looked like it came down to a popularity contest. A letter from Mami dated Jan 10th describes how it was in Camagüey.

"As you know from the press, happenings in Cuba precipitated the first of the year in a most unpredicted manner so that practically we spent a whole day without authorities or any persons who dared assume control. Then everybody put on the 26 of July armband and when the Fidelistas arrived in town even Triana (married to a cousin) was in the revolutionary uniform. Then Adolfo, helped by Alvarito, Roberto, Cuco Comas, John LaHerran, Oliverito Tomeu and other friends succeeded in having the culprits of the murders at Los Desengaños arrested. Today he went in front of a tribunal they have created for such cases and made a formal accusation. We will probably have the sad consolation that the guilty will be punished."

"Tell Chip that if he is not busy you can all spend some time with us whether you plan to return to live in Nicaro or not. We have been informed that everything is going back to normal. Disnalda has already left (she is pregnant!) and Elia Maria is leaving Sunday with all the children. You could go just to get your things.

"Lucy returned day before yesterday and says that in la Habana things were not as smooth as in Camagüey.

"Zoila Gallo (a distant poor relative who, in the Cuban tradition, is my grandmother's companion) was married and Mamá is temporarily in Zoila R.(Mami's half sister)'s house but after Z.G. comes back from their honeymoon she will return to live with Mamá and so will her husband who is a very nice person." Apparently abuela Consuelo has recovered enough to be moved from house to house.

Mami ends her letter with "Manolo just arrived in your car."

The companion letter from Papi had more details about Nicaro; apparently he just had a short conversation with Manolo as he came to trade cars. Albertson is the new Administrator but he is leaving and they don't know who will take his place. Anastasia is leaving also. Red Wells fell and broke some ribs. Wonder what is really happening there. Are the newly empowered rebels interfering in the operation or are the Americans free to run it as before? He ends the letter announcing that Miguelito and Maricusa, Miguel's children are having lunch with them. I hoped there was no table talk about their father's murderers going on trial. I always imagine that children are more sensitive than adults and must be protected, but have no evidence that it is so.

Here in St. Louis we have to reach a decision soon. Or rather, Chip has to make up his mind whether to return to his job or not. He has unsuccessfully looked for another job, but probably not as assiduously as he could. As for me, I want to get back to Cuba now more than ever before. Before I wanted to find a way to live in Cuba for selfish reasons, life was better there, as simple as that. Now I have no idea what life there will be like, but I think I can help my parents. Finally we decided to go to Camagüey to see for ourselves, once there Chip will give the Nicaro management the final word they want. He will sign a new contract or resign depending on what he learns on the ground. The press here has been following every move of Fidel Castro with unquestioning approval. To them he is the embodiment of Joan of Arc, Bolivar, Robin Hood . . . it is the Robin Hood part that is bothersome. If he starts making good on his promises of distributing riches, somebody will have to get hurt. But for now, the end of violence is enough reason to rejoice, and nobody wants to remember how the violence started.

The three of us arrived at the Miami International Airport the second week of January 1959 and the party mood was still on. Nobody is happier than a happy Cuban. They called across the room to acquaintances and talked to strangers nearby, smiling and laughing always. They were going back home. Cubans have a long tradition of running to the United States for a while, when they, or some of their countrymen, have made a mess of things. My grandparents did it last century when they rode out the war of independence in New York City. But we always keep our identity and we always return.

I would suspect that exiled politicians and revolutionaries returned to Cuba (most likely to la Habana) to jockey for position the moment Batista's plane was out of sight. There may be Fidelistas and collaborators in this cheerful crowd, who, during the six years of attacks and reprisals found it healthier to move to the safe haven of Florida. But my guess is that most in this crowd had not been engaged in sending arms to the rebels but, more like us, were staying out of the way of bombs and unwarranted arrests. If fear was part of the mix of emotions, I didn't sense it. Now all of us ordinary Cubans have accepted the idea that once the tyrant, both the target and dispenser of violence is gone, it is safe to return and wait for life in Cuba to resume its normalcy.

The more boisterous in the group took the flight to la Habana; a couple of hours later the rest of us boarded the Pan Am plane to Camagüey. We from the provinces, or el interior as they say in the capital, tend to be quieter. From Miami to the Rancho Boyero Airport outside Havana is a short and not too interesting flight: all you see is water and, there you are, descending over a city. Flying to Camagüey is worth fighting for a window seat. The water changes color a dozen times before we are over solid land: there are shallows, keys and submerged reefs protecting the north coastline. I always try, and fail, to identify what I am seeing. I never know for sure where we are until we are over the dry savanna and see the runway of Aeropuerto Internacional Ignacio Agramonte (courtesy of the U.S. Air force).

Unlike my last arrival, this time we had the welcoming family group I had always expected. Every arriving passenger was similarly received; these were not people returning from schools or shopping trips. Every family had lived stressful times and may have wondered if they would ever be reunited again. Papi was a little thinner; Mami was wearing dark glasses because she was recovering from an eye infection, but to me they looked good. Just the fact that they came out to the airport instead of waiting for us at the house meant, to me, that they have decided not to give up. They have no choice.

This city has not changed in three hundred years and it has not changed with the revolution except for the presence of milicianos. Where do they come from? It was estimated that at the height of the conflict there were three hundred rebels, but there must be more than that in uniform in Camagüey alone. There will be many questions later, but right now we are grateful to be together, besides, I don't know how much Papito can be trusted. I know that in the last two weeks some who previously had been one thing turned out to be another. Not that we have anything to hide. Our family has found itself out of necessity on the same side as the newly in charge by bringing the killers to trial but that common cause is over and that thin alliance can quickly dissolve.

At the house the usual visitors, Alfredo and Dora, tía Pepilla . . . all want to know if we are returning to Nicaro. The choice that seemed so difficult in St. Louis seems inevitable here. What else is there to do? Chip is a geologist and Nicaro may be the only place in Cuba where there is a job for him right now. Taking advantage of the newly repaired phone lines, he called Albertson, acting manager, and accepted his offer. Mentally I walked into our hilltop house: the philodendron in the living room planter had dried up and will have to be replaced, but the outdoor plants outside the window were thriving, especially the royal poinsettia tree that Chip went to so much trouble to transplant. I walked in the kitchen and found that Maria had emptied the refrigerator and left it open to avoid mildew. In the bedroom the bed was made; my clothes were in the drawers and in the closet. Jeffy's rubber play pool had been emptied and brought inside. The outside walls that had taken two hits from the Cuban Navy ship had been repaired.

If I have to sum up all the conversations taking place in my parents' living room, they will add up to "Let's wait and see." While our friends are relieved that the tensions of the days of unpredictable violence are over, the incertitude of what is coming is greater with every speech of the Comandante en Jefe. The new regime is moving into position at an amazing speed. Of all the groups that contributed to the fall of the Batista government it is obvious that the rebels from the Sierra have come out on top, and as much as they try to be known as the 26 de Julio movement, in the minds of the people it is Fidel, and only Fidel. While still in St. Louis we had seen on television the wild crowds in la Habana carrying placards of "Gracias Fidel." All the other heroes of the revolution are, at least in the United States, completely ignored. Why one individual is singled out above the others is a subject I have given a lot of thought. Why him and not, say, Armando Hart, who was one of many dedicated to the same cause, but only Fidel gave his name and his face to the movement. Who shall be credited (or blamed) with singling out that particular young man? Journalists did much to single him out, especially the international press. By following one glorified person instead of multiple leaders they simplified their job and made things easier for their readers or listeners.

In the United States the adjective charismatic is almost invariably attached to him as if they belonged together. I had to look it up and still could not understand the connection. Fidel or somebody near him is a genius at marketing. And nature played its part. First, he is taller than average. While Hitler had used being shorter than those around him to his advantage, it stands to reason than the tallest one in a group will be noticed. Some find him good looking because they don't remember the round-faced, chinless youth. Growing a beard transformed him, hiding his weak chin and drawing attention to the eyes. There was something about his eyes that mesmerized some people. Somehow I seem to be immune to their pull; I even see a touch of insanity in them. But our friends who listened to his four hour declaration of purpose at our Plaza de la Caridad are not talking about his words, important as they were, they noticed the person. A very respectable matron who, could not have avoided the famous speech had she tried since she lives in one of those houses with the connecting porches surrounding the Plaza, described Fidel to my brother in law. "You should have seen him," she gushed, "he looked like a Cristo."

I saw most people important to me without leaving my parents' but there was a visit I had to make. My grandmother was back at home after hospital stays and a time at my aunt Zoila's home. I was warned to be careful with my words: she had not been told that her grandson had been killed so I put on my happy face. Not that she can see it; abuela Consuelo had been almost blind for many years.

Years ago I had figured out why Abuela's house on Calle de Republica is so odd. It had not started out as a house but as the carriage entrance and service area to a large house, no longer in existence. Like many homes carved out of centuries old buildings, it took some detective work to figure out its ancestry. The street façade is half the width of the rest of the dwelling, just wide enough for a small door and street level balcony. After the seldom used living room and level with a sitting room and the stairs (yes, there is a long and narrow upstairs apartment) the home widens with a walled courtyard with a view of newer buildings towering over this old one. Behind the yard is the open dining area shaded from the afternoon sun by a hanging canvas and behind that, the kitchen with its charcoal stove. Each of the three connecting bedrooms has a small window with a broad sill opening to the yard. The bathroom facilities in the back have evolved over the years and by now even include a flushing toilet.

Abuela has lived here in dignified poverty since before my days, but she no longer is able to greet her visitors in the sitting room by appearing regally from her inner sanctum hanging on to the arm of her companion. I had to go to her in the middle bedroom where newly married Zoila Gallo announced me. Abuela is a fraction of her former volume and it took me a while to realize why she is so changed: She is not wearing her dentures. The broad jaw characteristic of her family is not there. Still, she has her clear voice, knows who I am and even has some sense of humor. I am not her favorite grandchild, which would be Lucy who everybody says looks like her, but she has enough affection for all of us. She made me promise to come more often. I explained that I will be living in Nicaro once again and road trips along the Carretera Central were again easy and uneventful. Abuela was no stranger to the hardship of life during rebellious uprisings— she was married during the war of Independence and one of her more prized wedding presents was a box of matches. She had also had a brother killed during that distant war, only she had three others and I had none. I don't understand why the family has decided that she should be protected from grief now, she has buried two husbands, a son, a sister and who knows how many other relatives and friends.

The living room at my parent's home is again rearranged. Oli's pastel portray has arrived and needs to be placed with the best light. Papi's friend in Miami found the best way to send the crated picture to Camagüey without even having it opened for inspection. Even in a solid Catholic city like Camagüey there are small congregations of other denominations. One of them is the Episcopal Church which has been here forever and even has a school in the part of town known as La Vigia. The crate was delivered to their church, probably listed as "Religious Art." The minister himself brought it to my parents and it sat uncrated in a corner of the room for a few days until looking at it could no longer be avoided. Most portraits are painted with the artist looking day after day at an increasingly bored subject, (I know, I posed for one in Puerto Rico) but this color drawing was done using a snapshot as the model. It has the look of a happy moment frozen forever. We had to smile back when we looked at him and then, after a moment, when we thought about it, it was hard to look at it. It had been slightly damaged by the movement of the trip but nobody seemed to notice. Some of the chalk powder had come loose and migrated under the glass. It did nothing to spoil the general effect; if anything, it made it look more ethereal.

Thanks to the dry season Papi has been able to spend time in the north coast fincas. A driver can take him to Los Desengaños and from there he takes the long, slow, horseback rides to La Gertrudis and everywhere in between as he had always done in the past. It is probably too painful for him to stay in the family house in Los Desengaños, but at the other end he has his utilitarian cement block house and taciturn Ernesto to inform him of sick cows and dry ponds. I haven't gone with him yet. We are waiting for word from Nicaro any time now and want to be ready to go on a moment's notice.

We had been prepared for anything but what came from la Nicaro in one thick envelope: termination papers, an apologetic letter from the acting manager, and a copy of the most amazing document I had ever seen. Chip threw it away but I retrieved it and kept it. Not for planned revenge — we had had enough of that, but I could sense that there was a lesson there that may serve us, and others, in the future.

Here is a translated copy of that document. The names of the signers are not included because it would not add anything to the impact of the letter. Serve only to note that they were friends, regular visitors to our home; one had been my brother's childhood friend. They must have known that the only reason we thought we should stay in Cuba was to try to be of some comfort to our parents after his death. We had thought of Nicaro as our last opportunity to stay.

Letter to Albertson-English Translation
Nicaro. Oriente
26 January 1959
Mr. Floyd E. Albertson
Acting General Manager
Nickel Processing Corporation
Nicaro, Oriente
Estimated Mr. Albertson:

We are addressing you in your capacity of Acting General Manager of Nickel Processing Corporation to inform you of our concern motivated by the rumor that Mr. Martin S. Tischler is returning to his job in this Company.

Mr. Tischler created a great general antipathy against his own person in the course of his work at Nicaro and in his social contacts; as if that was not enough, Mr. Tischler, in various occasions that we were able to verify, dared use negative and completely undeserved qualifiers on comments referring to "The Revolutionary Movement 26 of July" and to the Cuban people, of which we could testify if you consider it convenient.

Given the current situation and the creation of a healthy nationalism by the Revolutionary Government we are afraid that the return of Mr. Tischler will create labor relation problems and general discontent detrimental to the good will of the personnel of this Company.

We are sure that the service of Mr. Tischler will be more satisfactory in a place where he would not have to work in the middle of mutual antipathy.

Yours truly,

(Ten Printed names and signatures follow)

cc.   George F. Wonder   President
Rafael Gonzalez Cardenas   Vice-President
Carl T. Linderholm   Resident Engineer G.S.A.
Martin S. Tischler

The company, after caving in to pressure, was generous. They offered to pack up our household furniture, appliances and anything we had left behind and ship it to any place we specified. Having no place else, and without even asking them, we had everything sent to Chip's ever-helpful parents in St. Louis. By the time they were informed, they had no choice but to give up their basement for as long as needed.

I read and re-read that letter. We all passed that piece of paper around trying to see hidden meaning in it. Mami was angry; she wanted to do something, call relatives of the signers and question them. We wondered which one of the signers initiated the petition and which ones went along out of fear or self preservation. There has always been jealousy, intrigue and all the baser instincts in the workplace, but this was different. This was an action that marked the start of a new era. We saw it as a declaration of purpose more explicit than all the speeches we had heard or been quoted so far. It said that from now on, loyalty to the government (in this case "The Revolutionary Movement 26 of July") would be a requisite for employment and if management tried to ignore that, other employees would step in and remind them. It also made clear, if not in words but in purpose, that old friendships had ceased to exist. The days of friendly political arguments, at one time less heated than arguments over the merits of baseball players, were over. The only question remaining was, is this a temporary phenomenon resulting from the trauma of the violent times we have lived so recently, or is Cuba permanently changed.

The target of the written attack accepted it better than the rest of us. He may have even welcomed the insult as an excuse to exit this nightmare that he had innocently wandered into. Chip was ready to move on to a fresh start.

But, you don't look for employment as a geologist in the classifieds, if there was such thing here. The geologists' world is known only to other geologists, but fortunately he has stayed in touch. He saw no hope in trying to get back with the Geological Survey but through membership in a professional organization he learned of a convention in San Francisco. That's where he headed with a stopover in St. Louis to buy a suit. Jeffy and I stayed in Camagüey for now.

I must admit that I had never appreciated this three hundred year old city as I should have. I see no beauty in the narrow grey streets with not a tree in sight except the few puny ones at the parks. All the beauty is hidden in private gardens in the middle of the houses. Maybe I would appreciate it more if we had lived in the center but we had never lived in the town itself except for the short time, two years at the most and out of my memory. Many of my friends have lived all their lives in those houses with doors opening to the sidewalk and loved the experience. As children they had played with others in the park and visited at their homes nearby, the reason why they probably have better social skills than I do. We did find playmates outside of town in the Garrido neighborhood so the lack of them cannot be my excuse for not being more attached to the city of Camagüey. As a child I always cried on the return trip from la finca, partly on anticipation of school but mostly because I considered Los Desengaños home and had never found a way that I could stay there. Now less than ever. It is time to say good bye again, but this time I am not even sure what I am leaving behind.

The city has taken a new feel. With a child in tow I can't do much wandering but I had walked along the Calle de Comercio the day I visited Abuela, expecting to see younger versions of myself and my friends — the young women parading along the narrow street, and the young men standing in front of the Gran Hotel — but there was nothing of that. Maybe the months of bomb threat had cured them of the tradition we called pepillar. People on the street now seemed to know where they were going. The conversations had shifted from sidewalks to homes. My parents' home one of them. There was much talk but I missed my father's laughter and wondered if it could ever come back. My cousin Roberto, who had also lost his hearty laughter, was with him often. It was business talk but not completely business as usual because there was always an underlying gloominess. One day when they were talking about repairs to the family house at Los Desengaños which had been listing since the 1932 hurricane — we had become accustomed to doors that stuck and windows that didn't close — Papi said half meaning it, "I hope the next hurricane finishes it off." That, about a place that he had loved more than any other.

In the current mood it was fitting that we visited the cemetery. The youthful angel guarding over the Sanchez family was still there, his folded arms holding something against his chest. I had never wondered about that before. The whole flat square of marble had been recently cleaned. A framed photograph of this burial place, completely hidden by flower wreath, had been on the wall of my father's home office during my childhood. I was told that the photo was taken the day his mother was buried but nobody commented much on it. It was one of those things like trophies and a lacrosse ball that had always been there. I spent much time in that office with the door closed pretending to practice my guitar lessons (a wasted effort) so I know exactly what was there, but when we moved to the new house, with the larger home office, with a built in safe and bookcases, the framed tomb photo disappeared.

There are several burial places in the Camagüey cemetery that are visited often. Not by grieving relatives but by locals who appreciate history and tradition, and even by the occasional outside visitor. One such place is near the entrance. It has an inscription that most Camagüeyanos know by heart. Being not one of them I can only repeat the first two lines:

"Aqui Dolores Rondon finalizo su carrera"
"Ven mortal a contemplar las riquezas cuales son."
Here Dolores Rondon ended her career.
Come mortal one and contemplate what riches are.

And the last line:

"El mal que se economiza y el bien que se pudo hacer,"

The evil that was spared and the good that was done.

Chip returned from San Francisco optimistic about a job prospect in California. While waiting to hear from at least one of the contacts he had made, he became Papi's driver. They went to El Destino where he reported having a more successful experience with a horse than he had in Los Desengaños. I think it was a mare named Cuca that almost made him think that he could adjust to this life, flies, ticks and all. Titino, the Galician casero, at El Destino is much more than a cook. He is the person who stays

230

alone around the batey all day while everyone else is out , does whatever needs to be done, and of course, greets visitors. He had loved Oli and had been his biggest fan. Now he has a room made as a monument to his memory: the polo boots, straw hat, even tools, that to Titino meant Oli and he didn't want anybody else to use. I never saw the room; I never went back to El Destino either.

The road north to Nuevitas is passable, but with the usual potholes that provide a livelihood to enterprising boys. They stand on the side of the road and wave a shovel. Most people stop; they are forced to by the deep holes, and contribute a coin to the volunteer road crew. We had Adriana and Jeff with us on one of those trips to Los Desengaños and they were not amused by the slow trip with many stops and detours. One thing I have learned, Adriana rides in front, she had already vomited on the back seat of our new car when nobody warned us of her car sickness.

I don't know if any of us will ever be at peace at Los Desengaños. Papi looks so solemn and business like when he talks to the new people. I didn't even walk to the otra casa to meet the family living there. This is a place to live in permanently, not to visit as a tourist or absentee owner. Since I am not going to live here there is no time or need to get to know the new encargado and his family. I felt I was intruding. The children didn't have such problems. Papi commented that Adriana was his father's daughter, "she likes pigs better than cattle." We just spent a couple of hours, took the children with us, and went on to stay at Mami's little house at Playa Santa Lucia instead of staying in the old house. Papi got on his fat horse and rode slowly to La Gertrudis by himself, followed only by a favorite dog.

It had been three years since Chip and I faced the endless waves, sand, and the start of a life together at this beach. It was another January but with the unpredictable winter weather of this island, in 1956 there was a cold wind blowing, the kind we knew simply as a Norte, and now there was just a cool breeze and a clear sky. A few vacation houses have been built but the only place to eat out is still La Concha, restaurant and motel, with the same owners but a different waiter. They had managed to survive long months without customers when fear kept people away from the area. The Santa Lucia murders cannot quickly be put out of mind but the talk now is all about what is coming, not what had gone. To the great majority of civilians who stayed out of the conflict and were not touched by personal tragedy, life should pick up just where it stopped just a few months before, only better.

In the original plan, Mami's funny little house was intended as a place to spend the day, with no bedroom, just an open common room, bathroom and kitchen, since presumably we would be spending the night at the house in Los Desengaños. When Papi saw the project under construction he objected, if he was to visit there he had to have a siesta room where he could take a nap out of sight so an enclosed bedroom was added. Of course, he takes a nap on a hammock on the front porch of Los Desengaños, but that is different. Privacy there extends at least as far as the road. At the beach it is common ground just a few feet away. The house is not on the water front; Mami bought a waterfront lot later just in case this one proved inadequate, but since nothing has been built yet on the sandy stretch between the beach house and the water the children can step outside and have the whole beach as their front yard. And so they did. I have not mentioned Jeffy's little shovel; it was just one of many toys he acquired during our stay in St. Louis and the only one he has kept. Not only kept, but it has become a sort of hard, cold metal security blanket, he is never without it. It was originally part of a set, but the accompanying bucket was ignored as were all the other toys. The little shovel, held firmly in his hand, had tested the consistency of any surface he found along the way. So far the sands of Santa Lucia have proven the best digging grounds.

Back in Camagüey, I found very few useful things to do. No point getting involved again in the bookkeeping part of the business since I didn't expect to be around long. Strangely, this "wait and see" attitude was not just ours, who were facing an imminent move. Everybody around us had it. Words like Agrarian Reform were enough to freeze any long term project. In this upside-down world reforms were promoted by those who would be the losers if land redistribution would be implemented. Who are the so called "landless peasants" that revolutions are supposed to help? If they are landless, they are not peasants, I say. They are certainly not the guajiros. I could not imagine Ernesto feeding chickens in his own little plot. Angel Nuñez rode to San Miguel to hear what they had to say at one of the many public meetings. His explanation for going was "para que no me cuenten." Roughly translated as "to see for myself" but if he brought home anything from the meeting, he isn't saying.

In the middle of April, Chip received the offer he had been waiting for. Southern Pacific, the railroad company, was putting together a team of geologists to map lands they own in California and Nevada. It is the kind of work usually done by geologists fresh out of college not encumbered by family. Or by those who purposely chose a gypsy life style. The project will be completed in two or three years and during that time we will move every few months, living in trailers, motel rooms and rented houses. I immediately started restyling my mind to accept, and even look forward to this new future. After all, this was more like what we had envisioned when we married three years before. It would be good for Chip to go back to the kind of work he had once loved, without the mining camp intrigue and the violence around him.

We made several quick visits around town to say good bye to friends. One was to Brooks, head of the Function Four agricultural project. He seemed genuinely sorry to see us go "we will be left alone", he said. Five years in this city of over a hundred thousand people and apparently he has not made a friend.

Early in the morning on our final day in Camagüey I selfishly skipped downstairs with nothing but a new life in my mind, and there, by the front door, Papi turned away, but not fast enough. I saw him crying, something he does easily now, but until a few months ago I didn't think he was capable of doing.

We drove to la Habana in our blue De Soto with Jeffy standing on the front seat between us. His only prized possessions were on the back seat: his little metal shovel and a stuffed toy named Tigre. The soft cuddly tiger was the night time companion but the shovel was the daytime favorite toy. Every time we stopped, he grabbed it and found a soft spot where he could test it. He is not violent in nature or that shovel could be a fearsome weapon.

There are no road blocks on the Carretera Central, but still there are more uniforms than I like to see — now it is milisianos in olive green with black arm bands instead of soldiers in kaki. There were a few detours but not as many signs of destruction as we expected. Not as many major bridges have been blown up here as they were in Oriente and Camaguey Provinces.

I should be able to report something out of the ordinary — not that Havana is ever ordinary — at this historic moment of April 1959 but I saw nothing but the usual awe inspiring old city. An unpopular government has just evaporated and a motley collection of young people, unaccustomed to governing, are moving into every position of authority. There are circus-style trials taking place and people are being stood against a wall and shot right across the harbor at the old Cabaña fortress. Prisoners are been held in antique dungeons below the water line of that fortress at whose massive walls so many tourists had aimed their cameras. But one is more likely to learn about what is happening in this city sitting in front of a T.V. in

Philadelphia than driving along the Via Blanca into Havana. Describing the mood and condition of a city at a particular time brings to mind the story about the blind men describing the elephant: it all depended on which part of the animal's body they happened to grab. On one street, people may be going about their routine workday while their neighbors a few streets away are being arrested or are going into hiding.

You don't have to know your way around la Habana to find the FOCSA building. There is nothing else like it here or anywhere in the world. It is the pride of Cuban architecture and several architects have their name connected to its design. The name is an acronym for the name of the project which originally was intended to house members of a certain industry but the concept changed before the building was finished and now the apartments are owned as condominiums. My brother in law, Gonzalo, owns one (J on the tenth floor) where we plan to spend our last days in Cuba. Approached from the East, the block of apartments looks like a giant open book sitting on top of the two story high city block of commercial and office space. The tower is really shaped like a Y but the two open arms are where the 373 apartments are located. On the flat rooftop of the lower building there is a landscaped park and swimming pool which is what the residents see if they look down from their balconies. If they look straight across, they face the view of the ocean beyond the sea wall known as El Malecon, and the city which, to many, is one of the most beautiful in the world. I am not going to weigh in, since I am not familiar with that many world cities to use as comparison and, besides, I fail to see beauty in any-thing made by man. The very top of the tower is where a private club-restaurant is located, named, of course, La Torre. It is for those who must see farther than anyone else. I believe the name of the game is "King of the mountain." Months ago my mother had written that my cousin Walter had been hired as manager of the club La Torre. Now I understood why that was newsworthy.

One could live a lifetime on the FOCSA and never had to go across the street. We parked on the parking level and went downstairs where Gonzalo has an office, but didn't find him there. The secretary informed us that he and Lucy were not at the apartment either but were expected any moment. We wore out our welcome quickly when Jeffy used his shovel to empty a sand urn so we decided to take a walk in the great outdoors: the park-like level right under the towers. It was a good idea. After sitting in a car for nine or ten hours a walk in the park was just the thing. Ours was a familiar sight: a child running around with his little shovel and the two adults enjoying the cool of a late afternoon. That we were two stories above the street in the busiest part of a city that had recently hosted the most gruesome spectacle that our generation was to see, could be forgotten. The Havana coliseum known as El Palacio de los Deportes had been televised world wide as a stage to display the worst traits of the human race.

When Fidel met with international criticism for the summary executions that were taken place, he responded in his typical over-the-top style by saying, they want trials, and we'll give them trials. Chosen for the first public trial was an Army Major whose name, Jesus Sosa Blanco, was familiar to us from our time in Nicaro. He may or not have been guilty of at least some of the charges but his guilt or innocence was not what came out at the trial, it was the nature of the mob watching it. Those present could not be excused in their behavior as hungry for vengeance because the accused had operated at the other end of the island and this city crowd had never heard of him until that day. Still, they clamored for blood and had a wonderful time doing it.

We had been admiring the landscaping of the rooftop as much as the view. The FOCSA was only two years old, it had opened in 1956, and yet the small trees and shrubs looked like they were firmly rooted. I wondered how deep the soil went and what happened to the water run-off. We were pondering those matters when I saw Lucy and Gonzalo walking toward us.

I had time to study my sister from a distance. I think she has changed more than I have. Standing tall next to her husband in high heels and simple elegant dress she looks settled and dignified, not a struggling housewife without a house, like me. I feel so insecure while she looks so self confident and sophisticated. By marrying a man out of her age group, she has skipped a generation. And the amazing part is that they look like they belong together. I wonder how the wives of her husband's friends see her. Do they resent her youth and good looks? When we had time to talk was when I became aware that she has entered a different world from the one where we grew up. But then, so have I. She and Gonzalo mention people whose names are only vaguely familiar to me. I am not in the habit of following Havana society news since I have never gone to school in the capital, and have visited so few times that I know nothing of the people they mentioned. Most of our friends and relatives in Camagüey are not as proud of being guajiros as I am and take some interest on what goes on in the capital. I may have made a conscious effort of ignoring the capital, but I truly don't know anybody in la Habana outside of my aunts and cousins, and at this point I am not interested in getting to know them. My life has moved in a different direction. The name dropping may have been for my benefit, but I don't think so. Those are her friends now and this is her world.

We spent two days with them mostly holed up in their apartment. Havana is safe and secure, or so we are told, but why take chances. On another time we would be visiting relatives, shopping, or touring the city with our hosts but, here, like in Camagüey, the feeling is of increasing concern. Gonzalo repeated the latest joke (we Cubans console ourselves from the gravest misfortune by repeating stupid jokes), this one goes like this: Do you know why this is called La Revolucion del callo? A callo is a corn, or callus, one of those painful growth people get on their toes from wearing cheap shoes (according to Mami). The answer is that people are happy with the Revolucion until it affects them personally; until it steps on their corn. When it happens to others, one can rationalize that they had it coming to them; when it happens to you, you yell. The problem is that the stomping is getting closer and closer to home; affecting people that were not even connected with the overturned regime. We also heard what is only a light-hearted way of discussing a serious issue: he called this "The Watermelon Revolution", green on the outside and red on the inside. This last was more of a concern up North where the word communist sets up alarm bells. Around here we care less about what they call themselves than what they do and how it affects us.

You don't have to be a builder or an architect to admire the interior arrangement of the FOCSA. Havana is full of modernistic buildings that use architectural details for purely aesthetic reasons. Here it is function that is paramount. It took me a while to figure out why if I went out of the apartment by the front door I ended up on a hallway and if I went out the kitchen door, I was in a different, a service hallway. Jeffy's interest was on the balcony. He was fascinated by gravity; how he could open his hand over the edge and the item he was holding would disappear out of sight. After he threw down a box of band aids, a pencil, and who knows what other small items, we kept the door to the balcony closed before he tried his experiments with something more valuable.

It was probably not too soon for any of us that we said our dry-eyed goodbyes. We tried to be casual, while not knowing when and if we will be together again. Then we loaded the DeSoto and headed for the ferry. As things often go, The Havana – Key West ferry doesn't leave from Havana and doesn't land at Key West either. It will cross the ninety mile stretch of water and take us to a port just north of the city of Key West. Come to think of it, it is not really a ferry but a World War II landing craft where the automobiles and the passengers ride separately.

We left Havana going East through the tunnel under the bay and found the ferry dock on the separate township of Regla where we joined the slow moving line of cars being driven into the cavernous hold of the huge craft. Once we relinquished the car to be secured in its place, we walked upstairs with the other passengers. Most of them seemed to be Cubans or Americans who had been living here, and had become Cubanized, but not tourists. We all wanted to be on deck for a final look at our island. I tried to remember a poem by Gertrudis Gomez de Avellaneda, the favorite poet of Camagüey, titled Al Partir, (On Leaving) where she describes the sounds of the filling sails of a ship that took her away from her country and to another exile of years ago. This time there are no flapping of sails and no gentle creaking of wood. I listened for some special sound to remember.

I heard the giant door close with a loud metallic Clank.

Epilogue. Remembering the end and moving on

I didn't want to open my eyes and wake up all the way so I let the rhythm that entered my brain in my sleep go around and around. At first there were no words attached to it. Just tarara, tarara, tarara, but finally it became words. I repeated them like a mantra:

> *Yo se un himno gigante y extraño.*
> *Que anuncia en la noche del alma una aurora.*

Poorly translating the Rimas into English it would be:

> "I know a hymn, gigantic and strange,
> That in the night of the soul announces a dawn."

Now I know what Becquer meant. A dawn has arrived.

Reflecting on the wonder of waking up to beautiful words it hit me. The nightmares are gone. Have been gone for a long time and I didn't even notice.

They were not always the same. They took place on locations of my youth or in places I have never visited; locales probably borrowed from movies or other make-believe scenes. There may have been other people involved, but the central figure was always Oli. He was not wounded, or sick, or in any apparent distress, but somehow I knew that he was doomed. And, this is what made it a nightmare; he wanted me to help him and I couldn't.

Some of the earlier nightmares were a repetition of a scene that really happened but was more comic than tragic. I was sitting on the porch of the house in Los Desengaños. Can't call it the front porch when there is no street, but it was the long side and since the house was about five feet off the ground it was a good look out. But I was not looking at anything but a book or magazine in my hands when I heard Oli call: "China, help me." Not loud or frantic; just the kind of "help me; I need an extra hand in this project." I was aware that he was nearby doing some carpentry work, moving boards around, something not urgent. I didn't even look up. What is it? The second time he called it did sound urgent. I jumped down from the porch and went to help. A stack of lumber had fallen on him as he was trying to pull out a board, and he was pinned down under a mountain of rough-sawed boards. He was not hurt. It was the sort of ranch incident that provides a source of jokes for a while then is filed away. But the words "help me" somehow became permanently engraved in some inaccessible part of my brain.

Did he call for help a few years later in November 1958?

Cuban expatriates of my generation, and maybe some Cubans who quietly stayed in Cuba for whatever personal reason, can tell exactly the moment when their world collapsed: a visit by a couple of armed militia (made more hurtful if they were personal acquaintances before they donned the black arm bands and weapons), a goodbye hug from a friend at the airport, a public announcement from the new regime ... For me the end had come with a phone call from tío Julian.

And moving on

At the time, my anchor to life was still holding firmly in Camagüey, family, friends, and in particular, Los Desengaños. Those were still there and presumably forever. Now, as I write this, fifty years later, all that is gone, it has been gone for a long time. People my age become accustomed to loosing and replacing parts of our lives and so have I. But the loss of 1958 left a permanent wound that changed me for all time. With my young family I moved many times, saw many wonderful places, and made many friends. My second son, Daniel Oliverio, was born in California in 1960. My marriage ended, as it should, since the reasons that brought us together no longer were valid.

A truckload of armed militia arrived at Los Desengaños in 1961 and they told my father, in front of his wide eyed six year old granddaughter, that he had twenty four hours to leave. He tried to convince friends not to go into exile: his argument was "They can't kill us all." But house by house the neighborhood emptied out; Marta took Oli's children to live in Bogota with her brother. Eventually, my parents felt so isolated that they gave up and took a plane to Mexico and from there to Florida. My father, amongst other things, was a partner in a fertilizer business in Belle Glade, sold it, and later was not too proud to mow lawns, his and his neighbors, in Miami. My mother, who had interrupted a career at age twenty four, went back to school and worked into her eighties. Both Lucy and I did well in our working life as was expected of us. But Marta, who eventually joined the exile community in Miami, surprised those who didn't know her well, with her strength and resilience.

There is nothing left of Los Desengaños. My sons had trouble locating the site. Santa Lucia Beach is now an international tourist destination with world class hotels and an airfield. The only identifiable ranch in the area was El Cafetal, the grand experiment of the Texans from the King Ranch. Why it was spared (confiscated, but not destroyed) when the Cuban owned ranches were eradicated must have some explanation that eludes me.

The road to the beach, now paved, has been relocated and now doesn't go past where our front gate once was. By sheer luck, they took the turnoff by a sign marked "El Cafetal". No towers were in sight. A few houses down the dirt road they asked an amiable old guajiro for directions. They were led to a gate of what would have been "Los Desengaños" and within sight of the solid old two-arch bridge. Only by the sight of that bridge which they had seen in photographs they were able to deduce that this was the right place. Where the ruins of the old sugar mill once were, they found only rubble. The ruins had been dynamited; possibly because of the persistent myth that there was gold buried there. In spite of broken bricks everywhere, somebody had planted plantains but there are no cattle, no windmill, no corral, just the bridge. Their guajiro who acted as their guide was living with his family pretty much as country people had lived in my days except that his livestock consisted of a herd of goats. Goats can eat anything, including marabou, that invasive plant that was our nemesis and now has taken over. On my older son's last visit, the old guajiro was unchanged, but his goats were gone, stolen by thieves who will never be caught. His wife, chickens, yuca and the well maintained hut remained.

—I don't want to see what is there. Let the same location become another place for other people and other times. As long as I don't see it, in my mind it will always be as it was and it will always be mine.

Splendor in the grass

This is not about the guinea grass that fed the animals that fed us. Or the grass that grew over and around the ruins of El Desengaño. It is my favorite few lines from the much longer poem:

"Ode on Intimations of Immortality from Recollections of Early Childhood":

> What though the radiance which was once so bright
> Be now for ever taken from my sight,
> Though nothing can bring back the hour
> Of splendor in the grass, of glory in the flower;
> We will grieve not, rather find
> Strength in what remains behind...

Thank you to William Wordsworth for saying it so much better than I could.

Glossary

Here are some of the Spanish, local slang, or words of native American origin that I have used, and their English translations. Some have other meanings, but this is the way they are used in this text.

a la zanca— riding on the horse's rump behind and holding on to the rider on the saddle.

a piso – boarding cattle for a fee

Algarrobo –carob tree

Alpargatas- canvas shoes with rope soles from Spain. Right and left shoes are identical.

Arroyo — stream, brook

Atascadero – a place to get stuck in the muck

Bachillerato — equivalent to High School; not university bachelor degree

Balneario— bathing beach inside enclosures

Barbudos— bearded men with rifles

Batey — native american word for village; housing compound at ranch or sugar mill

Beneficeo – our use: yearly round up of calves for branding, vaccinating, castratíon, etc.

Bolas — gossip going around.

Botellas — not just bottles. Political appointments

Caballeria — land measure equivalent to 33.5 acres.

Cachanchán — slang, sidekick, unskilled assistant, go-for.

Calle — street

Callejón — alley

Callo –callus, usually painful and on the toes.

Canastilla— layette for a baby. From canasta, basket

Caneca – glazed clay bottle

Cangrejo — a crab. Cangrejeros are people from Nuevitas or other coastal towns.

Carboneros –the men that make charcoal -carbon

Carreta de bueyes — ox cart

Casero— employee, who stays in the batey, cooks and feeds the chicken.

Cayo— islet, key

Central azucarero -- sugar mil

Glossary

Chapear—to cut grass or brush with a machete

Cojo – a man that limps

Colonia — sugar cane plantation connected with the Central.

Corrales — compound of enclosed yards for animals.

Criada— a house maid.

Criollo — native breed of animal.

Cuartel — army post

Derramadero — flood plains. Low land near a river.

Destajo – work done under contract. Usually land clearing.

Empanadillas – our wonderful fried pastries.

Encargado – person in charge. Called capataz elsewhere.

Encargo – a request to take or bring something

Estancia – Independent farm or a farm within a large finca.

Finca – ranch, combination farm and ranch, country home

Fotingo – old car, a clunker

Gallego – man from Galicia-gallega-woman from Galicia.

Gallinero — poultry yard

Ganado –commonly used only for ganado vacuno: cattle

Garabato—hooked stick; my father's nickname

Golpe de estado— coup d'etat.—Is there an english word?

Guajiros – country people—the best!

Guanales — area with mostly guanos; not suitable for   pasture.

Guano –cabbage, palmetto or Sabal palms, their fronds

Guardaraya — clearing along a fence to serve as a fire break

Guayabal — area where guava trees, guayabas, grow

Jibaro — wild, feral dog

Jiqui — tree with extremely hard, durable wood.

Jobo —a large tree with fruit resembling a yellow plum

Lechero — milkman , piñon lechero, a poisonous milky seedpod.

Mambises — Cuban insurrects in the war with Spain.

Marabú or marabou — an invasive bush that escaped from yards

Mondongo— means tripe at home was a dish made with pigs'viscera.

Monte — forest, also countryside

Mulata —mixed race woman, white and negroe.

Parvulas — little ones, before first grade at Las Teresianas

Palmiche — berries from the royal palm trees

Pepillos and pepillas — flirty teenagers

Piñon – trees used as living fences

Platanos — plantains; large bananas used as cooked vegetables

Platanitos —not small plantains; bananas eaten as fruit.

Playa – waterfront; with or without sand beach.

Potrero—a fenced pasture

Quinta— recreational country home

Rastrillo— a rake,also a gate that has to be dragged to open and close

Recogedor— smaller than a potrero and larger than a corral

Reses – cattle in general

Taburete—a rustic chair with seat and back of untanned hide.

Tienda—the store

Tranvía—trolley car

Tumba—clear cut woods to be burned.

Vale — a piece of paper guaranteeing payment.

Yagua—the frond casing of the royal palm

Yerba de guinea—our favorite pasture grass.

Zafra – cane grinding season at a sugar mill

** ** **

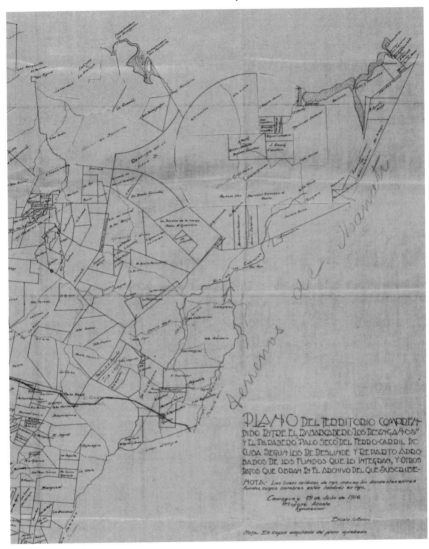

Section of a map from the Cuban collection at the University of Florida, Gainesville.

About the Author

Angela Sanchez Tischler left Cuba with her husband and small son for the last time on May 1959, which is where the narrative of the book Los Desengaños ends. For the next fourteen years she followed her geologist husband to job locations in California and Nevada. Their last location in California was in Cambria, a beautiful village on the coast near the Hearst Castle where they lived for nine years. She took small part time jobs to supplement the household income and, later, to help her parents who had arrived in Miami with thousands of other Cuban refugees.

She did anything, made pies for a local café, worked as assistant at a daycare for preschoolers, and park aid at the Hearst Castle. This last was a dream job that included the use of the swimming pool after the tourists had left.

"I took the Postal entrance exam and was surprised when I was hired. At first it seemed like a bad move; better pay but more difficult work. As it turned out, it was the best move I ever made. The job gave me security and confidence in myself.

"My next, and hopefully last, relocation was to Crescent City, Florida. I stayed with the Postal Service for thirty years and retired as Postmaster of Pierson, Florida in the year 2000. During my many years listening to customers from behind a counter I learned that so many people want to talk and many have interesting things to say. That gave me an idea. When I retired, I went to the editor of the Courier Journal, the Crescent City weekly newspaper, and offered to write a column. I argued that local people only get in the paper when something happens to them. This column would give them an opportunity to air their opinions and make themselves known. We agreed to call it "It's your turn."

" For five years I interviewed, photographed and wrote about all sorts of people, not just the well known. I actually did very little writing, I mostly quoted my subjects. Eventually the idea came to me that it was only fair that if other people trusted me with their personal stories, I should trust them with mine. That was the start of this book of memories."